R0061528501

012

A
Kidnapping
in
Milan

Also by Steve Hendricks

The Unquiet Grave:
The FBI and the Struggle for
the Soul of Indian Country

A
Kidnapping
in
Milan

The CIA on Trial

STEVE HENDRICKS

W. W. Norton & Company
New York · London

For information about permission to reproduce selections from this book,
write to Permissions, W. W. Norton & Company, Inc.,
500 Fifth Avenue, New York, NY 10110

For information about special discounts for bulk purchases, please contact
W. W. Norton Special Sales at specialsales@wwnorton.com or 800-233-4830

Manufacturing by RR Donnelley, Harrisonburg
Book design by Charlotte Staub
Production manager: Devon Zahn

Library of Congress Cataloging-in-Publication Data

Hendricks, Steve.
A kidnapping in Milan : the CIA on trial / Steve Hendricks. — 1st ed.
p. cm.
Includes bibliographical references and index.
ISBN 978-0-393-06581-7 (hardcover)
1. War on Terrorism, 2001-2009—Secret service—United States.
2. United States. Central Intelligence Agency. 3. Intelligence service—Italy.
4. Nasr, Hassan Mustafa Osama, 1963- 5. Trials (Political crimes and
offenses)—Italy. I. Title.
HV6431.H435 2010
363.325′16—dc22

2010020788

W. W. Norton & Company, Inc.
500 Fifth Avenue, New York, N.Y. 10110
www.wwnorton.com

W. W. Norton & Company Ltd.
Castle House, 75/76 Wells Street, London W1T 3QT

1 2 3 4 5 6 7 8 9 0

To

Rocco Chinnici, Giovanni Falcone,

and Paolo Borsellino,

who, to borrow from the last,

died but once

while others die every day.

Carlyle said "a lie cannot live."
It shows that he did not know how to tell them.

—*Mark Twain*

Contents

A
Kidnapping
in
Milan

Prelude

NEAR THE BASILICA di Sant'Ambrogio in Milan stands a column of rough stone erected by the Romans in the time of the Caesars. It is Corinthian in style, a fluted cylinder topped by leaves and scrolls. The flutes have not weathered the ages well, the leaves are chipped, the scrolls broken. On the lower part of the ruin are two holes a millennium and a half old and a hand's breadth—or, to the point, a head's breadth—apart. The Milanesi say that if you put your nose to either hole, you can smell sulfur. Put your ear to one, and the roiling of Hell's flames and the cries of its sufferers can be faintly heard. The holes were created by the horns of Satan—that is agreed. Beyond that, stories diverge. By one history, Satan came to Milan to lure Saint Ambrose, patron of the city, into deepest sin, but Ambrose would not be tempted, and in a fury *il Diavolo* sunk his horns into the column. Another story says the encounter between good and evil was more muscular, that Ambrose and Satan locked arms in a cataclysmic grapple and Ambrose threw Satan off with such force that his horns were lodged in the column. Another claim—completely scurrilous, the Milanesi will tell you—is that the contest with Satan took place in the Holy Land, that its protagonist was not Ambrose but Christ, and that many years after Christ threw Satan headlong into the column, the column was imported to Milan.

In Milan a known fact is always explained by competing stories, more than one of which will be plausible. Some of the stories will be frivolous, even absurd. With time, the elements of all will mix, their separate origins becoming unclear. With time enough, even the one fact once known with certainty will become all but unknowable.

Chapter 1

A Kidnapping

MILAN IS COLD in winter. December slips over Monte Rosa from Switzerland, down the massif of the Pennine Alps and across the wide plain of the river Po, where Milan sits exposed. The winter lifts a dampness from the rice fields around the city, and the dampness makes the chill the ruder, but the Milanesi, conditioned by two millennia of incursions, meteorological and otherwise, ignore the season. In January the sidewalk tables of the coffee bars on Corso Vittorio Emanuele II are filled with citizens and their guests, their dark coats buttoned to their necks, their hands, gloved in pliant leather, wrapped around espressos as if it were the normalest thing to be taking a *caffè* out of doors when other liquids begin to freeze. To be Milanese is to declare the business of life more important than a mere assault from God.

It was unremarkable, then, that on a cold day in the winter of 2003 a man passed a portion of his lunch hour on an inhospitable bench in a sad Milanese piazza named Dergano. Dergano once marked Milan's northern frontier but was now lost in the city's rambling, uncertain transition to suburb. The center of the piazza was asphalted, and thirty or forty cars were parked in rows orderly even by the standards of Milan, which believes itself less chaotic than the rest of Italy. Humanity, which is to say vivacity and interest, had been relegated to the piazza's periphery. There were a few benches, which had been retouched by artists of the street and which sagged. There were a few trees, which, barren this time of year, added to the piazza's sorrow. On two of the piazza's sides stood unadorned modern buildings, their fronts covered in cheap marble of the kind known to the floors of discount stores worldwide, their occupants a large chain bank and larger chain grocery. The piazza's other sides had escaped the crime of modern architecture. Their buildings were simple but charming—plastered in gentle pastels, linteled in great blocks of stone, cheerfully inferential of lives they had seen. A bakery, a wine shop, and a small mobile phonery were housed there.

The man on the bench was of the indeterminate age between youth and decline, perhaps forty. His forehead had begun to wax, his scalp to wane, but gracefully; not for some years would he face the choice of shearing what hair remained or combing it over a bare dome. His build was casually athletic but with a padding of flesh bespeaking a desk job. When he smiled, which was not often today, the left corner of his mouth tugged slightly downward, as if a piece of him refused to surrender entirely to joy. His aspect was altogether ordinary, save in one respect: he had sandy, almost blond hair, a minor oddity in dark Italy.

Colleagues knew Luciano Pironi by his nom de guerre Ludwig. That he had a nom de guerre did not imply distinction. Ludwig was a mere *maresciallo*, a marshal, in the Carabinieri, a branch of the Italian Army once important but no longer. The Carabinieri take their name from the horseman's sidearm, the carbine, which likely takes its name, in corrupted form, from Calabria, in Italy's south. The Calabrians learned early that men with rifles light enough to be used at a gallop could give the next duchy over a good whacking. Today the Carabinieri only police Italy's cities, and that only partly. The State Police, what Americans might call the National Police if they had one, share the job. Each force pursues its own cases, interrogates its own suspects, and makes its own arrests. In theory they divide their jurisdictions amicably, but sometimes one force withholds leads and witnesses from the other. There are two emergency phone numbers in Italy, 112 for the Carabinieri, 113 for the State Police. In a time of crisis, a citizen can pick his rescuer, and 113 is regarded the wiser choice. Other police agencies supersede the Carabinieri and State Police in certain fields, like the Finance Guard, which has jurisdiction over money laundering and smuggling. The multiplicity of police is a legacy of Mussolini, who slept poorly in his ducal bed if he thought he had given one force too many guns or too much opportunity to use them. He carved off authority and built rivalries with the same fevered inefficiency with which he built oversized train stations. The multiple forces survived because they fit the Italian condition: Italy was not unified until the late nineteenth century, and then only grudgingly. Italians have never trusted their national government nor, in the main, each other. The political birthright of the Italian is suspicion.

The most visible of the Carabinieri are foot patrols. They wear uniforms of black with red stripes down their pants and white sashes across their chests that shine at a distance but are dingy up close. They patrol in pairs so that, as Italians say, there will be one who can read, one who can write. *To be a carabiniere*, in idiomatic Italian, is *to be a martinet*. That life, however, was not for Ludwig. He belonged to a unit of plain-clothed Carabinieri detectives, the Raggruppamento Operativo Speciale, the Special Operations Group, which had been created in 1990 to combat the Mafia and terrorists. In Milan, the ROS was concerned mainly with terrorists. The ROS might almost have been considered elite, except that little that was attached to the Carabinieri bore elitism's happy stigma. Hence the noms de guerre, originally adopted to make it harder for criminals to harm lawmen but maintained, in part, to give an air of importance to a job that lacked it. Luigi had become Ludwig because of Teutonic origins: his mother was German, his father Italian; German had been his first language. He had colleagues who had taken the names Hyena and Brasco, as in Donnie Brasco, the undercover FBI agent played on screen by a virile Johnny Depp. "Ludwig," shading to the commonplace, suggested a calmer temperament.

Like any carabiniere with talent, Ludwig believed he had been misplaced. He thought his rightful home was SISMI, the Servizio per le Informazioni e la Sicurezza Militare, or Military Intelligence and Security Service. Like ROS, SISMI fought terrorists, but did so with more prestige. The officers of SISMI were spies, not police, and they worked against enemies both at home and abroad—a burden which in America was shared by the CIA, FBI, Secret Service, and others. It was not easy for a carabiniere to join SISMI. Merit mattered, but merit was rarely enough, and it helped to have a patron or friend on the inside.

As it happened, Ludwig had a well-placed friend, an American named Bob, who was highly regarded by the director of SISMI's Milan office and who was also known, favorably it seemed, at SISMI's headquarters in Rome. Bob could expect that any recommendation he made would be looked on with respect. He was a spy. It also happened that Bob needed a favor, the subject of which he first raised with Ludwig, glancingly, in August of 2002, five months before Ludwig came to the cold bench in Piazza Dergano. April may have been the cruelest month in Eliot's Europe, but in Milan it was August. The Milanesi, like certain Amazonian tribes, hardly know the air conditioner, and in high summer those who do not decamp to Liguria to fight for a towel's breadth of sand stay home and roast *au jus*. Criminals are among those who stay, so lawmen do too.

That August, while their wives were in diaspora, Ludwig and Bob often met for lunch or dinner in Piazza Risorgimento, which was in a more pleasant quarter than Dergano. They favored a pizzeria named Tosca, whose virtues included tables that, unlike in most Milanese restaurants, did not abut conjugally. At Tosca a gentlewoman might venture to the powder room without having to choose between sucking in her intestines or becoming intimate with the shoulder blades of six strangers, and a cop and a spy could talk business without holding a town hall meeting. At one of their lunches, Bob told Ludwig that an informer had tipped him to a terrorist plot. The leader of the plot was Osama Mustafa Hassan Nasr, more commonly called Abu Omar, an Egyptian who lived in exile in Milan and had a violent interpretation of the Quran. Bob believed that Abu Omar ran a terrorist network that recruited and sent men from northern Italy to the Middle East to wage jihad. He was also plotting to hijack or in some other way attack a bus from the American School of Milan, where children of the American and European diplomatic and plutocratic classes were educated. (Their campus was located, with not a little irony, on Via Karl Marx.) Ludwig had heard of Abu Omar before but had known only that he was being investigated by yet another arm of Italian justice, the Divisione Investigazioni Generali e Operazioni Speciali, the Division of General Investigations and Special Operations. DIGOS, another counterterrorist agency that was more prestigious than ROS, was something like a big-city detective unit with the national reach of the FBI. Bob said little more of Abu Omar at that lunch and not much about him in succeeding lunches, but in December he told Ludwig he was assembling a team to seize the Egyptian, and he asked Ludwig to join it. Ludwig asked what he would have to do.

Bob explained that Abu Omar was a man of regular religious habits and rarely missed the noon prayers at his mosque. Nearly every day he descended from his apartment on Via Conte Verde, walked the couple of blocks west through Piazza Dergano, turned south onto Via Ciaia, which angled into Via Guerzoni, then turned west onto Viale Jenner, where his mosque stood. The entire walk took five or six minutes. Most days Abu Omar left his apartment a few minutes before noon, although some days he left earlier. Ludwig, if he agreed to help, would go to Piazza Dergano at ten o'clock on a morning that Bob would name and would wait for a call on a mobile phone Bob would give him. When the call came, he would walk to Via Guerzoni and wait for Abu Omar, who would be easy to spot. An Arab with a long, bushy beard, he always wore a light-colored *galabia*, the traditional tunic-like garment of his people, and a *taqiyah*, or skullcap. Ludwig would stop him, show his police credentials, and ask to see his identity papers. Because Ludwig was a cop, he would know how to make the stop seem real, and should passersby or another cop happen along, Ludwig could shoo them away with authority. Ludwig needn't worry, however, that Abu Omar would be under surveillance by DIGOS that day. Bob would see that he was not being followed. While Ludwig inspected Abu Omar's papers, others on the team would "collect" the Egyptian and take him elsewhere for interrogation. Bob hoped his people would get "actionable intelligence" from Abu Omar, but not only that. They would also try to convince him to become their spy, which would be quite an accomplishment, since Western intelligence agencies had failed badly at recruiting moles from among the Islamic terrorists of Europe. Bob did not say what might convince Abu Omar to turn coat on his fellow terrorists. He also said he might need to send Ludwig to Piazza Dergano more than once because conditions might not be right for intercepting Abu Omar the first time. Maybe there would be too many people on the street, or maybe Abu Omar would have the flu and stay home. In such an event, Ludwig would receive no call on the mobile phone, and at one o'clock he could leave Dergano. Bob would send him back another day.

Bob, Ludwig knew, had already spoken well of him to the SISMI chief in Milan, and now Bob let Ludwig know that if he took this assignment, SISMI would learn even more about his worth. It was a deft pitch, fit for a CIA manual: a small task, easy in itself but part of a more important whole and sweetened with a personal incentive. Ludwig did not need much convincing. He accepted, asking only that, if possible, the job take place on the weekend because during the week it would be hard to explain an absence of three or four hours to his superiors. (Ludwig knew without Bob's saying that he was not to explain his noonlighting to his superiors.) Bob said he would try for a weekend but could make no promises.

After lunch, Ludwig went to the ROS office, looked up the file on Abu Omar, and found his picture as Bob had described him. The file was otherwise unremarkable and made little impression on him.

In January, Bob gave Ludwig the cell phone he had mentioned, and a few days later he told Ludwig to go to Dergano next Monday, January 27, 2003. Come the day, Ludwig excused himself from his office and drove to Dergano on his scooter. He found a neighborhood bar, which in Milan is a place that sells both stimulant and stupefacient—coffee and alcohol—and in its typical form is barely wider than an aircraft lavatory and furnished almost as minimally, although occasionally there will be a flourish of something dramatic like a table or chair. A Milanese takes his coffee standing up, at the bar proper, where a brass foot rail takes the place of a seat. A drinker who sits doubles his price, and the workaday Milanese refuses to pay for real estate when he needs only caffeine. Ludwig took his place at the footrail, ordered his drink, and drew it out as long as he could. He may have been reduced to ordering from the sandwiches that in Milanese bars have been dressed years in advance and are heated when ordered—a gastronomic improvement, but just, over cardboard. Eventually he left and strolled about, never straying more than a few blocks from the piazza. Later he took to the bench, where the entertainment was slim and the minutes expired slowly. At one o'clock, no call having come, he returned to his scooter.

A week later Bob asked Ludwig to go to Piazza Dergano the coming Sunday. Again Ludwig went, but again there was no call. And so the following Sunday.

AT THREE in the afternoon on January 13, 2003, a man whose name was not Massimo but who will be called that here, was ruing the start of the week. The radiator in his office was, in the Italian phrase, going a thousand, and the air was as dry as the inside of a sauna but without the cedary charm. The day had been monotonous, even for a Monday. He had made a few appointments that he cared little about, had attended to a few (but not enough) of the papers that had been sitting too long on his desk, and had weighed and re-weighed which of his remaining tasks was the least unpleasant. When his mobile phone rang, he figured it for another start-of-the-week nuisance—there were always plenty after a quiet weekend—and he thought he might let it go. Reflex, however, impelled him to glance at his caller ID, which read "Call 1," a hidden number. His curiosity slightly piqued, he answered.

If Massimo may be believed (and it is hard to say when he may and when he may not), a man's voice greeted him in Spanish, which Massimo spoke fluently. The man, who was unknown to Massimo, was not given to pleasantries. He said a sentence that Massimo knew by heart, a few cloaked words that meant "There's a job to do." Massimo replied almost instinctively with a coded sentence of his own that meant *Ho capito*, "I understand." The code words dissolved the caller's abruptness into congeniality, and the two strangers talked as if old friends—a phenomenon that Massimo had noted on previous calls of this kind throughout the years. He and the callers were part of a fraternity that, once known, dissolved barriers between them. The caller today did not chat long. He said he would see Massimo tomorrow and did not need to say when or where, because unless there were superseding orders, the details were already fixed.

"*A domani,*" Massimo said and hung up.

He wondered whether the "Spaniard," as he thought of him, was the CIA's new antenna—antennae being local spy chiefs, so called because they picked up information low to the ground and transmitted it to their cortical headquarters. The CIA's chief in Milan had been replaced some time ago, but Massimo hadn't met the new man yet, which was not unusual. Many months often passed without Massimo's hearing from *la Cia*. The silences had daunted him when he was first recruited, more than twenty years ago. He had wondered if they meant the information he supplied was not useful, but he soon learned the silences meant nothing. New orders always arrived, and money too—in the quantity it should and at the time it should—which was sign enough that he was doing a good job. In the meantime, the less contact with the CIA, the better. It meant less chance of exposure.

Massimo spent his life guarding against exposure. He could tell a dozen stories about the attentive porter, the bored housewife, the curious waitress who had stumbled onto a spy by accident. If you remembered at every hour of every day to keep your guard around the banal observer, you would simultaneously protect yourself from the true hunters of spies. Vigilance, however, had its cost. For one thing, if you were truly vigilant, you would permit yourself no intimate relationships. He knew of moles who took lovers or wives, but to do so was to invite peril into your life. Long ago he had concluded that it was better to struggle with loneliness and ennui than to risk such danger. No one knew him, and he knew no one.

The reward for this isolation was the billow of adrenaline that coursed through him when he stole something and gave it to the CIA. That stolen something might influence the lives of many people, or even—why should he not say so?—of a nation. With the adrenaline came a sensation of power that, however brief, made the game worth it. The phrase was one Massimo liked to repeat: *vale il gioco*, the game is worth it.

In Milan there was plenty of game. The extremists of Islam—the mujahidin and would-be mujahidin—made their spiritual home in the city's two large mosques, and they hoped, like Massimo, to attain a permissive invisibility. Some of the Islamists were soapbox insurgents, more hellfire than gunfire, but others were organizers for al-Qaeda and kindred groups. For them Milan was like a stop on a caravan route of old, both a haven and a hazard—a place to gather supplies, knowledge, and allies, but also a place where they might be found by enemies. Among their enemies were intelligence agents from their Middle Eastern homelands. The agents came to Milan, watched the Islamists, and sometimes accomplished other ends. The Syrians, for example, trafficked in cigarettes and stolen cars. The Iranians shopped for forbidden technology. The Libyans— well, it was hard to say about the Libyans: they might be behaving themselves, or they might be doing as the Iranians. The Israelis were in Milan too, and their willingness to assassinate and kidnap had long inspired the deepest fear in Islamic terrorists. Then there were spies from beyond the Middle East, like the Chinese "business-men" who sought industrial secrets and counterfeitable formulas, or the Russians, French, or Koreans who came to town for any number of reasons. In Milan, the game was all around you, if only you knew where to look.

The day after the call from the Spaniard, Massimo left for the meeting. It was his precautionary habit with such meetings to spend at least two hours beforehand *a piedi*. The likelihood that he would be followed was small, but it took patience to make sure, or at least it took patience not to be crude about it. You could, inel-egantly, walk down a street, double back, and note the faces, hair, coats, hats—whatever struck you—of the people you passed. Shoes were especially good; a person might shed a coat or a wig, but it was hard to change shoes on the go. Later, you could double back again, and anything familiar about the people you saw would give away your pursuer. Or you could hop on or off a bus just before it departed and see who else did the same. It was the stuff of movies, but sometimes Hollywood did not lie. These methods were not, however, the best for spotting a tail. If you were hunted with more than the mildest determination, you would have more than one follower, and when you "burned" the first by doubling back, a sec-ond would take over, and perhaps a third, a fourth, and a fifth, if the pursuers valued you enough. You could not double back for-ever. And even if you had only one follower, you marked yourself as having something to hide, a fact that might have been unknown to your pursuers, who maybe had been only a little suspicious of you. What you wanted was to convince them of your unexception-ality. To convince them took methods less crude. Walking was good and in Milan was easy since the city was as flat as Nature allowed and the streets had grown organically, Europeanly. A man could stroll, say, from the Convent of Santa Maria delle Grazie, where Leonardo's *The Last Supper* was sheltered, across town to the castle of the Sforzas, or in the other direction to the Navigli, the canal dis-trict, without laboring for breath and choosing from any number of smallish streets that would make spotting a follower easy.

So Massimo walked. The afternoon was cold, but there was no rain and even a bit of sun, an aberration for hibernal Milan. He enjoyed the fading light for a time, then, having seen no one of note on the street, he turned into a bookstore. He browsed, pulled a book off the shelf, and became to all appearances absorbed in it, but the door was never beyond his peripheral vision, and he noted everyone who entered. He watched to see whether any eyes flit-ted over him or worked too studiously to avoid him, but none did. Everyone gave the bland, aging man the small due he deserved. He left, walked some more, and entered a clothier's, where he exam-ined a shirt. Then it was a grocery, then an electronics superstore, then a sexy shop, as Italians call their stores for erotic assistance. Massimo enjoyed sexy shops, professionally speaking. They made people, even spies, uncomfortable, and a discomfited spy was one who made mistakes. At one or two stores he bought a bauble or two, which added a degree of realism to his errands. Amateurs never bought anything; they were too agitated. Now and then he caught a tram or a bus and rode it a few stops.

Long after day had turned to dark, he reached Piazzale Loreto, where Mussolini and his mistress had been hung from the canopy of a gas station after their encounter with Partisan bullets. Mas-simo descended into the Metro and boarded the red line. Five stops later he alighted and emerged at Piazza del Duomo, where Milan consents to be wantonly glorious. The Duomo is one of the largest houses of Christendom, yet its edifice is like a bride's mantilla—

unimaginably intricate but not burdensomely so, and productive of the feeling, even in Massimo, that it is good to be alive. He skirted the cathedral and across from its north transept passed through the glass doors of La Rinascente, a department store of the prospering middle class that could have been uprooted and dropped at Fifty-ninth and Lexington without the shoppers of Bloomingdale's ever noticing the difference. He rode up successive escalators past perfumes and stockings and cravats and tureens to the seventh floor, where he got off, bypassed the aisles of haute foodstuffs, and entered the modernist café and solarium, which might better have been called a nimbarium at that time of year. He took a table an olive's throw from the brilliantly lit rooftop of the Duomo and ordered a beer. The café was filled with its usual polyglot mix of tourists and shoppers whose conversations—German here, Japanese there—made it a good place for foreigners to meet without drawing attention. He tried to guess who among the patrons might be his contact. This was just for sport since his contact would recognize him. He sent a passport photo to the CIA every three years for this purpose.

He checked his watch: 19:15, a quarter of an hour to go. Punctuality was an obligation in this fraternity, even in Italy, where time is a fluid rather than a solid. If your contact did not arrive within a few minutes of the agreed-upon time, you left. There was a fallback arrangement in such cases, usually a return meeting the next day at the same time. Massimo sipped his beer, scanned the crowd again, then turned and looked at the Duomo's hundreds of lit spires and uncountable gargoyles and curlicues. He had seen them any number of times, but he still could not look at them without thinking of the thousands of men over five centuries who had strained to create them. When he turned back to the café, two men stood before him, smiling, apparently pleased at having caught him unawares. He cursed himself for his mental digression.

The men offered their hands, and one introduced himself in Spanish as Bob. He was stout with a smile that seemed to rise from his rounded belly. As soon became clear, he was serious about his work, but he did not appear to be encumbered by its seriousness, and one might even have called him merry. He was, as Massimo had guessed, the chief of the local CIA office. Massimo would later decline to describe Bob's companion, except to say that he apparently had no Spanish. In any case, Bob shifted the conversation to English, which the other man did understand, and explained that he needed help with a terrorist named Abu Omar. He did not linger over the details, nor would Massimo later. A spy prefers to share only that which is to his benefit, no more, and much of what he shares will not be true. This presents a conundrum for those who would understand espionage: Trust spies not at all, and one learns nothing. Trust them too much, and one might as well have learned nothing. It is probable that Massimo, who told his story to Guido Olimpio of *Corriere della Sera*, Italy's largest newspaper, aggrandized many and fabricated some of the details about his involvement with Bob. But he was verifiably honest about some of his work, and it is certain that something very like what he described occurred.

The three spies concluded their business in the café and left. They had work to do.

MASSIMO LEFT MILAN early the next morning for a city in whose police station he sometimes worked. When he arrived at the station, he gave his magnetized ID card to a guard, who scanned it and waved him inside. It was early, and the office was empty. He seated himself at a desk, turned on a computer, and glanced at the summary of news bulletins that greeted officers at the start of the day—nothing interesting this morning. Then he navigated through the computer network, entering passwords as needed, and came to the files he intended to steal. The office had safeguards to prevent the theft of data. For example, the computer on which he was working was offline so that documents could not be uploaded to the Internet, and to get printouts past the guards at the exit required signatures and stamps from superiors. But there were loopholes, and by exploiting one of these, Massimo was able to transfer the files to a computer with an Internet connection and upload them to an e-mail account. Then he shut down the computers and the rest of the day went about his regular duties, a model officer of the law. When he got back to Milan, he downloaded the files, whose subject was Abu Omar, and passed them to Bob.

Bob had also asked Massimo to establish a few prepaid mobile phone accounts that would not be traceable to "our men." For this task Massimo turned to a man at a phone company whom he had paid regularly over the years. The man arranged the accounts, and Massimo gave their subscription cards to Bob. As he got to know Bob a little, he learned that he led with pats rather than prods, that he made people feel as if they were one of his band, not merely under his dominion. Massimo began to trust Bob a little, which was pleasant although unnecessary. He would have played the game no matter who at the CIA called the plays.

As Massimo told the story, Bob eventually sent him to apply his research in the field. The day was Friday, February 14—St. Valentine's Day in the United States, though not in Italy, where the citizens do not need a holiday to declare their passion. Per Bob's instructions, Massimo went to Piazzale Maciachini, a large crossroads a few blocks from, and even more graceless than, the smaller Dergano. Maciachini's architecture was an homage to the line and box and the merciless efficiency of capital. Its establishments included a tattoo shop, a discount shoe store, and a gas station. Its denizens were mostly Arab and Asian, a reflection of the demography of the quarter, and the twangy strands of Middle Eastern music sprang gaily from a couple of storefronts. Massimo waited at a specified corner, and soon a small white station wagon drew alongside him. He nearly laughed when he saw the driver. Giorgio, as the man might be called, had worked with Massimo on another job some years earlier. He seemed pleased to see Massimo, and Massimo, knowing Giorgio was trustworthy, did not mind seeing him. It could be small, this world of spies.

Massimo got in the car, and Giorgio drove a few minutes, then stopped near Via Giuseppe Guerzoni, a narrow street of only a few blocks whose namesake had fought with Garibaldi in the Resurgence before retreating to a professorship of literature, where the battles were as contested but usually less bloody. A hundred meters of Via Guerzoni were lined by high walls on both sides. Behind one wall lay the grounds of Parco Bassi; behind the opposite wall, a plant nursery. It was a good block on which to encounter someone without witnesses. It was not, however, perfect. There were a couple of breaks in the walls through which people came and went, and Via Guerzoni terminated into Viale Jenner, a major ring road from which cars and pedestrians turned onto Guerzoni with some frequency. Worse, inside Parco Bassi stood a police station, and although the station's entrance lay on the opposite side of the park from Via Guerzoni, it was still disconcerting to think of the number of officers who sat a few meters away who could step out for a noon stroll and stumble onto the confrontation with Abu Omar in which Giorgio and Massimo were to take part.

As they waited for Abu Omar to arrive, Giorgio told Massimo that others on the team were keeping watch along his route and would alert the rest of the team when he passed by. But though Giorgio and Massimo waited several hours, the spotters never gave the alert. Abu Omar, the man of habit, had not been habitual. Eventually Giorgio and Massimo left.

The next day Massimo returned to Maciachini and was picked up by an affable American named Leon. They took a short drive around what Massimo liked to call "the operational area" and passed a couple of parked, occupied cars, which Massimo suspected were part of the operation. He would have liked to get a good look at their occupants, but he had no desire to be seen by anyone who didn't need to see him, so he turned his head. Leon stopped the car near Guerzoni and told Massimo that the team had already had a couple of near misses with Abu Omar. One time the job had been blown by a *gattara*, one of the old women of Italy whose self-imposed duties included the care of stray cats. On that occasion, just as Abu Omar was approaching his snatchers, a gat-tara stepped out of her doorway up the block with food for a *gat-tino*. This amused Massimo: a terrorist saved by a kitten. Leon also told Massimo that some of the spotters on the team were women, which Massimo found curious, possibly because his views on the female sex could not be called enlightened or possibly because in the Italian secret services relatively few spies were women. Now and then Leon exchanged calls with the other sentries, but again Abu Omar did not show, and after several hours the day's work was called off.

Before they parted, Leon asked Massimo to come to a certain address later that night for a meeting, and Massimo agreed. He thought he was being invited to a small conference, but when he arrived, he found to his horror that he was at a dinner party. A large group of spies about whom he knew nothing had "marked" him on entry, and among them were women—women!—whose pres-ence suggested frivolity even if they were part of the snatch team. His face reddened, and he might have cursed Leon and walked out had not Bob arrived at his shoulder, jovial and calming. Bob made a short speech to the group praising their work, then gave the floor to Leon, who talked about plans for the next few days, which included a break for everyone tomorrow, Sunday. When the speeches were done, Massimo did not linger.

He would later claim he was back on the stakeout Monday, which might have been true, and that he participated in the climac-tic events of that day, which was not. Although he talked a good line about soldiering away without recognition, the truth was that invisibility gnawed at him. He wanted his quarter hour of fame, even if the fame had to be obscured by anonymity, and he lied to get it. He did so on the assumption that the facts could not be veri-fied. The assumption was presumptuous. As it would turn out, it was shared by his co-workers.

THE FOURTH TIME Bob sent Ludwig to Abu Omar's neighborhood was Monday, February 17. This time, however, Bob said that rather than go to Piazza Dergano at ten o'clock, he should go to Piazzale Maciachini shortly before noon. Ludwig went as instructed. He was chaining his scooter to a post when a dark-colored Volkswagen, a Polo or Golf, he would later recall, stopped beside him. The driver was a man of about forty, short and stocky, even pudgy, with black hair. Lowering the passenger window, he said in Italian, "Ludwig, I'm Bob's friend. Get in!"

Ludwig stepped into the car, and they drove in silence through Dergano. At the intersection of Via Guerzoni and Via Bonomi, steps from a plaque that honored Partisans who died fighting Fascists in the Second World War, Stocky stopped the car. He told Ludwig, as Ludwig already knew, that Abu Omar would be walking toward them from Piazza Dergano, which lay to the east. When he came to the intersection where they were waiting, he would turn south onto Via Guerzoni. Stocky would let Abu Omar get a head start, then would essentially follow him down Guerzoni. He would not precisely follow him, because the first block of Guerzoni was one-way the wrong direction. So Stocky would loop around to the two-way portion of Guerzoni, overtake Abu Omar, and stop halfway down the block. There between the high walls a white cargo van would be parked on the sidewalk. Ludwig would get out, stop Abu Omar, and keep him by the van. Stocky said all of this briefly and then said no more. He was a rationer of words and had reached his quota. His Italian was flawless, which led Ludwig to think that if he was a foreigner, he was a well-practiced one.

Some minutes later, a call came on Stocky's phone. He said little to the caller—"Yes," "Alright"—and hung up.

"The subject is approaching," he said to Ludwig.

Ludwig looked at the clock on his phone and saw that it was ten or fifteen minutes past noon. A minute later, Stocky started the car, and a minute or two after that, Abu Omar appeared, long of beard and galabia. He passed briskly through the intersection, and just then Ludwig's phone rang. It was his personal phone, not the one Bob had given him, and the ringing, at that moment, was as jarring as if it had occurred in a movie theater. Stocky snapped at Ludwig not to answer it, which Ludwig did not have to be told, but the phone's silencer button was temperamental, and he had trouble working it, so he popped open the back of the phone in a fluster and after some fumbling yanked the battery out.

Stocky put the car in gear, circled around to Via Guerzoni, and drove past Abu Omar to the white van he had described. It was parked almost crosswise on the right-hand sidewalk, its nose nuzzled up to the wall. Ludwig stepped out of the car and was relieved to find the street deserted, save for the approaching Abu Omar. He hailed him, flashed his Carabinieri identification, and asked to see his papers.

"I don't speak Italian," Abu Omar answered in thickly accented English.

This surprised Ludwig, but he recovered and repeated his request in English. Abu Omar got out his passport, residency permit, and identification card and handed them over. He did not seem surprised at being stopped. Ludwig walked him toward the wall and stood facing the van with Abu Omar facing him, so that the Egyptian's back was to the van's sliding cargo door. Ludwig did not notice anyone in the cab up front. The back was windowless.

He quickly saw that Abu Omar's papers were in order, but he leafed through them slowly to give Bob's men in the van time to act. Several moments passed. He drew out his perusal further, giving each line of the documents as much scrutiny as it would bear, but still the men in the van did nothing. A minute crawled by, maybe two. Later Ludwig would not be sure whether his perception of time had been accurate or had become elongated, as happens to some people in car wrecks. He pulled the phone without a battery from his pocket and pretended to call a Carabinieri dispatcher to verify Abu Omar's information. This too he dragged out, but for some time still nothing happened.

Then, suddenly, the passenger door of the van's cab blasted open—or so it seemed—and a man leaned out and screamed in Italian, "*Hey!* What are you doing?" Notwithstanding that Ludwig had been hoping for something like this, he was caught completely by surprise. He jumped, and Abu Omar did too. In the next moment, or maybe it was the same, the sliding cargo door of the van tore open with a great rip and crash, and two men leaned out of the hold, grabbed Abu Omar by the shoulders and torso, and heaved him from the ground. They had him inside the van in a second— two seconds at most—and the door slammed shut as quickly as it had opened. A moment later the van's motor started and the van jerked back into the street, then sped north up Via Guerzoni.

Ludwig remained on the sidewalk, slack-jawed, Abu Omar's papers in one hand, the cell phone in the other. This was not what he had expected. Later he would not be able to say quite what he had expected, but the abruptness and ferocity were such a shock that his mind's ability to receive information seems to have been rattled out of him. Of the man in the passenger's seat, he would later be able to say only that he was puffy-faced and very tan or dark-skinned—Arab, if he had to guess. The men who had grabbed Abu Omar were nothing but heaving arms—faceless, incorporeal, more force than human. Abu Omar, he thought, had neither resisted nor shouted. There simply hadn't been time.

Stocky recalled him from his bewilderment by shouting, "Come on! Get in!" Ludwig got in the car, and Stocky U-turned, or maybe he had already U-turned—Ludwig was not attending to the details— and drove back north on Via Guerzoni. The van, already far ahead of them, was soon out of sight, and Stocky did not follow. He turned the car toward Piazzale Maciachini, and they drove in silence. Ludwig took the phone Bob had given him from his pocket and set it and Abu Omar's papers on the dashboard and left them there when he got out at Maciachini. Neither man said goodbye.

He unchained his scooter and rode to his apartment in Piazza Tricolore, named for the Italian flag. The green of the Tricolore is said to symbolize Italy's fertile valleys, the white its snow-covered Alps, the red its warriors' blood, spilled in the wars of Resurgence that freed Italy from foreign tyranny. Ludwig fed his dog, then himself, then went back to the office, just another carabiniere.

Chapter 2

A Sirocco

THE PROPHET MUHAMMAD gave the name Hassan, meaning "handsome" or "pleasant," to his first grandson. According to the *hadith*, the body of sayings that Muslims attribute to the Prophet, in the after-life Hassan is to lead the children of Paradise. "Osama," famously after September 11, 2001, is Arabic for "lion." "Mustafa" means "the chosen one." "Nasr" was the name of a house of the medieval Saffarid Dynasty in Persia and means "victory" in Arabic. A child born in Alexandria in 1963 and given the name Osama Mustafa Hassan Nasr did not want for decoration.

Alexandria is not what it once was. Founded by Alexander the Great as the port of supply for his Persian campaigns and the new capital of Egypt (replacing Memphis, which returned the snub by refusing to bury Alexander after his death), it became a city of Hellenic splendor and learning and remained so for nearly a thousand years. There Euclid fathered geometry, Herophilos begat anatomy, and Archimedes forwarded his theories on levers and screws. The intellectualism begat tolerance, and people of different creeds lived alongside one another in relative ease. Jews so thrived that for a time the Jewish community was the world's largest. The Septuagint was produced in Alexandria. Christians were later made welcome, albeit after a rough start: Mark the Evangelist was dragged through the streets until hardly enough was left of him to make a reliquary.

(A Coptic church in Alexandria still has what is purported to be his head, but the rest of his remains were smuggled to Venice in 828 to reside in St. Mark's Basilica.) It is a commonplace in the West that the town degenerated when the Arabs took it in 642 in the great wave of conquest that Muhammad began and his successors continued. But in fact by the time the Arabs arrived, Alexandria's Greco-Roman, Judeo-Christian institutions of knowledge, including its vast library, which was collected by copying the texts of every ship that called at harbor, had already dulled and decayed. The Arabs only accelerated the decline, principally by moving the capital to Cairo. The denouement continued for a millenium, and when Napoleon intruded into Egypt briefly in 1798, staying no longer than a Romantic poet on holiday, he found Alexander's mighty port a negligible fishing village.

Alexandria, like all Egypt, dates its encounter with modernity to the Ottoman invasion of 1801 and particularly to the rule of the first Ottoman pasha in Egypt, Muhammad Ali. The pasha's power knew few limits. Early in his reign, he invited hundreds of Mamluks, the former slave-soldiers who had come to dominate Egypt, to his citadel and, after fêting them, had the lot of them murdered—a precedent for dealing with opponents that later rulers of Egypt would appreciate. But Muhammad Ali was no mere brute. He built foundries and factories, hospitals and schools, canals and ports, bridges and railroads, and he turned the valley of the Nile into an immense cotton plantation. Alexandria became a great port once again, cotton flowing through its harbor to the world, and machines and experts to build a nation flowing in. The trade gave rise to subsidiary institutions, and Frenchmen, Ottomans, and Britons sailed to Alexandria and built resplendent banks and accounting firms and mansions in high colonial style. When the British relieved the Ottomans of their rule in 1882, the flavor of Alexandria became more European yet, and by the turn of the century, 100,000 foreigners lived there. They came for money but stayed for other reasons, like the tolerance that still prevailed among the citizens. Alexandria's Christian and Jewish communities, although reduced during the Arab and Ottoman reigns, had been well accepted by the Muslim majority, and the ecumenicalism continued under the British. Foreigners were also drawn by the Corniche, the graceful palm-lined promenade with the broad bay to one side and handsome cafés and clubs to the other—a sanctum in the heat and poverty of North Africa. After World War I, the British nominally returned control of Egypt to the Egyptians, but Britain retained an enormous influence over the country, and the Europeans who ran the nation's telegraph companies, railways, and trading houses remained. They continued to make their symbolic capital in Alexandria, which by the middle of the twentieth century was a pleasant bustle of a million beings.

So, at least, did Alexandria seem to Europeans—and to a minority of Egyptians who had profitably attached themselves to the Europeans. Most Egyptians had long held a different view, as Europeans could have seen if they had but looked. Flaubert, on visiting Alexandria in the mid-nineteenth century, observed complacently, "We have had bands of ten or twelve Arabs, advancing across the whole width of a street, break apart to let us pass," and he quoted his traveling companion, "Whatever happens, I'll be able to say that once in my life I had ten slaves to serve me and one to chase away the flies." Egyptians were less sanguine about chasing away their colonizers' flies. Among the many other debasements they endured, one for which Alexandria became known was sexual depravity. For a hundred years starting around the time of Flaubert, a class of Europeans came to Egypt generally and Alexandria particularly on what amounted to whoring safaris. Boys rented their mothers to tourists for a few pence, jesters had themselves buggered by animals for public amusement, and ghastly child brothels operated in Alexandria without censure into the middle of the twentieth century. A protagonist in a Lawrence Durrell novel famously synopsized the city "Alexandria, princess and whore. The royal city and the *anus mundi.*" This state of affairs did not endure.

IN 1952 a postman's son from Alexandria who had risen to a colonelcy in the army led a coup that overthrew King Faruk, the playboy descendant of Muhammad Ali and bootlick of Britain. Gamal Abdel Nasser soon expropriated nearly all of the property of Europeans in Egypt—their factories, their farms, their banks—some of which he gave to the people and some of which he reserved for the state. The foreigners bayed, but their governments were not ready to war with Nasser, and in the end the bayers left like concertgoers denied an encore. Their departure left a large economic and, in some ways, cultural void, particularly in Alexandria. Nasser thought he could fill it with a nimble socialism. The profits of Egyptian labor that had once passed to foreigners would be redirected to schools, hospitals, and other infrastructure, which would be built and run by and for Egyptians. There would be electricity, clean water, sewers, literacy, and jobs. Of course, there would be costs. Political opposition would have to be forbidden for a time, lest opponents hinder the young socialism, and persistent opponents might need re-education of a forceful, highly unpleasant kind. But Nasser was confident that once Egypt prospered, few would complain.

Had the oil of Kuwait lain beneath him or genius within him, he might have succeeded. Instead, in his eighteen years in power, his economy soured for want of natural resources and intelligent investment. The poor increasingly lived ten or twelve to a room, took unclean water from a tap down the block, endured open sewers where sidewalks should have been, and sent their illiterate or barely literate children into the streets to sell cigarette butts to supplement the family's meager income. The government meanwhile became an all-fingering oligarchy. Its elite, who grew fat skimming the national pot, gave thick contracts to cronies, sent their children to the best schools at home and abroad, and built sporting clubs and villas that outdid the superfluity of their colonial predecessors. The corruption trickled down to the lowest levels of government, and bakshish was required for even the smallest of services. To open a business, an entrepreneur had to grease the police and other protectors, and for a bright young graduate to find work often required similar lubrication. The bright and young who could leave, did. (The trend continues today: Mohamed Atta, before finding his calling in aeronautic murder, had taken a degree in architecture from Cairo University but left for better opportunities in Germany.) This all would have been bad enough with a stable demography, but in Egypt, as elsewhere in the Third World, the people were multiplying beyond the land's ability to sustain them and crowding into cities. One million Alexandrians in 1950 were four million by century's end.

Nasser's failure was God's opportunity. The instrument through which He seized it was a young teacher named Hassan al-Banna, who espoused the view that Muslims had succumbed not merely to the West's armies but, worse, to its worldliness. The Westerner, al-Banna said, worshipped wealth and put ambition over humility, individual over community, and the desires of the body above the needs of the soul. Centuries of colonialism had so contaminated Arabs that they desired little more than to be Westerners themselves. They claimed to be Muslim, but the Islam they practiced was a bastardization, and the wages of their sin were manifest: God had let His people wither under the rule of the corrupt. But al-Banna preached a cure: undiluted piety, which was to say a return to the true Islam of the Quran and hadith.

In 1928, a quarter of a century before Nasser's coup, al-Banna gave his developing philosophy (it took decades to fully flower into the above) a practical form by founding the Society of Muslim Brothers. "Society" was meant not in the cramped sense of a group or association but in the larger sense of a whole community: a neighborhood, a village, a nation. Al-Banna's Society offered not just religion but services the government had either failed to provide or provided badly. Where the government left people illiterate, the Brothers held night classes to teach them to read.

Where the government left people malnourished, the Brothers sold them meat at cost. Where the government neglected the worker who lost his job, the Brothers pooled wages into unemployment-insurance collectives. As the Brotherhood grew, it founded hospitals and schools, textile factories and labor unions, apartment co-ops and mosques, newspapers and magazines. In its totality, it approached the society al-Banna had imagined, and it was less corrupt than the government. If you stepped into a taxi with a Brother behind the wheel, you could be sure of getting to your destination without being cheated. If you applied for a loan from a Brother's bank, you need not pay a bribe; often you need not even pay interest. By the time Nasser took power at mid-century, the Brotherhood had grown to 2,000 chapters of perhaps 500,000 members, in a nation of 20 million.

The religion on offer from the Brothers was stern. *Islam* may be translated "surrender" or "submission," and a Brother's submission was expected to be complete. Centuries of Islamic study of the Quran and hadith had determined how a Muslim should dress (baggily, for one's sex should be hidden), what he ate (no swine, no carrion, no elephant), what he drank (no alcohol), what he read (mainly the Quran and hadith), the songs he sang (not many), the pictures he hung on his wall (also not many), how he prayed, how he played, to whom he talked. Sex, as in other authoritarian religions, was a fearsome power, and the Brothers dealt with it by obliterating woman, who was a trap to ensnare the male believer as he walked Islam's path. A woman in Brotherly society covered her hair, neck, trunk, arms, legs, feet, and ideally her face and hands. In schools and in hospitals, in mosques and in cafés, women were sequestered, often with back-of-the-bus care, when they were not banned outright. (Many women found comfort in these "protections," and a few were allowed positions of prominence in the group, provided they did not question man's preeminence—somewhat as women are in the Catholic Church.)

The Brotherhood held that those who strayed beyond the true

Islam were enemies of God, to be won back to Islam if they could, to be condemned if not. It followed that Egypt's government, which was far more secular than religious, would have to fall to *sharia*, the body of law based on the Quran and hadith that is best known in the West for the severing of thieving hands and of blasphemous heads. The most extreme of the Brothers wanted sharia not just in Egypt but in all the lands of the medieval caliphate. They envisioned a single holy kingdom, without individual states, stretching from North Africa to South Asia. The Brothers were divided on whether God's rule should be brought about peacefully or forcefully. Those who argued for peace said that if the Brotherhood continued its good works, fallen Muslims would see the superiority of piety and return to the true Islam, that over time the numbers of the pious would so increase that the governments of men would have to yield to that of God. Those who argued for force said no government would let the Brotherhood (or any other group) threaten its power and that Egypt in particular would crush the Brothers long before sharia arose. If the Brothers wanted to see God's kingdom on earth, they would have to put it there by the sword, as Muhammad had in Arabia and as his followers had across the Mediterranean and Near East. For authority they cited the Quran, which said, "The punishment of those who wage war against God and His Messenger and who strive with might and main for mischief throughout the land is execution, or crucifixion, or the cutting off of hands and feet from opposite sides, or exile from the land." And, "Fight in the cause of God those who fight you, but do not transgress limits; for God loves not transgressors. And slay them wherever you catch them, and turn them out from where they have turned you out."

Al-Banna wavered between violence and peace for several years, but at last he created a militia known as the Secret Apparatus, which might be thought of as the godfather of the many Islamic terrorist groups that have disturbed the world since. At its peak, the Apparatus probably had a few thousand militiamen and was hidden even from much of the Brotherhood. The Apparatchiks bombed hotels and restaurants frequented by the godless and murdered Egyptian officials and British soldiers. In 1948 the Apparatus assassinated King Faruk's prime minister, but Pyrrhically: six weeks later, the regime assassinated al-Banna. The Egyptian populace was as divided on the violence as the Brothers themselves had been. On the one hand, the people had little sympathy for the decadent autocrats who ruled them—they had got what was coming to them. On the other, murder was appalling, particularly of civilian innocents. For the next half century the Egyptian mood would wander between these two poles, now a little nearer one, now the other.

Although Nasser had given the Brothers a small role in his coup in 1952, once in power he signaled that his modern Egypt had no room for their archaic cause. Two years later a Brother tried to assassinate him as he addressed the nation from a square in Alexandria. (The would-be killer thought God would guide his bullets, but if He did, He was a poor Marksman: eight of His eight shots went awry.) Most Egyptians, still grateful to Nasser for liberating them from the kings of Egypt and England, deplored the attempt, and the liberals of Alexandria were aghast. Nasser responded by banning the Brotherhood, hanging six of its leaders, and sending nearly a thousand of its members (many innocent) to long terms in desert prisons. But an idea is hard to destroy, and the Brotherhood, though banned, did not die. Many of its activities continued underground, and some Brothers cautiously formed groups similar to the Brotherhood. The momentum behind sharia grew.

As Nasser's socialism faltered, it was his misfortune to bungle wars against Israel in 1956 and 1967. The failure of 1967, which he shared with Jordan and Syria, was so thorough that Arabs generally and Egyptians particularly asked how they had come to such desolation. Many throughout the Arab world found convincing the Brotherhood's argument that God was punishing them for leading wicked lives and leaving wicked men in power. They were also comforted by the Brotherhood's simple cure for these ills. Piety could be achieved by anyone, and collective piety, whether forcefully or peacefully expressed, was easier to understand as a national remedy than, say, improving the balance of trade or entering wiser geopolitical alliances. After 1967 a large subset of Muslims gravitated to the Brotherhood's hairshirt Islam like down-and-out Pentecostals to snake-handling.

NASSER DIED in 1970 of a bad heart. His successor, Anwar Sadat, wanted little of his socialism, and to balance the leftists who had multiplied under Nasser, he negotiated a détente with the Brothers. They renounced violence, and in exchange he paroled great batches of them from prison and let them preach and organize politically. Officially the group was still banned, but unofficially it was tolerated. Perhaps more important, other Islamist groups were given greater freedom to proselytize, and they gained members quickly. (An Islamist is a Muslim with a fundamentalist view of the Quran and a desire to share it. Some, but by no means all, Islamists believe violence is the best means of sharing.) Sadat seems not to have fully appreciated the power he was dealing with. He apparently thought Islamism was something like an unruly camel that could be pacified with a few dates and bridled, but it was much more akin to a virus, and he had just let it out of quarantine. In 1981, after making peace with Israel, he was assassinated by members of Jihad, one of several extremist groups that had evolved under his détente. Jihad had hoped the assassination would inspire a popular uprising that would culminate in sharia, as had happened in Iran in 1979, but the Jihadis overestimated the Egyptian enthusiasm for both blood and Islam.

Sadat was succeeded by Hosni Mubarak, who reverted to a Nasserian intolerance and imprisoned so many thousands of Islamists—some after trials but many not—that he had to build new prisons to house them. Many of the prisoners were tortured, and nearly all were brutalized in one form or another. They defended themselves with prayer and solidarity and found in their persecution a stigmata of their faith. Men who came to prison relatively moderate Islamists became zealots. Zealots were won over to violence. Some of the violent came to support not just insurrection but terrorism. These last reasoned that a government so barbaric could be defeated only with barbarity and that those who enabled the government, whether by action or inaction, would have to suffer. Mubarak had meant to pulverize the movement, but his maul had forged a stronger metal.

Jihad profited from these developments but not as fully as it might have. The group's leaders remained more interested in trying to decapitate and seize the state than in winning over the millions who might demand more enduring change, so Jihad remained a relatively small group. Not so al-Gamaa al-Islamiyya, whose bland name—the Islamic Group—belied its wallop. Founded in 1973 during Sadat's liberalization, Gamaa flourished among students at Egypt's badly underfunded and overcrowded universities. Its founders had learned from the Brotherhood's provision of services, and they offered tutorials, cheap textbooks, lecture notes, and rides to classes. Within a few years, Gamaa was powerful enough to force colleges to adopt Islamist curricula, segregate classes by sex, and silence heretical professors. Eventually, Gamaa expanded its work beyond universities and became more critical of government repression and corruption, thereby earning a more diverse, less educated membership. After Sadat's assassination, Mubarak imprisoned so many Gamaa militants that it took the group most of a decade to rebuild. When it did, the fire of the prisons was inside it.

In 1992 Gamaa began a campaign of terror against the godless, bombing liquor stores, video stores, and discos and murdering Jews, Copts (the Christians of Egypt), anti-Islamist intellectuals, policemen, mayors, judges, and, most spectacularly, the speaker of Parliament and the head of the counterterror police. In 1995, working with Jihad, Gamaa nearly killed President Mubarak in Ethiopia. In five years in the 1990s, Gamaa and its allies killed more than 1,200 people. Egypt was terrorized.

Mubarak's trouble in stopping Gamaa was that it consisted of hundreds of unhierarchical cells, one of which was no sooner undone than another struck. His eventual solution was to kill whom he could and terrorize everyone else. When his security services learned a terrorist was in a certain house, they might assault the whole block. When a terrorist wasn't found, his family might be tortured. After Mubarak's near assassination in Ethiopia, his security services kidnapped the thirteen-year-old son of a Jihad leader, sodomized him on camera, then blackmailed him to spy on Islamists by threatening to show photos of the sodomy to his family. He was made to recruit another child, who was abused in the same way. (When Islamists discovered their spying, Ayman al-Zawahiri, Jihad's leader and soon to be second-in-command of al-Qaeda, had the boys executed on videotape and distributed copies as a warning to would-be traitors.) In his crackdown, Mubarak killed at least several hundred people and probably thousands. His interior minister, Zaki Badr, said that if he had his way, he would kill every Islamist militant in Egypt. "I only want to kill one percent of the population," he explained moderately.

By 1997, Mubarak had crippled Gamaa, and a large faction of its leaders struck the same deal with him that the Muslim Brotherhood had with Sadat—renouncing violence for parole. Not all of Gamaa's leaders supported the accord. In particular those who had fled Egypt urged their brothers not to surrender, then condemned them when they did and thereafter saw themselves as the last repository of resistance to Mubarak. In November of 1997, several months after the accord, exiles of Gamaa and Jihad organized the slaughter of fifty-eight foreign tourists and four Egyptians at the Temple of Hatshepsut in Luxor. As the terrorists had intended, Egyptian tourism was devastated for years. As they had not intended, Egyptian opinion turned on them for good. What little popular support Gamaa had retained through the years of bombings and murder evaporated, and terrorism as a political solution was thoroughly discredited. In 2003 another set of imprisoned Gamaa leaders would be persuaded to renounce violence, and Mubarak, for the moment at least, could claim to have won the fight against terrorism. But for an Egyptian set on violence, there were other places to practice it.

THE ALEXANDRIA to which Osama Mustafa Hassan Nasr was born in 1963 was in some respects unrecognizable even from the Alexandria of nine years earlier, when the attempt on President Nasser was made there. The Muslim Brotherhood had thrived in Alexandria—an equal and opposite reaction to the city's extreme Westernization—and when Westerners were banished from Alexandrian society in the late 1950s and Nasser failed to fill their place, Islamists did. There followed several merciful changes, like the closing of child brothels and the extension of aid to the poor. But there were less welcome changes, like subordination of women and attacks on Jews and Copts. By the end of the 1950s, the Jews were forced to flee en masse, and a community that had survived millennia was, suddenly, gone. Over time nightclubs and beach huts closed, swimsuits yielded to robes and headscarves, and many inland Egyptians who once summered in the city's cool, literal and metaphorical, stayed away. The city's boulevards fissured with the national and local economies. Its edifices turned scabrous. In a generation, multicultural, polyglot, and (for some) prosperous Alexandria was remade unicultural, monoglot, and shabby.

The family of Osama Nasr belonged to Alexandria's remnant upper middle class. His father was a public prosecutor, his mother a housewife. They were Muslim, but they wore their religion without ado, as one wears socks. The young Nasr was a small, sickly child with a slightly deformed femur and was preyed on by schoolyard toughs, whom he learned to fight off. He also learned to take refuge in introversion and long hours of reading in the municipal library. In high school he became enamored of Marxism and its photogenic propagator Che Guevara, and he decided politics was the life for him. Since Egypt was short on parties of the revolutionary Left, and since his breeding was more liberal than Communist anyway, he joined New Wafd, a reformist party that called cautiously on Mubarak to hold fair elections, restore civil liberties, and guarantee human rights. He took to writing articles for a party organ called *Wafd Youth* and thought he had a way with words. But as his involvement in Wafd deepened, he became repulsed by its internal power struggles. After watching party members throw fists and chairs at one another at one caucus, he resigned his membership and looked elsewhere for answers to Egypt's problems.

He found them in the Islamism that was thriving all around him. Its devout solution, he saw, was cleaner and more empowering than Wafd's messier politics. He attended Islamist lectures and read the Quran with new eyes and had soon made a political conversion so complete that he declared himself a Salafist. Salafism might be thought of as a fundamentalist's fundamentalism. It holds that Islam was perfect during the Prophet's generation and the two generations following and that everything added to Islam has been, in essence, rot. He felt no queerness about replacing his previous liberal, democratic view with a conservative, authoritarian one. He felt, he later said, as if he had come home. His parents felt differently. They said his increasing fundamentalism could end only in trouble, and they urged him to desist. His father even locked him inside the house one night to keep him from going to an Islamist gathering. But he persisted, and in the end they let him be. Later his younger brother Hitham chose the same Islamist path. It was symptomatic of the movement's power that it could draw both sons of a comfortably establishmentarian family.

Nasr enrolled at the University of Alexandria and, his religious rebellion notwithstanding, elected to study law as his father had done. But his passion for Islam was a distraction, and he failed several classes. He almost certainly joined the university's very active chapter of Gamaa, although he would later sometimes say he did not. He also attended a smallish, radical mosque that was less regulated than the larger mosques at which the government appointed imams and supplied sermons. To keep the less regulated mosques in check, the government sent informers and police to watch them. In 1988, when Nasr was in his third year of law school, he was invited to give a sermon at the mosque, and he chose for his topic political repression in Egypt. As he spoke, he warmed to his subject and denounced several high officials by name. After the service, three policemen in plainclothes met him at the door.

"You got enthusiastic," one said. "You are under arrest."

Years later he would say he did not realize he could be arrested for vigorous sermonizing, a perhaps plausible claim since at that moment, several years after Sadat's assassination and several before Gamaa's campaign of terror, Mubarak's government was arresting extremists with some discrimination. The policemen put him in a car and drove him to an office of the State Security Service, where he was made to sit on a chair and blindfolded. An officer started screaming questions at him: When did he begin attending Islamist lectures? Who did he know in the mosques? Why did he speak against the government? Who told him to do it? The officer punctuated his questions with blows—first with fists, then with a stick. After some hours, the questions stopped, and Nasr was driven to a different office and the questions were repeated, only this time the punctuations were shocks with an electrified rod. At the end of the interrogation, he was driven from Alexandria to Tora Prison, outside Cairo, where he was held without trial for six months. During that time he met many Islamists, including members of Gamaa and Jihad, whose piety and commitment to achieving sharia impressed him. Probably he was further radicalized under their influence.

At the end of his term, he was returned to the State Security office in Alexandria, and an officer said he hoped Nasr's adventure had taught him a thing or two about public speaking. He also said that, having met a lot of members of Gamaa, Nasr would make a useful spy, and he offered him a job as a paid informer. Nasr would later say that he refused, that even had he been tempted by money or fear, Islam forbade him to betray his brothers. He would not be untrue to Islam. But the officer insisted, and when Nasr hesitated, the officer said he would jail his whole family if he did not take the job. Nasr asked for two weeks to think about it—a play for time, he later said—and the officer granted his request and sent him home.

He resolved to flee. He got a student passport, which was not hard to do, but getting across the border was another matter because he was probably now on a registry of political criminals forbidden to leave the country. He heard, however, that a new port of entry had been opened at Nuweiba, on the Gulf of Aqaba, and that either it had no computers or its computers were not yet linked to central computers in Cairo. He decided to try it. He shed his Islamist clothing for Western wear, trimmed his beard, and left Alexandria without telling anyone, not even his family. At Nuweiba he passed through the border station without incident. Either the stories he had heard about the computers were true, or he was lucky.

He traveled by ferry to Jordan, which was not the destination he ultimately desired but would have to do for the moment. His ultimate desire was Europe or, better still, America. He would later say that at the time he practically worshipped the United States and that he had earlier applied for visas to study there and in Europe but had been turned down. Evidently he was untroubled by the contradiction between his admiration of the West and Islamism's critique of it—a contradiction not entirely unusual in Islamism, several of whose luminaries were educated in or took refuge in the West.

Nasr had chosen Jordan as expedient because it was nearby, because an Egyptian did not need a visa to enter, and because it was poor enough that one could live there on little money. His plan was to work, save, and make his way to Europe to resume his legal studies. But Jordan turned out to be much poorer than he had thought—startlingly so to a bourgeois Alexandrian—and jobs were scarce for a young man who not only knew no trade but had never held a job in his life. The job he finally found was carrying rocks at a construction site, but he was too delicate for the task and soon quit. When he failed to find other work that appealed to him, he asked his Jordanian acquaintances where else he should look, and they told him Yemen. The Yemenis, they said, had a large, uneducated population and were hiring Arabs from abroad to teach their children the Quran. Egyptians did not need a visa to get into Yemen, so after two or three months he quit Jordan for Sanaa. Yemen, however, proved to be already awash in Egyptians teaching the Quran. He managed to find work at a school library, which was more agreeable than hauling rocks, but the pay was slight and he could save nothing. Again he asked the natives where he might find a better life, and this time he was told to go to Pakistan. Pakistan, the Yemenis said, is the place for a man like you. After four or five months in Yemen, he went.

PESHAWAR IS the capital of Pakistan's North-West Frontier Province. From its tin-makers' shops and wool-spinning factories, it is a short and not particularly steep climb to the Khyber Pass, beyond which lies the chaos of Afghanistan, battlefield of greater powers since history began. Afghanistan's modern convulsions started in 1978, when the country fell into civil war, which prompted the Soviet Union to invade and the United States to arm the opposing rebels, some of whom, notoriously, saw in their struggle not merely a resistance to empire but a jihad. The war was—is, depending on how one defines it—nasty, brutish, and long, and millions of shelled and pauperized Afghans sought refuge over the Khyber Pass. With them came holy warriors who set up headquarters in Peshawar, from which they raised money, bought arms, launched raids into the motherland, and in some cases trained terrorists for attacks beyond Afghanistan. The noncombatants who overfilled Peshawar lived in sweeping tent cities whose pitiful sight moved governments and individuals across the Middle East to send money for their relief. For a time Peshawar was, if not quite soaked, at least damp in riyals from Saudi Arabia and Yemen, dinars from Algeria and Jordan, and pounds from Egypt and Syria. Much of the money went to schools, clinics, and charities of the food-and-shelter variety, but much also went to jihad. For terrorists, it was convenient to smudge the line between humanitarian and military aid, and so charities arose that gave long-grain rice with one hand and long-range sniper rifles with the other.

Arabs sometimes traveled to Peshawar with similarly smudged intentions. A man might start from Jeddah for a madrassa and end in a Tora Bora tunnel. Sometimes the madrassa had been a ruse all along, but sometimes the man had been moved to fight only after arriving. Or maybe he had known he would fight but not that he would become a terrorist. Some Arab governments, eager to be rid of their zealots, paid their way to Peshawar. Egypt even released a few extremists from prison on condition they enplane for Pakistan. Evidently the governments assumed that the zealots would be killed in the war, or their zeal would shrivel in the Afghan wastes, or the rich among them—Osama bin Laden being the epitome—would run through their fortunes arming God's battalions. The Arab governments thought little, and the American government less, about the men who would survive the Afghan wars. They did not foresee that the zealots' passion for sharia might be intensified or that they would become practiced in guerrilla warfare and connected to an international network of terroristic financiers, recruiters, and plotters. The blowback, infamously, would concuss the Hudson and Potomac.

Peshawar had many exiles from Egypt, in large part because the repression by Mubarak after Sadat's assassination sent many Islamists fleeing at just the time when Peshawar was most in need of humanitarians and soldiers. One Egyptian who came to Peshawar, for a few months in 1980 and a few years from 1986, was Ayman al-Zawahiri. A surgeon, he dressed the wounds of refugees in a Red Crescent hospital but eventually developed an enthusiasm for mass murder. From Peshawar (and elsewhere beyond Egypt) he rebuilt Egyptian Jihad, allied the group with bin Laden's al-Qaeda, and plotted a righteous apocalypse, which was partially realized with the massacres at Luxor in 1997 and in the United States in 2001.

Nasr would later say he went to Peshawar strictly as a humanitarian. In his telling, he found work teaching the Quran and Arabic in a school run by a Kuwaiti charity. The charity also disbursed food and clothes but, Nasr said, no arms. It was one of the happiest periods of his life, but it did not last long. The Islamists of his acquaintance in Peshawar often had energetic discussions about whether violence should be used as a political tool, and he, so he said, took the negative view. When there was a terrorist attack, he would speak out against it. Word of his opposition to terrorism spread, and the extremists on the other side of the argument eventually told him he must join the jihad. He, more lover than fighter, refused. They threatened him with death, and in 1991 he left, an innocent run out of another country.

He flew to Tirana, the capital of Albania, which was not the Western Europe of his dreams but which was, at last, Europe. He was given a grant of asylum on grounds of his persecution in Egypt. It was a convulsive time in the Balkans. The Berlin Wall had fallen only two years earlier, the Iron Curtain was being dismantled fold by fold, and ugly, austere Albania, one of the most closed of the Warsaw Pact nations, was moving from the stifling impoverishment of Communism to the unruly impoverishment of frontier capitalism. Meanwhile, next door, Yugoslavia was rending itself to tatters, and the rumbles of the nearby war shook Albania uncomfortably.

Nasr chose Albania because it was predominantly Muslim—the religion was a legacy of long Ottoman rule—although Albanians tended to exercise their faith more lightly than he. One of the country's poets had written, "Churches and mosques you shall not heed. Albanism is Albania's creed." And indeed the Muslim majority and

Christian minority had got on well enough over the years. Muslims and Christians overseas, however, thought that half a century of godless Communism had been detrimental to Albanian spirituality, and on Communism's fall they sent missionaries to share their gods. Most ministered pacifically, teaching the Quran or Bible and digging wells or plowing furrows in hope of showing the goodness of their faith. But some Islamic charities, particularly those staffed by exiles from Gamaa and Jihad, had designs beyond winning converts.

A dozen or so of the Islamic charities were funded on Saudi wealth, and at one of these, the Human Relief and Reconstruction Agency, Nasr found work, the nature of which is not known. (Years later he would not be talkative about his job there.) He attended a mosque and in its chaste environs met an Albanian woman, Marsela Glina, whom he married after a brief courtship. He did not speak Albanian, and she did not speak Arabic. Their shared language was pidgin English. Theirs may have been one of those marriages, not uncommon among Islamists, in which a few phrases of male command and female assent made up much of the conversation. Glina apparently was not as fervent in her Islam as he, but when he insisted she wear a veil, she assented. He was thirty years old, she eighteen.

In 1994 the Human Relief and Reconstruction Agency ran out of money, and Nasr decided to establish himself as a man of commerce in the anarchic market. A photo from the time shows him cutting the figure of a businessman in a suit of double breast and effulgent sheen, his head cropped as close as a kiwi, his cheeks, which were starting to hint at chubby, smooth as gourds. An excellent mustache made the man. It was full and dark and wider than the lip on which it sat, in the style of men of the Levant and firehouses of West Virginia, and suggestive of virility. If he had worn a beard and galabia in Pakistan, as was likely, he had got rid of them somewhere along the way. He intended to open a grocery, but he ran into some sort of difficulty and abandoned the idea. He then settled on a sausage factory, which got as far as a $20,000 expenditure for equipment. Where the money came from is not clear, though perhaps from Arab entrepreneurs abroad. The factory, however, also ran into problems and never ground a gram of meat, and he seized next on a bakery. Not long before the ovens were to be fired, in August of 1995, he was visited by a police officer who told him he was needed at the station for a small matter—it would take only five or ten minutes. Nasr assumed one of his workers had gotten into trouble, and he was happy enough to help straighten it out. But on arriving at the station, he was transferred to the custody of the Shërbimi Informativ Kombëtar, the State Intelligence Service, or SHIK, and interrogated. As he told the story later, SHIK's officers asked what he was doing in Albania, what he had done in Pakistan, why he had left Egypt, whether Islamists in Albania planned to attack Egypt's foreign minister when he visited Tirana that week, and much else besides. It was obvious to Nasr that the officers knew a lot about him, which surprised him. He had thought the post-Communist government was barely functioning, and yet here it had conducted what seemed a very competent surveillance of him. He was questioned for days, often repetitively, he assumed to catch him in a mistake, and when his answers displeased, the officers struck him with fists or the handle of a gun.

In the end they told him they knew he was clean. He was not sure whether they had known so all along or had concluded so from the interrogation. They then said that as a businessman he commanded the respect of many people and would make a valuable informer. They asked him to be their spy and said that in return they would help him with the application for citizenship he had recently submitted. The pitch was not much different from the one he had been given in Alexandria six years earlier. He refused this one too (so he later claimed) and somewhat to his surprise they let him go.

When he got home, he told his wife he had been detained

because of a mix-up at the station: the police had thought he was using his business as a front to smuggle drugs, and it had taken time to convince them of their error. Evidently husband and wife did not discuss the topic in detail because years later Marsela Glina would be able to say little more than that the arrest had soured him on Albania and he decided they should leave. A few weeks after his release he traveled to Romania and, liking what he saw, applied for residency for himself, Glina, and their daughter Sara, who had been born a year or two earlier. Another child was on the way. The Romanians were apparently inclined to grant Nasr asylum on grounds of his persecution in Egypt, but they had no need for another housewife and two more children, and the application was denied.

Nasr devised another exit strategy. At the end of 1995 or the start of 1996 he bought tickets for the family to fly to Cairo via Munich. He was told that to change planes in Germany, they would need German visas, so, as he later told the story (with possible embellishment), he bribed an officer to let them through the emigration checkpoint. He had also been told that Glina was too far pregnant to be allowed on a commercial flight, so he had her dress in thick, baggy clothes to disguise her state. Nobody stopped her as they boarded. Later, when the flight began its descent to Munich, Glina pretended to go into labor, on Nasr's instructions. She must have been convincing, because when they landed an emergency crew was waiting at the jetway. A German officer came aboard and said Glina would be taken to a hospital but since Nasr and his daughter had no entry papers, they would have to stay on the plane. When Nasr refused to be separated from his wife, the airline crew begged him not to make a scene. They were in enough trouble, they said, for transporting a woman in so advanced a pregnancy. He ignored them and demanded asylum. Under German law, he was permitted to remain in the country while the government evaluated his claim, so the whole family was taken to the hospital, where doctors discovered that Glina was only seven months pregnant and not in labor. They were sent to a refugee center outside Munich to await the outcome of their plea.

While they waited, Glina gave birth to a boy, whom they named Omar. In history, Omar was a seventh-century caliph who evicted Christians and Jews from Arabia and reserved Mecca and Medina for Muslims ever after. The production of a male heir earned Nasr the honorific Abu Omar, Father of Omar. Technically speaking, he was also Abu Sara, but that title would not have been considered a decoration; Glina, on Sara's birth, had become Umm Sara, Mother of Sara. Some months later Germany denied their request and they appealed. By the time the denial was finally affirmed, they had spent nearly a year and a half in the refugee center. What Abu Omar, forbidden to work, did with himself while Glina attended to home and children remains a matter of speculation. Confinement, however, was not good for their marriage. They quarreled often, and after one tremendous fight, they divorced in the fashion permitted by some schools of Islam—the husband solemnly declaring himself through with his wife, whereupon God recognizes their partition. For reasons unknown, they did not also dissolve their civil marriage in Albania. When their final plea was denied, Glina returned to Tirana with the children, but Abu Omar's future lay elsewhere. He would, he determined, slip into Italy.

THE IMMIGRANT to Milan travels with the arc of history. Over the millennia, bands of strangers from the North battled their way through Gaul, stopped in Milan with little more intention than to repair mail and plate, and ended up staying centuries. From the South warriors also came, meaning to fill their carts with grain before crossing the Alps, but they stayed too, and their blood still runs in Milanese veins. Strangers have often ruled, but not, historically speaking, for long. Thus the Celts supplanted the foundational Ligurians and were defeated in turn by the Romans, who succumbed to Hannibal and the Carthaginians, who were beaten in a return match by the Romans, who were followed, in loose succession, by Attila, the Goths, the Lombards, Barbarossa, the Spaniards, the Austrians, Napoleon, and Silvio Berlusconi. This crossroads history is reflected in the city's name, which probably comes from the Celtic "Mid-lan," or "place in between"—what we would call a hub—and has made a hash of Milan's culture, so that one may enter a Milanese trattoria and find both *pomodoro a strica-sale*, which is salt-rubbed tomato, a legacy of the South, and *cotoletta alla milanese*, a breaded veal cutlet that any Northern European would recognize as wiener schnitzel.

The greatest immigration in Milanese history began just after World War II, when the U.S. Marshall Plan and newly liberated Italian capital remade northern Italy. Milan had been a seat of industry before the war—there was a saying that while Rome had a church on every corner, every corner in Milan had a bank—but after the war Milan was *the* seat of Italian enterprise. Breda made trains in the city, Falck forged iron and steel, Alfa Romeo built its sinuous coupes (the company's logo, the serpent and red cross, was the coat of arms of Milan's Visconti), and Pirelli, the colossus, made tires. Italians called the nation's economic rebirth *il miracolo*, and "the miracle" became a byword for Milan. To man the enormous factories, Milan imported a proletariat of hundreds of thousands. Most came from Lombardy and other regions of the North, but a large minority came from the Mezzogiorno, the land of the Midday, which was to say south of Rome. In Italy, the cultural split between North and South approximates that of the United States. Northerners of that era called Southerners *terroni*, which was derived from *terra*, "soil," and could be translated as "clodhopper." In the Northern stereotype, terroni were indolent, dirty, clannish, and slow. Northerners liked to say that Africa began at Rome, and even that great urb irritated many Northerners with its inefficiency and bureaucracy. The Milanesi believed themselves mislaid in Italy. Their city, they said, was an international capital in search of a country.

The migrants who powered the miracle were greeted in Milan with wretched apartments in sunless streets, the worst of schools, and the blackjacks of police. Long after the miracle went bust, a haphazard jumble of tenements might still be called a *Corea*, because so many of them had been built during the Korean War, which coincided with the miracle. The bars where Southerners drank, having been kicked out, sometimes literally, of "Northern" bars, were called *le casbah* or *i suq*. The neighborhood of Dergano, where Abu Omar would settle, had its share of *le Coree*, *le casbah*, and *i suq*.

The immigrants helped make Milan the richest city in Italy and one of the richest in Europe. Milan faltered a bit in the early 1970s, when the factories were boarded up and the jobs sent to places where workers did not ask for union wages and Sundays off, but the recovery was quick. Other industries had flourished during the miracle: banking, technology, publishing, television, and above all the one with which Milan became synonymous—*la moda*, fashion. Since at least the sixteenth century, Europeans had appreciated Milan's skill with gloves and hats, ribbons and point lace, leather and jewelry. Sellers of these wares in England were called Milaners, and the English, with their genetic oblivion to the foreign accent, pronounced and eventually spelled the word "milliners." (Later the meaning of "milliner" was restricted from a general haberdasher to a maker of ladies' hats.) Toward the end of the miracle, Milan's small fashion workshops transformed themselves into great manufacturers, and Armani, Versace, Dolce & Gabbana, and Prada became global clichés for taste. To visit Milan was to know this. The shoes of the Milanesi were a little pointier than those of other metropolitans, their heels were a little higher, their pants a little blacker, their stockings runless, their hemlines revelatory of neither too little nor too much leg. Their glasses were isosceles.

The workforce of the more sophisticated second boom required a supporting proletariat as the first boom had, and many of the janitors and maids and nannies again had to be imported. The immigrants were poor, unskilled, and from families that had until recently worked the land, only this time the land was not metaphorical Africa but the thing itself: Morocco, Tunisia, Egypt, Ethiopia, Senegal, and Mali; also Albania, Ukraine, Turkey, Syria, Pakistan, Bangladesh, Thailand, and China. The newcomers found Milan no more hospitable than their predecessors had a few decades earlier. Hundreds, perhaps thousands, made their first Milanese homes in abandoned factories or idled trains. When these quarters became an embarrassment to the city, the local government steered its guests into metal, container-like shelters that broiled in summer, froze in winter, and were ringed with barbed wire and uplifting rules, like bans on card-playing and women.

In time, some immigrants established themselves in cheap apartments and lent their floors to newer arrivals, some of whom in turn established themselves and lent their floors. A few opened businesses. Because their neighborhoods tended to be run-down and their clothes not *alla moda*, many Italians associated the new residents with shabbiness and crime. The same Italians tended also to be disturbed when they emerged from certain Metro stops into a welter of Indo-Aryan and Semitic languages spoken by men socializing on the hoof outside kebab shops where not long ago pizzerias had been. Politicians saw opportunity in such changes, and mean, small-minded parties of the Right rose to power in Lombardy on "the immigrant threat." Their hysterics about the contamination of the culture, the language, and the race were exactly those of such parties everywhere. By the end of the 1990s, residents of foreign extraction made up just ten percent of Milan—chicken scratch by the standards of major American or British cities—but to hear the xenophobes, one would have thought it was forty-nine percent and counting. For immigrants, the result was hostility, discrimination in housing and jobs, and stops by police on the street to check their identification—dark skin being cause enough for suspicion.

These affronts came to be symbolized in a homeless Moroccan named Driss Moussafir, who in 1993 was killed, along with four policemen and firemen, by a Mafia car bomb that exploded near a park in which he was sleeping. From the reaction of many Milanesi, one would hardly have known Moussafir was among the dead. The mayor's eulogy of the victims omitted him, high officials paid their respects at the coffins of the Italians but ignored his, and police and news reports listed him last, when mentioning him at all, and usually referred to the others by name but to him only as "an immigrant." There were protests of this neglect, and the city grudgingly agreed to name a school for him where immigrants were taught Italian. The sign on the school misspelled his name "Woussafir." *Moussafir* meant "traveler."

To the devout Muslim, Milan presented additional trials, not least of which was a constant assault by the human, particularly the female, form. In Milan one inhaled sex as in Alexandria one inhaled sea air. The prevailing advertising strategy—for clothes and perfumes, cars and stereos, dishwashers and paper clips—could be summarized in the word "cleavage," if cleavage were no longer associated with the naturally occurring breast. The breast of advertisual Milan was watermelonious, demanding, and seemed to spring from every other billboard and shop window. There were buttocks to match, their display meant to give a dromedary assurance that in this desert of life a man could mount such as those and ride a long time before reaching the next oasis (where, apparently, he bought paper clips). Ten minutes' residence in mammarian, gluteal Milan could prove a trial for the devout Muslim. The city made manifest what came of a people who deadened themselves to God, and the newly arrived Islamist was not surprised to learn that the country's great cathedrals were filled only when a Nobel laureate or a foreign philharmonic visited. Many a pious Muslim dove for cover in Milan's mosques.

ABU OMAR CHOSE Italy partly because he knew a few Islamists who had settled there and partly because Italy, notwithstanding the growing hostility to immigrants, was still relatively liberal with grants of political asylum. Italy was also easy to get to. The refugee center outside Munich was not much policed, nor were voyages by train, so he simply bought a ticket on the express to Rome and one day in May of 1997 was off. On arrival, he requested asylum from his persecutors in Egypt. Apparently he did not mention his fraternization with the mujahidin of Peshawar or his arrest by the SHIK of Albania. He was given temporary quarters and help with his petition by the Jesuit Center of Rome, which abutted Vignola's Church of the Most Holy Name of Jesus, not far from the Vatican—an irony for an Islamist with, as would later be discovered, a growing distaste for infidels.

It would take the Italian government years to weigh Abu Omar's petition, during which time he was free to move about. He settled in the town of Latina, south of Rome, where friends helped him find work of an unknown kind in the town's mosque and where he began to preach, apparently as a lay imam. From time to time he visited cities in the North. Milan did not exactly enchant him, but its Muslim community was large, many of its members were fervent, and he knew the imam of one of the city's largest mosques, a Gamaa man named Abu Imad, with whom he had been imprisoned in Egypt.

In the summer of 2000 he left Latina and settled in Milan. For an Islamist who had fled Egypt, worked for Islam in Peshawar, and been suspected of terrorism in Albania, it was not an innocuous time to go to Milan. Indeed, at that particular moment, Abu Omar could almost have settled in a training camp in Kandahar with less suspicion.

Chapter 3

The Enemy Within

IN FEBRUARY of 1993 a Pakistani-Kuwaiti named Ramzi Yousef, who had come to the United States on a plea of political asylum and was at large pending a hearing on his plea, blew up a Ryder truck filled with fertilizer under the north tower of the World Trade Center. He was driven by a loathing of American sponsorship of Israel on the one hand and the brutal semi-secular regimes of the Middle East on the other. He had hoped to topple the north tower into its twin and bring down both in a hail of death—an outcome that would have to wait eight years and other attackers—but he succeeded in killing six, injuring more than a thousand, and, unintentionally, impelling the police of Milan to take a closer look at the deranged Islam in their midst.

Yousef, it turned out, was a disciple of Omar Abdel-Rahman, known as the Blind Sheikh, who was perhaps the preeminent leader-in-exile of Gamaa. The Blind Sheikh had been expelled from Egypt for issuing fatwas condoning terrorism and had spent time among the mujahidin of Pakistan and the terrorists of Sudan. At one time he counted among his friends Ayman al-Zawahiri and Osama bin Laden. In 1990 he settled in the United States, notwithstanding that he was on the State Department's terrorist watch list. "We must be terrorists," he told a Brooklyn audience a few weeks before the Trade Center bombing. "We must terrorize the enemies of Islam to frighten them and disturb them and shake the earth under their feet." While Yousef plotted to blow up the Trade Center, the Blind Sheikh conspired to blow up the headquarters of the United Nations and bridges and tunnels into Manhattan. He was arrested in 1993, tried in 1995, and elected by a dozen infidels to life membership in an institution of correction. Yousef had by then fled to Pakistan, from which he advanced a plot with his uncle, Khalid Sheikh Mohammed, the future evil genius of the September 11 attacks, to blow up several airliners over the Pacific Ocean. Instead, Yousef was caught in Islamabad and extradited to New York, where he too received the sentence of a lifetime.

The FBI's investigation of Yousef and the Blind Sheikh turned up a tangle of connections between their cell in greater New York and fanatics abroad. Among the connections were phone calls to Milan. The calls would have been interesting in any case, but they were the more so because Yousef sometimes traveled on a falsified Italian passport. The men on the Milan end of the calls were parishioners of the Islamic Cultural Institute, which was the formal name of the mosque on Viale Jenner that Abu Omar would later frequent. The mosque had been founded only a few years before the Trade Center bombing, in 1988, by one Ibrahim Saad, a devotee of the Blind Sheikh and another Egyptian whose commitment to Gamaa had made him unwelcome at home. On coming to Italy, Saad had been frustrated that Milan, unlike other large cities in Europe, had no correspondingly large mosque and that its small mosques lacked the proper zeal. He got a stake from an Islamic businessman—an Eritrean named Idris Ahmed Nasreddin, who had become rich in Milan and Switzerland and whom the U.S. Treasury Department would later declare, for a time, a financier of terrorists—and opened the mosque in an old garage. Squeezed among low-rent *tabaccherie* on Viale Jenner, the garage was bland, modern, forgettable, and advertised by no sign. One passed through its iron gate and into another world, like entering a gay bar in Biloxi.

Saad set himself up as imam, but his power was soon eclipsed by that of another exiled Egyptian loyal to the Blind Sheikh and Gamaa. He, Anwar Shaaban, was a naval engineer of middle age whose appearance suggested a withered cornstalk: widen the nose of Osama bin Laden, set glasses on it, and there was Shaaban. He had waged jihad in Afghanistan, then had come to Italy a political refugee, ungratefully. Western godlessness and materialism disgusted him, as did the slumbering, as he saw it, of Milan's Muslims in the West's downy bed. He preached a brimstone Islam.

Not long after Shaaban became imam, the Bosnian War erupted in the former Yugoslavia, just across the Adriatic from Italy. The advantage in the war lay with well-armed Serbia (sometimes aided by Croatia, sometimes opposed by it), which set to brutally cleansing itself of Bosnian grime. Europe and the United States stood aloof, as if the Serbs were only spring cleaning, and embargoed arms to all sides—an act neutral on its face but in truth punitive to the weaker Bosnians. Muslim nations tended to be less numb to the Serbs' many atrocities (they did not mind the Bosnians' so much), because half of Bosnians were Muslim and nearly all of the Serbs were Christian. Many Muslims called for a defense of their brothers and sisters in Bosnia and Herzegovina, and Islamists of more malignant temperament saw in that defense a chance to establish a terrorist beachhead in the West. Bosnia, they believed, could become Europe's Afghanistan.

Shaaban was one of the earliest such visionaries. He had many allies in Europe, and together they began to marshal an army, first from the ex-mujahidin who had found sanctuary in Europe but soon from young men new to jihad. Shaaban's congregation—predominantly young, male, and immigrant—made a fine recruiting ground. Many of his parishioners were barely literate in their own language, let alone the new one, were bewildered by the differences from their homeland, and were further isolated by the slights and sneers of Italians. They turned to Shaaban for all manner of spiritual and practical guidance: how to keep one's faith among unbelievers, how to renew a visa, how to find a flat, how to import a bride. Their trust in him and their alienation from Italy made them receptive to his talk of holy war against the West and of the ennobling deprivations of battlefield camps. He enlisted many such men and began taking them to Bosnia and returning for more. His allies from other European cities did the same.

To pay for their travel, camp supplies, and arms, he raised money from rich Arabs in Europe and the Middle East and supplemented their donations by extorting halal butchers in Milan on threat of torching their shops. Some of the arms purchases were elaborate. According to one terrorist, Shaaban's circle bought assault rifles, grenades, and missiles from traders in Russia (where weapons circulated freely after the fall of Communism), shipped the arms by sea to Italy, and forwarded them to Croatia and from there on to Bosnia. Swiss corporations owned by Arabs and Pakistanis oversaw the logistics, and Swiss banks handled the payments, some of which were also filtered through charities like the Lucerne-based Mother Teresa of Calcutta Center. (In Milan, Shaaban had his own charity, Il Paradiso, whose relief also tended to ordnance.) The chain of supply for the arms shipments was, however, deemed too complicated, and simpler ones were established.

The army that Shaaban and his colleagues assembled in Bosnia was known as the Islamic Brigade. Although Shaaban consulted on battlefield strategy, his chief role when in Bosnia seems to have been more inspirational than strategic. He was something like the high priest of the mujahidin, and troops were apparently moved by his antebellum harangues. In combat they proved fearless or nearly so, but their first assaults were debacles. Men whose dearest wish is to be martyred are not necessarily assets under fire. They are wont to charge fortified machine-gun positions without a preceding artillery bombardment or covering small-arms fire. Their efficacy is then hindered by being cut in half. It would take time for the commanders of the Islamic Brigade to convince their men to sell their lives dearly.

Martyrdom, however, was good for recruiting. Hardly had a martyr, if martyred spectacularly, departed for his seventy-two wives than tales of him spread across the Islamic world. (The hadith, contrary to common report, does not specify that the seventy-two are virgins.) As such tales multiplied, Shaaban began to draw men from not just Milan but across Italy, then from other European countries, then from throughout the Arab world. There is a story of an Egyptian peasant, one Mahmoud al-Saidi, who desired to make jihad in Bosnia and asked his village elders how he might do so. Go to Milan, they told him, and seek out Anwar Shaaban. So al-Saidi sold his only cow to pay the airfare.

At its peak, the Islamic Brigade may have numbered five thousand men and was supported by tens of millions of dollars—by some accounts, hundreds of millions of dollars—that flowed through dozens of Islamic charities. Eventually the Brigadiers learned to fight. They won small battles, then larger ones, often with ugly consequences. After taking a village, they might smash the pews of its ancient church, burn its relics, and deface centuries-old murals by excising the head of a Madonna or modifying the genitalia of her Son. Worse might be in store for the villagers. When the Brigade took the Croat town of Miletici, with the loss of one of their fighters, they told their Croat captives that their dead comrade's life had been worth those of four infidels. They selected four young men of the town, tortured them horrifically (the face of one was sliced off), and slit their throats. As the blood rushed from them, the executioners caught it in bowls and ladled it back over their heads. After another battle, at Podsijelovo, they tortured several Serbian fighters, then paired them off, armed them with knives, and ordered them to fight each other to the death. Those who refused or who became injured were decapitated with chainsaws or cleavers. Those who survived were made to kiss the severed heads, which the mujahidin nailed to trees. The Islamists evidently videotaped some of the sport at Podsijelovo; recordings of it were reported to have circulated among the faithful. A witness to another battle said that afterward the holy warriors and their wives took turns shooting two Serbian prisoners, then decapitated them and played soccer with the heads.

"They like to kill," said a Bosnian soldier who fought with them. "Whenever they could kill with their knives, they would do so."

Shaaban's martial endeavors were not restricted to Bosnia. He also sent recruits to al-Qaeda's training camps in Afghanistan. He showed them how to get visas to Pakistan on religious grounds, then arranged their travel, often by way of an intermediate point like Geneva or Zurich so as to cloud their point of origin. In Islamabad or Peshawar, al-Qaeda would take charge of them. One recruit Shaaban directed in this manner was L'Houssaine Kherchtou, a baker from Morocco who had come to Milan to make money, not war, but who was won over to jihad by Shaaban. Sent to Pakistan, Kherchtou was tutored by al-Qaeda in surveillance, electronics, and the use of rifles, anti-aircraft guns, mines, and explosives. Some of the lessons supposedly took place at bin Laden's house in Peshawar. After a tour of duty in Afghanistan, al-Qaeda sent Kherchtou to Kenya and Sudan to become bin Laden's personal pilot, but when al-Qaeda cut off his flying lessons and refused to pay for an operation for his wife, he defected. His testimony in a U.S. courtroom helped convict some of the al-Qaedans behind the bombings of U.S. embassies in Kenya and Tanzania in 1998.

Shaaban also gave miscellaneous help to terrorists in Tunisia, Egypt, and the United States. One of those terrorists was Ramzi Yousef, who, it seemed, had spent time in Milan before bombing the World Trade Center and who may have received his false Italian passport from Shaaban or one of his lieutenants. This intercourse, along with the phone calls between Milan and the cell in New York, was among the earliest clues that all was not well behind the garage door on Viale Jenner.

THE POLICE of Italy were then, as today, the least encumbered in Western Europe when it came to tapping phones. They tapped about 100,000 a year, for a total of 1.5 million calls. The per capita rate, about 170 taps for every 100,000 people, was three times that of their nearest rival in Western Europe and orders of magnitude beyond the rate—1 for every 100,000 people—claimed by the United States. After the emergence of disturbing signs from Viale Jenner, the counterterrorists at Milan's DIGOS tapped the phones of Shaaban and his acolytes. What they heard disturbed them, and they opened an investigation they called Sphinx. For more than a year, they listened and watched.

They learned that a cornerstone of Shaaban's work was a document-forging enterprise that served terrorists across Europe and that may have created Yousef's false passport. When fully realized, the enterprise was highly compartmentalized: one team acquired blank documents, another team doctored them, another delivered them to the newly minted man. Often the doctorers did not know the true name of the client or his mission, and the client did not know who had made his papers. Where possible, the forgers supplied complementary papers: a passport and a visa, a driver's license and a residency permit. The best documents were stolen ones that had already been used and stamped and that the forgers altered only slightly—for example by inserting a new picture but leaving the name and other data untouched. If the client could pass for a European, say an olive-skinned Italian or Spaniard, he was given a European identity. If time and money permitted, he would test his new papers by traveling to an irrelevant country before going to his ultimate destination, which, if he were stopped, would not be discovered. Apparently the Milanese scribes were skillful, because their clients were not often stopped. The scribes' work refreshed the meaning of the "fine Italian hand," which term had arisen in the Quattrocento to compliment Florentine copyists of the Bible but which now applied to copyists guided by a superseding text.

Their raw material—the blank or stolen documents—generally came from abroad. One of their sources was a Serbian gang that burgled city halls in Belgium, which tended to be lightly guarded on weekends and which held hundreds of blank passports, driver's licenses, and official stamps. The Serbs sold the passports for between $700 and $2,300 apiece, and often they passed through several buyers before reaching Milan. Other documents came from purse-snatchers and hotel burglars, notably in Madrid, Toronto, and Cairo, and still others from officials in Yemen, Algeria, and Albania who sympathized with the terrorists or were persuaded to sympathy by a small consideration. Because no international authority kept a list of stolen passports, terrorists who needed to move across borders undetected could remake themselves again and again. After 2001, investigators would find terrorists who had changed their identities seventy times.

"Sphinx" is ancient Greek for "to strangle"—the sphinxes of Egypt may have been given their name for the way lionesses attack the throats of their prey—and in June of 1995 the investigators of Operation Sphinx moved to strangle the flow of documents and men through Shaaban's network with raids on six dozen premises across northern Italy. Ten Egyptians and a Palestinian were arrested, and more arrests followed, though not of Shaaban, who was in Bosnia at the time. At the mosque on Viale Jenner, the police found forgers' tools and documents in the process of being falsified: a Pakistani visa, employee ID cards for a Saudi "relief" commission in Bosnia, and, under a writing pad on Shaaban's desk, a doctored Danish passport for a Moroccan terrorist named Karim Said Atmani. In all, Sphinx yielded more than a hundred false documents.

Atmani's bogus passport was illustrative of the reach of Shaaban's network. Atmani was an Afghan War veteran and member of the Groupe Islamique Armé, which terrorized Algeria for roughly the same reasons Gamaa and Jihad terrorized Egypt. (The GIA's attacks were so indiscriminate that even Osama bin Laden recommended the group restrain itself, lest it tarnish the image of jihad.) In Italy, Atmani helped Shaaban shepherd his lambs from Milan to the Bosnian War, and he was himself a fighter in the Islamic Brigade. Afterward he conspired with GIA terrorists in France, some of whom robbed armored trucks to fund their terrorism, and others of whom carried out fatal attacks in 1995 and 1996 in the Paris Métro and elsewhere. He then stowed away to Canada on a Liberian-flagged cargo ship and with other exiles in Montreal dreamed up terror attacks, like the bombing of a Jewish neighborhood and the release of chemical poisons into the city's Metro. Though unrealized, the schemes were not all fantasies. Atmani's roommate was Ahmed Ressam, the would-be Millennium Bomber, who was caught while crossing the Canadian-American border on his way to attack Los Angeles International Airport in 1999. Atmani was also caught trying to cross the border, in his case at Niagara Falls some months earlier. He had been using a falsified Canadian passport. Canada, however, merely deported him to Bosnia, where, like other Islamic Brigadiers, he had been given citizenship for his service in the war.

Before his deportation, Atmani shared power in the Montreal cell with another GIA commander, Fateh Kamel, an Algerian naturalized by Canada in 1993. Kamel had trained in al-Qaeda's camps in Afghanistan, and from Montreal he jetted to at least a dozen cities in Europe to raise men and money for the Bosnian cause. He also served as a sometime commander of the Islamic Brigade. After the war, he worked with the same GIA terrorists in France with whom Atmani worked. One of his jobs was to supply them with false identity papers, some of which he may have gotten from his friend Anwar Shaaban. After the GIA's attacks on the Paris Métro in 1995, Kamel shuttled between Paris and Milan to stimulate more slaughter. Unfortunately for him, his visits to Italy overlapped with the investigations of DIGOS, whose agents listened as he ordered bombs to be built.

"What are you afraid of?" he said to one hesitant builder. "That everything will explode in your house? Tell me at least if Mahmoud has gotten the gas canister."

Another time, he boasted, "I do not fear death . . . because the jihad is the jihad, and to kill is easy for me."

These and other conversations moved the Italians, in November of 1996, to raid more apartments and arrest more Islamists, who were found to possess gas canisters, remote-control transmitters, and other materials in the bomb-making line.

Eventually Kamel was arrested in Jordan, and Atmani was arrested in Bosnia. Both were extradited to France and convicted of conspiracy and trafficking in false documents, but their sentences were short—eight years for Kamel, five for Atmani—and were further shortened for good behavior in prison. On release, they returned to Canada, which ruffled many Canadians, but since Canada had itself passed Atmani back to Bosnia, the nation's moral footing was, like its dollar, weak.

All of this was to say that until Operation Sphinx marooned Anwar Shaaban in Bosnia, he and the mosque on Viale Jenner were part of a web of terrorism whose filaments stretched around the globe. He made the most of his marooning by becoming more of a battlefield general than he had been. He apparently led the Islamists to victory at the battle of Vozuca, after which he magnanimously gave captives the chance to convert to Islam and tortured only those who refused. By some accounts, he took his eldest son, who was maybe twelve, into battle with him and trained his two younger sons for the day they might bear the familial arms. A few years later two of the sons may have been videotaped in Chechnya hacking the heads off Russian soldiers—"a way to harden them," said a terrorist who saw the tape and thought it was they.

Several months after being marooned, Shaaban planned a rendezvous with his good friend Talaat Fuad Qassim, honorifically Abu Talal, who was usually regarded as Gamaa's leader in Europe. Abu Talal was yet another expatriate of Egypt, which had sentenced him to death in absentia for plotting to murder anti-Islamist officials and intellectuals. He had spent time among the mujahidin of Afghanistan before seeking refuge in Denmark, and he was as important a creator and quartermaster of the Islamic Brigade as Shaaban. Shaaban had once brought him to Italy on a kind of violent guest-lectureship. "The Muslim," Abu Talal had told his audience, "has the duty to be a terrorist, in the sense that he has to terrorize the enemies of Allah to represent peace and security to the faithful. Terrorism against the enemies of God is a duty in our religion." Mubarak's Egypt had pressed Denmark to extradite Abu Talal, but the Danes were deaf to Egypt's plea, as they were to the pleas of every state that might murder a returnee. The Danes did not, however, leave Abu Talal to his own devices. After he and several followers were suspected of conspiring in the Trade Center bombing of 1993, Danish police arrested them and found in their apartments a chemical commonly used in bombs, formulas for building bombs, and sketches of what seemed to be bombing targets in Europe. Fingerprints on some of the seized items matched fingerprints on bomb-making manuals that had been seized in New York from one of the would-be Trade Center bombers. But Denmark, like most other countries, had no law against possessing such chemicals or formulas or sketches of buildings, and the fingerprints, while suggestive, proved nothing. The Danish police had to release the suspects. Insult to the police's injury, the ministry for immigration later granted two of them asylum on grounds of persecution in Egypt.

In September of 1995 Abu Talal flew on a false passport from Copenhagen to Zagreb, the capital of Croatia. He intended to continue overland to Bosnia to meet Shaaban and other leaders of the Brigade. Instead, he disappeared. He was the first subject—an honorand of sorts, although he did not live long enough to understand his place of honor—of a new American program that had been created for men just such as him.

IN 1883 a larcenist and embezzler named Frederick Ker, who had been indicted in Chicago for his sins, fled to Peru, and the U.S. government hired the Pinkerton Detective Agency to bring him back. Peru and the United States had recently signed an extradition treaty, and Pinkerton's agent carried the proper paperwork to extradite Ker, but when he arrived in Lima, he found it occupied by Chile, and there were no Peruvian officials to whom he could submit his papers. So he extemporized. With the help of the Chilean army, he kidnapped Ker and put him on a U.S. warship bound for Honolulu, then on another ship bound for San Francisco, then on a train to Chicago, where he was convicted. Ker appealed his conviction on grounds that his kidnapping and return violated the extradition treaty, but the U.S. Supreme Court ruled against him. In *Ker v. Illinois,* the court held that trial courts need be concerned only with trying a fugitive like Ker, not with how he had come to trial. It did not matter that Congress and the president had made law an extradition treaty that outlawed kidnapping. Mere law, the justices implied, was no match against the imperative of prosecuting a lawbreaker.

The better part of a century passed before the Supreme Court reconsidered *Ker.* In 1952 a murderer named Shirley Collins objected to having been kidnapped in Chicago (apparently association with that city was bad for fugitives) by Michigan lawmen, who took him home and won his conviction. On Collins's appeal, the Supreme Court upheld his conviction and said that nothing in the Constitution prevented such a kidnapping. What mattered, again, was that he came to trial, not how. Although Collins's case occurred entirely within American borders, the court in *Frisbie v. Collins* made clear that the same principle applied to international abductions. The principle and supporting ones became known as the *Ker-Frisbie* doctrine, which permitted bounty hunters to snatch suspects abroad and return them to trial in America. Later rulings very slightly limited the doctrine. For example, an appellate court (though not the Supreme Court) held that a *Ker-Frisbie* kidnapping might be invalidated if the kidnappers engaged in "conduct of a most shocking and outrageous character," like torture.

The doctrine seems to have been used only occasionally over the next few decades. Its most famous victim was a Mexican doctor, Humberto Alvarez-Machain, who, the U.S. Drug Enforcement

Administration alleged, helped Mexican drug lords prolong the suffering of a DEA agent whom they tortured to death in 1985. The DEA put out a bounty on Alvarez-Machain, and soldiers of fortune kidnapped him in Guadalajara and flew him to El Paso. At trial the doctor argued that he had to be set free because the DEA had violated the extradition treaty between the United States and Mexico. Unlike the Peruvian government in the case of Frederick Ker, the Mexican government had objected to the trespass on its sovereignty, which, along with other developments in international law and due process, seemed to give greater potency to the argument that it was illegal for U.S. agents to violate an extradition treaty. But in *United States v. Alvarez-Machain* the Supreme Court not only upheld *Ker-Frisbie* but expanded the doctrine by saying that Mexico had been aware of it for some time and could have demanded the treaty be changed to rule out *Ker-Frisbie* kidnappings. (The court had a fanciful notion of the balance of power between Mexico and the United States.) Alvarez-Machain was eventually acquitted at trial, whereupon he returned to Mexico, sued the United States, and won an award, which, however, was reversed by the Supreme Court. The U.S. government, the court ruled, could not be held liable for crimes it committed beyond its borders—a precedent with consequences decades later.

After *Alvarez-Machain*, governmental kidnappings of this sort came to be known in U.S. law enforcement circles as Mexican extraditions. More delicate law enforcers preferred the term "rendition," which rested awkwardly on the modern ear but which had a long pedigree. In his *Eikonoklastes* of 1649, Milton spoke of Charles I's "rendition afterward to the Scotch Army," and the *Encyclopædia Britannica* of 1860 spoke of the "rendition of fugitive slaves by the Northern States." "To render" shared a root with "to rend," *to tear*, and was kin to "to surrender," *to give up*.

The impolite term "Mexican extradition" did, however, accurately reflect that such kidnappings were reserved for the Third World. The First World would not tolerate them. In 1983 the U.S.

government charged billionaire Marc Rich with dodging $50 million in taxes, and he fled to Switzerland. The U.S. Marshals Service put together a plan to kidnap him, but the Swiss government got wind of it and warned, in a general way, that anyone who attempted a kidnapping in Switzerland would be arrested and prosecuted. The Marshals abandoned their plan. (Rich was eventually pardoned by Bill Clinton in the inglorious last hours of his presidency.)

An evolution in American renditions occurred in 1986. The year before, terrorists hijacked the cruise ship *Achille Lauro*, murdered a wheelchair-bound American, and extorted a plane to fly them from Egypt to Tunisia. On President Reagan's orders, U.S. fighter jets forced the plane to land at a NATO air base in Sicily, where Reagan demanded the hijackers be handed over to America. But the Italian government entertained the idea that Sicily was part of Italy and that consequently it had jurisdiction over the hijackers. Moreover, even if Italy had wanted to give them to the United States, the U.S.-Italian extradition treaty applied, which meant the hijackers had the right to argue against extradition in court and Italy had the right to consider the merits of the case. While the White House and Palazzo Chigi debated these points, armed Navy SEALs faced off against armed Italian troops on the Sicilian tarmac. In the end Reagan reluctantly agreed that Italy was not Mexico and backed down. Italy then enraged him further by releasing two of the hijackers (apparently to appease Egypt, which feared violence otherwise), but it tried and convicted the remaining three.

The *Achille Lauro* hijacking was not the only terrorist affront to American might in 1985. A few months earlier, terrorists had hijacked a TWA flight from Athens to Rome, killed a U.S. Navy diver onboard, and negotiated safe passage to Beirut, where they did not much trouble to hide themselves. They were not extradited, however, because the Lebanese government was devastated by civil war and could not exert its sovereignty.

Reagan responded in 1986 by signing National Security Decision Directive 207, which, lest *Ker-Frisbie* not be clear enough, appears to have authorized the CIA to capture terrorists abroad and bring them to trial in the United States. The directive has never been made public. At roughly the same time, the CIA founded a Counterterrorist Center, which over the next two decades would lead the American struggle against terrorism. Reagan's directive was a mixed blessing for the CIA. Most of the agency's officials seem to have been pleased by the authority to render, but many of them did not look forward to trying the renderees in court. The CIA was not in the habit of gathering evidence in a way that would hold up at trial, and even if it had been, its officers had no desire to make their evidence public, to say nothing of how either the evidence or the defendant had been collected.

A way around these problems was for the CIA to collaborate with the FBI, which was used to gathering court-worthy evidence and to having its methods made public. There were drawbacks, however, to such a collaboration. For one thing, the two agencies had an old and caustic rivalry, and many of their principals detested one another. Previous attempts at cooperation had fared badly. For another, FBI director William Webster had reservations about kidnappings à la *Ker-Frisbie* by the FBI or anyone else. Although the FBI had been given authority by Congress to arrest terrorists anywhere in the world, Webster believed Congress had meant the FBI to make those arrests only with the approval of the countries where the terrorists were found or, lacking such approval, to make them in international territory. Webster may also have reasoned (and as a former judge, was in a place to know) that *Ker-Frisbie* had survived so long because it had been invoked infrequently. If the CIA and FBI began rendering alleged terrorists willy-nilly the Supreme Court might reverse parts of the doctrine. He also believed, correctly, that a rendition from a country with a functioning government was a violation of international law, whatever U.S. law had to say about it, and that it would be politically foolish to outrage other countries with renditions unless they were absolutely necessary. He said he would let the FBI help the CIA but only on his terms. The CIA agreed, perhaps reluctantly.

Their first collaboration was Operation Goldenrod. The reference—botanic? chromatic? phallic?—is unknown. Their prey was Fawaz Yunis, a Lebanese terrorist who in 1985 had hijacked a Jordanian plane and blown it up after releasing its passengers and crew. Yunis had since been seen in Beirut, where he had taken up drug dealing. In 1987 the CIA and FBI lured him to Cyprus and from there to a yacht offshore. The bait was a narcotics deal and two female FBI agents whom the bashful American press later described as "casually attired"—they were wearing shorts and halter tops. Once in international waters, the FBI put cuffs on Yunis, transferred him to a Navy munitions ship, and flew him to Andrews Air Force Base. He was tried in federal court on evidence the FBI had collected and was sentenced to thirty years. (He served half that before being deported to Lebanon in 2005.)

Although the operation had come off well, for the next few years the United States seems to have rendered minimally—partly because it was not every day that horny, avaricious terrorists could be lured to international waters and partly because Reagan appointed the cautious Webster director of the CIA. In 1992 Reagan's successor, the first President Bush, issued National Security Directive 77, which apparently clarified and may have expanded the CIA's authority to seize alleged terrorists abroad. NSD-77, however, remains secret. President Clinton, succeeding Bush, not only let NSD-77 stand but put it to work immediately. His national security adviser, Richard Clarke, later wrote, "The first time I proposed a snatch, in 1993, the White House Counsel, Lloyd Cutler, demanded a meeting with the President to explain how it violated international law. Clinton had seemed to be siding with Cutler until Al Gore belatedly joined the meeting, having just flown overnight from South Africa. Clinton recapped the arguments on both sides for Gore: 'Lloyd says this. Dick says that.' Gore laughed and said, 'That's a no-brainer. Of course it's a violation of international law. That's why it's a covert action. The guy is a terrorist. Go grab his ass.' " It is believed that Clinton ordered the guy's ass grabbed but that the CIA did not succeed in the grabbing. Clinton clarified his rendition policy in Presidential Decision Directive 39, which he issued in June 1995, shortly after the bombing of the federal building in Oklahoma City. The directive said that when the CIA, FBI, and other law enforcers wanted to bring alleged terrorists to trial in the United States, they should first seek the help, or at least the consent, of the nations where the terrorists were found. The FBI had captured Ramzi Yousef with such help from Pakistan a few months earlier. If, however, those nations did not cooperate, Clinton authorized U.S. officers to seize and render the terrorists on their own.

At about the same time the staff of Clinton issued his directive, his National Security Council conceived a new kind of rendition. Rather than catch a man and take him, as ordinarily, to the United States, the CIA could catch him and take him, extraordinarily, to a third country—an "extraordinary rendition." The third countries would be dictatorships that could imprison or execute the victims as they chose. They might also interrogate the victims with more success than the CIA since they knew their homegrown terrorists well and could also be more savage in their questioning. Savagery, according to some (though not all) advocates of extraordinary rendition, could produce better intelligence than more-decorous questioning. But getting intelligence seems to have been a far subsidiary goal to getting rid of terrorists without due process. The promise of extraordinary rendition was that it would be swift and neat. The CIA had only to get a tip about a terrorist, snatch him, ship him, and walk away. Clinton approved, and the first victim was Abu Talal.

WHEN ABU TALAL left Denmark for Bosnia in September of 1995, an intelligence service tipped the CIA that he was on the move. It is not known which service gave the tip, although it seems not to have been Denmark's. The Danes' views on the rights of man—to wit, that every man had them—had long been a frustration to the CIA. A more likely source was Egypt's Mukhabarat, which monitored Abu Talal closely. The CIA had been interested in Abu Talal because of the links between his cell and the World Trade Center bombing and because he was suspected of having had a hand in the near assassination of Mubarak in Ethiopia earlier in 1995. His role atop Gamaa also made him a prize. When the CIA recommended his rendition to the National Security Council, the NSC, Clinton chairing, approved. The United States seems not to have told Denmark that it was about to kidnap one of its wards.

After arriving in Zagreb, Abu Talal met with an interpreter and retired to his lodgings, where, next morning, he was arrested by Croat police. He was never heard from again. When his associates asked the government why he had been taken and what had come of him, the Croats said he had been arrested for entering the country on a false passport, had been held for six days, then had been deported. They did not say from which port. Narrowly speaking, the Croats were not lying, for they did indeed hold Abu Talal for some days, after which they deported him—to the custody of the United States. Precisely what happened next has never been discovered. Officials in the Egyptian government later said off the record that Abu Talal was taken to a U.S. warship in the Adriatic, interrogated for two days, then passed to Egypt. If it was true that the Americans held him only two days, they almost certainly had little interest in getting information from him. A thorough interrogation would have taken several days at the least and probably, given how devoted he was to his cause, weeks or months. A brief detention suggested the United States wanted him only to disappear. Whatever the case, he was given to Egypt, and Egypt advertised the fact, both to threaten other terrorists and to chide Europe for harboring them. Abu Talal's fate is unknown, but almost certainly he was interrogated, brutalized, and destroyed. Egypt never

said more about the affair, and the United States never said anything at all.

A month after Abu Talal disappeared, in October of 1995, a suicide bombed a police station in the Croatian town of Rijeka. The
assault was poorly executed. The station was perched on high
ground, above Victims of Fascism Street, and the bomber could
not get his homely Fiat Mirafiori with Italian license plates close
enough to the building to bring it down. He wounded twenty-
nine people but succeeded in killing only himself. Next day, news
bureaus in Cairo received a fax from Gamaa saying the bombing
was a retaliation for the capture of Abu Talal. "Close the gates of
hell which you have opened upon yourselves," the facsimilists
warned. "Otherwise you will be starting a war the end of which
only God knows."

When investigators sifted through the remains of the suicide's
car, they found shreds of a Canadian passport, which, with other
clues, enabled them to identify the disintegrated bomber as one
John Fawzan. Fawzan had been a member of Gamaa employed by
an Islamic relief agency that was later found to have paid for the
training of Ramzi Yousef's Trade Center bombers. Fawzan was also
a follower of Anwar Shaaban; he had lived outside Milan and frequented the mosque on Viale Jenner. DIGOS had investigated him
in Operation Sphinx, but he had left Italy before they learned much
about him. His suicide had been orchestrated by another Gamaa
member from Milan, Hassan al-Sharif Mahmud Saad, a favorite of
Anwar Shaaban. Like Shaaban, Saad traveled often between Italy
and Bosnia. It was Saad's Fiat Mirafiori that Fawzan had used,
Saad having upgraded to a Mercedes from which he watched the
bombing. Investigators also learned that the device Fawzan used
to blow himself up was similar to ones with which Ramzi Yousef
had meant to blow up airliners over the Pacific—another sign, perhaps, of the internationalization of the Milanese network.

After Fawzan's bombing, Shaaban and Saad aspired to another
attack, probably against NATO peacekeepers, who were arriving in

Bosnia because the war was at last drawing to a close. NATO's calls for the Islamic Brigade to disband, just when it was finding its fighting form, infuriated Shaaban, who would no longer be able to train terrorists in Bosnia with impunity. As NATO moved in, some of the Brigade's fighters left for the next great holy war in Chechnya, while some, like Karim Atmani and Fateh Kamel, settled in Western countries and others, like Shaaban, stayed in Bosnia to continue the fight. Those who remained prepared a truck bomb, apparently for NATO, but it discharged prematurely outside the Brigade's headquarters, and other plans were made to strike NATO. Before they could be realized, however, Shaaban and other high commanders of the Brigade made a fateful road trip in December of 1995. After passing through two Croat roadblocks without incident, they were stopped at a third, ordered out of their trucks, and machine-gunned into their reward. It was the last day of the war, and the decapitated Brigade collapsed. Some Islamists speculated that the United States or another Western power had urged the Croats to execute the Brigadiers in order to obviate the hassle of arrests and trials, but it was just as likely that the Croats had retaliated on their own for the Rijeka bombing.

Hassan Saad, the tactician of the bombing, was not among the executed. He remained at large until 2001, when the Bosnian government finally arrested him and extradited him to Egypt. He too was never seen again.

MAHMOUD ABDELKADER ES SAYED, familiarly Abu Saleh, arrived in Milan after, it seems, forging documents for al-Qaeda in Yemen, leading a cell of Jihad in Sudan, playing a supporting role in the slaughter of tourists at Luxor, and running guns in Syria for use against Israel. He once claimed the Syrian minister of defense helped him with the gun-running. (The minister, a man of culture, was the author of a book that explained how Jews used the blood of gentiles to make matzoh.) Abu Saleh was entrusted with expanding al-Qaeda's operations in Milan. His entruster, by one account, was Ayman al-Zawahiri; by a different account, Abu Zabaydah, another al-Qaeda chief. On arriving in 1999, Abu Saleh asked the Italians' protection from his native Egypt.

"I told them," he said to a friend within hearing of an Italian bug, "that my three brothers were in prison, that my wife had had a road accident—an act of fate really, but I told them it was orchestrated by Egyptian intelligence."

"That's beautiful," the friend said.

"The whole thing corresponded to their idea of persecution, and consequently I was granted asylum. . . . Now there is a law in Italy that requires asylum claims, even those that have already been approved, to be reviewed every three months to see if the initial conditions are still in place."

"This is a form of terrorism," his friend condoled.

"Of course it is terrorism. Italy is a terrorist country. . . . The intent of the government is to take advantage of the Muslims living in this country."

In the three or four years between the departure of Anwar Shaaban and the arrival of Abu Saleh, Milan's terrorists had thrived. Operation Sphinx had merely slowed, not stopped, them. New cells had formed, some of which were also broken up but were succeeded in turn by other cells, some of which the police broke up too, only to see them succeeded by others. The terrorists—Egyptians, Algerians, Moroccans, Tunisians—were replicable. They were also growing savvier.

"Do you see this?" the police heard an instructor of sorts lecture his terrorist pupils in Milan. He was holding up a mobile phone. "This was created by an enemy of God. You can't imagine how many operations this has made fail and how many arrests it has caused. . . . It's nice. You can use it to communicate. It's fast. But it causes you huge problems. They created it, and they know how to intercept it."

Increasingly the terrorists avoided phones, and when they had to use them they tended to divulge little and to prefer either pay phones or mobile phones that they could discard after a few calls. Sometimes they communicated via e-mail or instant-messaging Web sites in short, coded phrases. To minimize the number of times their e-mails bounced from server to server (each bounce giving eavesdropping agencies a chance to intercept them), a terrorist might save a message in the draft folder of an online e-mail account, which terrorists elsewhere would check. After reading the drafts, they would delete them, then save their own drafts of reply. The system was an advance on the traditional dead drop, in which spies left messages for one another in the hollows of trees or niches of buildings. If the terrorists needed to speak in person, the smarter ones took a walk in a wide park or sat on the back of a bus with a roaring engine. On the sidewalk, they stopped abruptly to let potential tails pass them by or dropped scraps of paper while hidden comrades watched to see if anyone picked them up. If a meeting was in progress at a safe house, a lookout might loiter among the hangabouts in a kebab shop or pace the street hawking cheap umbrellas. To indicate to meeting-goers that a building was not under surveillance, a towel might be hung out a window or a shade half drawn. Some of the terrorists had learned their tradecraft, as spies call their techniques, from jihad manuals, while others had learned in the training camps of Afghanistan or Bosnia or from veterans of those camps. Austere experience had also taught veterans to reduce life to what was strictly necessary for the cause. Their apartments often had neither chairs nor tables, they slept on prayer mats or bare mattresses, they did not dress their walls or equip their kitchens, and they had no books, save *the* book. They were the heirs of Sparta not Athens.

Their work continued and extended Shaaban's. They falsified documents, recruited and sent warriors to training camps, and laundered millions of euros. In the home of one abettor of terrorism, police found €200,000 in cash. The terrorists of Milan did not seem primarily interested in attacking Italy or even Western Europe, but there were exceptions. A young Tunisian later told police that the leaders of his cell had him scout half a dozen potential targets in Italy. One was a U.S. military barracks in Mondragone, near Naples, which he watched for two weeks to learn how a truck with explosives might be driven inside. He was also ordered to assess whether it would be better to attack a particular Carabinieri station in Milan or the city's police headquarters. To study the former, he picked a fight with the doorman of a nearby building, then called the Carabinieri emergency number and asked for help. The Carabinieri took him to their station to make a statement, which gave him the chance to see how cars were admitted to the central courtyard, where floor upon floor of offices stood exposed. He decided that although the target was tempting, the turn into the courtyard was too tight for a car bomber to get up enough speed to ram his way in. The police headquarters, on the other hand, sat on a street well suited for bombing. On another assignment, he was sent to a disco to see if he could enter with a loaded backpack. He could. Another time, he and a friend were assigned to deposit three suitcases, each filled with sixty or so pounds of electronics and camouflage clothing, at the baggage check of Milan's central train station. When the bags aroused no suspicion, the leader of their cell mused aloud about which days and hours the station would be most crowded and estimated that fifteen checked bags could do the work of a truckful of explosives. The cell also discussed murdering Italian politicians and talk-show hosts and flying planes into the Italian Senate or landmarks in Milan.

Other terrorists in Milan had their hands in plots elsewhere in Europe, including a plot that was led by a German cell to bomb the Strasbourg Christmas market in 2000. The terrorists in Milan plotted a similar attack for Italy but were arrested before they could carry it out. Still other Milanese terrorists seem to have played a supporting (but unclear) role in the Madrid train bombings of 2004.

Until the end of the 1990s, nearly all of Milan's Islamic terrorists worshipped at the mosque on Viale Jenner, and several of them worked there. In time, the mosque's imam, secretary, librarian, cook, barber, and janitor would all be arrested on charges of terrorism. Notwithstanding such taints, membership at the mosque multiplied, eventually to two or three thousand. At noon prayers on Friday, the holiest day of the Islamic week, supplicants spilled out of the old garage and onto the sidewalk on prayer mats in orderly rows of seven across. Shoeless, bent on hand and knee, they made a cordillera stretching the better part of a block toward Mecca—a human topography of Islam. Not all of the parishioners dreamed of heroically murdering receptionists in their office towers and five-year-olds in their kindergartens, but many sympathized with the terrorists among them, and others were indifferent. Thus Abu Imad, the head imam, could ask at one gathering without fear of giving offense, "Is it alright to kill a person who prays and fasts but who agrees with the ideas of secular, democratic, and Communist people?" One of his guests could declare, with equal inoffensiveness, "Between us and the unbelievers there is hatred. The enmity and hatred will reign between us and them forever, until they believe in Allah alone."

The mosque on Viale Jenner so prospered that in the late 1990s Milan's radicals founded a second large mosque. It stood on the southern edge of Milan, on Via Quaranta, geographically distant from but architecturally and ideologically of a piece with with the mosque on Viale Jenner. Its superstructure was a disused factory, its piety bellicose. The formal name of the new mosque was the Islamic Community in Italy, but as this was similar to the formal name of Viale Jenner (the Institute for Islamic Culture), the mosques were usually identified simply as "Via Quaranta" or "Viale Jenner"—bad luck for the memories of Bernardo Quaranta, excavator of Pompeii and Herculaneum, and Edward Jenner, inventor of the smallpox vaccine. Via Quaranta, investigators would soon learn, was meant to supplement rather than supplant Viale Jenner's terrorism.

It was at Via Quaranta that al-Qaeda's Abu Saleh set up shop, quickly establishing himself as one of the mosque's leaders. Of his work, he told a disciple, "If the brothers want to hide, we hide them. If the brothers want documents, we take care of their documents. If the brothers want to move, we move them. If they need a weapon, you give them a weapon." He seemed a good recruiter, able to inspire young men but wise enough to test and restrain them. He clearly knew the waste of money and time and the risk to security of sending to jihad either a tenderfoot who might have a change of heart or an enthusiast whose indiscipline might wreck an operation.

"I am curious about one thing," he said to one recruit who wanted to martyr himself immediately. "Don't you like this good life? Do you want to die?"

"Listen, sheikh," the young man said, "if I liked this life, I would have gone to my cousin who is waiting for me in Germany and wants to marry me. In five years I would have the German passport and I would live in peace."

"If God wills it," Abu Saleh responded, "I am the first person to wish you to die a martyr," but, he explained, there were many unglorious tasks before a glorious martyrdom, and he told the story of a man in an Afghan training camp whose cadre was ordered to wash their feet each night because blisters hinder jihad. Not all of the warriors obeyed, but this man did because he had jihad in his heart and he never neglected even the smallest tasks. He became a martyr. "You may be ready to eat the stones of the desert," Abu Saleh told his recruit, "but you must know the meaning of it"—the meaning, that is, of the sacrifice jihad demanded.

The eternal dilemma of the counterterrorist is when to arrest: Spring now, and he may get five terrorists, but five others may flee. Wait till later, and he may get all ten, or he may get an obliterated train with human limbs scattered over the countryside. The police of Milan believed Abu Saleh posed no immediate risk, so they watched and listened to see where he would lead.

In August of 2000 he drove to the Bologna airport and picked up a Yemeni named Abdulsalam Ali Abdulrahman al-Hilal. By title,

Abdulrahman was an officer in Yemen's Political Security Organization, which was roughly equivalent to the FBI, but his more important office was carrying water for al-Qaeda. He and Abu Saleh had worked together in Yemen forging documents, and they had once teamed up to entrap an al-Qaeda defector. (Abu Saleh had secretly videotaped the defector telling Abdulrahman, who was acting in his state capacity, the hiding places of al-Qaedans in Yemen. Abdulrahman then alerted the al-Qaedans, who fled. Later al-Qaeda tried, unsuccessfully, to lure the defector to his death.) When Abu Saleh picked up Abdulrahman in Bologna, it was in a car DIGOS had bugged.

"I am studying airplanes," Abdulrahman announced on getting in the car.

"Which airline?" Abu Saleh said.

"If God wishes, I hope next time I will bring you a window or a piece of an airplane." They laughed. "I flew Alitalia. There is no security—Sanaa's airport is more secure than Rome's."

"And what of Operation Jihadia?"

"In the future, listen to the news and remember these words: *above the head.*"

"You make me dream," Abu Saleh said. "I dream of building an Islamic state."

"If God wishes it, we will, because the government of Yemen is weak. Sooner or later we will dominate it. But the big blow will come from another country—one of those blows that can never be forgotten. . . . Our focus is only on the air. . . . You will find it a good plan, but don't get specific—otherwise you'll dig your grave. . . . It is a terrifying thing and will move from south to north, from east to west. He who created this plan is a madman but also a genius. It will strike everyone dumb. You know the verse: 'He who touches Islam or believes himself mighty before Islam must be struck down.'"

"They are dogs. Every one of them will burn."

"We marry the Americans"—terrorists often called an attack a wedding—"so that they will study the Quran. They think they are lions, the power of the world, but we will hit them, and afterward they will know love."

"I know brothers who have gone to America with the trick of mail-order-bride magazines"—that is, by marrying American women who had run ads seeking husbands. They laughed again.

Abdulrahman said, "We can fight any power using candles and airplanes. They will not be able to stop us even with their most powerful weapons. We must hit them. And keep your head up. . . . Remember: the danger in the airports."

"Rain," Abu Saleh said cryptically. "Rain."

"Oh yes, there are big clouds in the sky. In that country, the fire is already lit and awaits only the wind."

"Jihad is already high."

"If it happens, every newspaper in the world will write of it."

This was thirteen months before September 11, 2001. At the time, several of the hijackers were already in the United States—the fire lit, awaiting only the wind. But neither DIGOS nor the FBI, which eventually received a copy of the conversation, fully understood what it was hearing. The idea that airplanes themselves would be used as weapons was then abstruse, although it was becoming less so. Some months later, Egypt warned Western states that Osama bin Laden might try to crash an airplane filled with explosives into the G8 summit in Genoa, in July of 2001. The Italians erected anti-aircraft batteries, but Genoa, of course, was not bin Laden's target. Even had DIGOS and the FBI understood what they were hearing, they probably could have done little since Abdulrahman did not say what the targets were or when they would be struck.

The Italian police heard nothing more about the plan until February of 2001, when a Tunisian apprenticed to Abu Saleh asked, apparently in reference to falsified documents, "Will these work for the brothers who are going to America?"

"Don't ever repeat those words, not even joking!" Abu Saleh

rebuked him. "If you have to talk about these things, wherever we may be, come up and talk in my ear, because these are very important things. You must know . . . that this plan is very, very secret, as if you were protecting the security of the state."

On September 4, 2001—so DIGOS would learn later—a computer at Via Quaranta downloaded a photograph of the Twin Towers from the Internet. It was an unlikely coincidence. The photo was soon deleted, but after September 11, DIGOS raided Via Quaranta and recovered it. Other computers at Via Quaranta also held deleted photos, mostly of political leaders (Yasser Arafat and George W. Bush were two) and of pornographic tableaux. Some of the photos appeared to have been altered steganographically—steganography being the art of hiding messages in another medium so that observers do not know they are there. A steganographer might change the color of every hundredth pixel in a digital photo, with each color corresponding to a letter of the alphabet. No one looking at the picture would notice the changes, but the right software would reveal their coded message. (The idea was an old one: In antiquity, Herodotus reported, rulers shaved the heads of slaves, tattooed messages on their scalps, and, after their hair had grown back, sent them across enemy lands to allies, who shaved them again and read the correspondence. Afterward, as in modern steganography, the files could be deleted.) DIGOS's recovery of the deleted photos was only partial, however, and the investigators could not say what messages they might have contained.

On September 6, Abu Saleh's Tunisian apprentice, Adel Ben Soltane, who was by then in jail on terrorism charges, received in the mail an envelope containing nothing but a wrapper from a stick of Brooklyn gum. Ben Soltane's jailers were puzzled about the wrapper's significance—until five days later, when they understood that he had been told the attacks in New York were imminent. That same week, a prominent priest in northern Italy named Jean-Marie Benjamin was warned by a Muslim acquaintance that the United

States and Great Britain would soon be attacked with hijacked airplanes. Benjamin told the authorities, but since his acquaintance had named neither cities nor dates, the claim was hard to assess.

That so many of Milan's terrorists knew in advance about the attacks of September 11 beforehand was a testimony to the city's importance in al-Qaeda's network. After the attacks, the U.S. Treasury Department, whose responsibility it was to freeze terrorists' assets, declared Viale Jenner "the main al-Qaeda station house in Europe."

A month or two before September 11, Abu Saleh left Italy and traveled to Iran, then on to Afghanistan, apparently to prepare for the American invasion. He is believed to have been killed in that invasion. (His Yemeni friend Abdulrahman fared only slightly better. He disappeared on a trip to Cairo shortly after September 11 and turned up again many months later at Guantánamo, having, it seems, spent an unpleasant interim in a U.S. "black site.") After Abu Saleh's disappearance, the Milanese police arrested many of his colleagues, but others carried on. One of them was Abu Omar.

Chapter 4

Beloved by God

AMADEUS VI, the fourteenth-century Count of Savoy, was over-fond of dressing his person and his retinue in green and so came to be called Conte Verde. At the urging of Pope Urban V, the Green Count gathered a force of holy warriors and sailed to Byzantium to save Christendom from the Turks. He drove them from Gallipoli and returned home to a victor's due, which, in time, included the naming of a street for him on the northern rim of Milan. Six centuries later, a portion of his street was taken over by the spiritual heirs of his opponents, who had come to his homeland on a violent religious mission of their own. History's revenge is slow but sweet.

The men who ran the mosque on Viale Jenner kept a flat on Via Conte Verde for use as a kind of extended-stay quarters for their extremist guests. Abu Saleh stayed there while looking for a residence, and Abu Omar followed him by a year or so, in the summer of 2000, and eventually decided to make the flat his permanent home. He was helped in his transition to Milan by the imam of Viale Jenner, Abu Imad, formally Arman Ahmed El Hissini Helmy, whom he knew from his imprisonment in Egypt, and by Abu Saleh, whom he had perhaps met in previous trips to Milan. Abu Imad apparently gave Abu Omar work in the mosque's library and in the small market the mosque ran to help pay its overhead. Eventually, however, Abu Omar shifted his spiritual and professional home to the mosque of

Abu Saleh on Via Quaranta, where he was named deputy chief imam. Abu Saleh had great confidence in Abu Omar. "If you have need of anything," he advised two terrorist followers, "go to Abu Omar." One of the followers referred to Abu Omar as either a *qaid* or a *dabet*—a qaid being a high commander, a dabet a lesser one.

Abu Omar earned a reputation as a passionate parson. "He gives some very spicy lessons," one terrorist said; "they're nuclear bombs." Said another terrorist, "I and all the other people in the group I hung out with were indoctrinated above all by the Egyptian imams of the mosques of Viale Jenner and Via Quaranta—that is, Abu Imad, Abu Saleh, Abu Omar. Thanks to these lectures, we were convinced to give our willingness to die dragging our enemies down with us, . . . to take even suicidal actions. . . . I believe the most dangerous people known to me before my arrest were Abu Saleh and Abu Omar because they had the capacity to inculcate extremist thought." Abu Omar's sermons are not preserved, but their themes were the sins of the West, of the sycophantic Arab governments that did the West's bidding, and of the Muslims who did not submit to the one true Islam.

In February of 2001 Italy granted Abu Omar's request for asylum, although it is not clear why. Probably the left hand of the Italian government that gave sanctuary did not know what the right hand that investigated terrorism was learning. The photograph on his asylum papers showed a change of aspect from his days in Albania. From his once-smooth chin, a beard of several pious inches now hung. In place of Western attire, he wore a galabia. His *zabiba*, or raisin—the endearing name for the forehead callus that devout Muslims earn from thousands of salaams to Mecca—seemed more pronounced, although that might have been due to the near disappearance of his hairline, which had been merely recessive in Albania. Asylum did not propel him to assimilation. In nearly four years in Italy, he had not learned more than a few words of Italian, and never would. His ignorance might be construed a declaration of sorts: his home was in the mosques, not the great wasteland around them.

A few months after acquiring asylum, he acquired a wife. Officially speaking, he was still not divorced from his first wife, but Islam allows a man more than one of these useful appurtenances, and the second marriage proceeded. His bride, Nabila Ghali, was a fellow Egyptian who had been in Italy for about a decade and who taught an Egyptian curriculum in the Quranic school at the mosque on Via Quaranta. The Egyptian consulate helped design the curriculum to ensure that Egyptian children abroad retained their culture—which was ironic, since many of the Egyptians who worshipped at Via Quaranta thought their government should be destroyed. Ghali's customary dress was a head-to-toe draping of black and gray, with the merest slits for her eyes. It is possible Abu Omar did not see a square centimeter of her during their courtship. They were married at Via Quaranta.

After it became clear to the counterterrorists of DIGOS that Abu Omar was a leader of some kind, they endeavored to put a bug in his office at Via Quaranta. Doing so took some time, perhaps until the late winter or early spring of 2002. The bug that was eventually emplaced was by one account a sliver of a thing, thin as a pin, and slipped inside a religious text—by whom is not known. Like every bug in the history of espionage, it recorded much banality, but amid hundreds of hours of conversational emptiness, there were minutes of interest.

IN THE FIRST week of April, a brother named Hammadi came to Abu Omar in a furor and said that one of the directors of the mosque was stealing money that was supposed to be used for jihad. He was ready to do violence to the director.

"Hammadi!" Abu Omar cried. "I don't understand you. I don't understand your hatred against the brothers. Why not use it against the Jews? Or the enemies of God? . . . Stay calm."

"How can I stay calm?" Hammadi said. "He is a thief, because the charitable money is needed for the mujahidin brothers."

"How is he stealing the money for the mujahidin brothers?"

"He changes the collection box too much."

"You're not the manager of this. This is my job. . . . You can't blame people just because they change the bins. Maybe they're full and they're changing them because they're full. I have it all under control."

"Where are the donations from last Friday?"

"Half is here, and the other is already on the road," Abu Omar reassured him. "We all have the same objective and the same cause. Our desire is to leave these cursed countries. . . . The wish is that we will all die martyrs."

Hammadi left, somewhat mollified, and returned a few days later. He had come from a meeting with, it seemed, another terrorist, and he said to Abu Omar, "I am supposed to tell you that he could use some blank documents."

"It's difficult to get them blank!" Abu Omar said. "You ought to be satisfied with some duplicates."

"Will you give them to me now?"

"There aren't any in this area!"

"He asked me for Libyan papers."

"For who?"

"For Hassan."

"I'll bring you a duplicate soon."

"*Original?*" Hammadi asked in French.

"Don't be so fast."

A little later Hammadi said, "I have good news for you. This morning in Tunisia they made an attack and several people were killed." He was referring to a bombing of an ancient synagogue in Ghriba that left twenty-one dead.

"The authors of this attack," said Abu Omar, "are beloved by God."

ON ANOTHER DAY in April, an Egyptian rushed into Abu Omar's office shouting about the need to attack Israelis.

"So are these attacks going to be made or not going to be made?!"

"What?" Abu Omar said.

"I'll explain it to you clearly. I want us to hit inside, outside—in whatever part of the world, all the establishments, . . . Israeli interests, . . . everything that concerns the Jews in the entire world."

Abu Omar laughed. "Use your head—ah, ah!"

"Listen, we'll make an attack that will teach them what force is. . . . These armed groups—don't they exist? It's a duty for every one of us."

"Every attack has its rules," Abu Omar counseled, "and there are also instructions that come from afar."

"Listen, I don't believe anyone from there. . . . Even these cassettes that you see from there are all bullshit, lies."

"They will do them"—by which Abu Omar seemed to mean the attacks. "They will do them."

"When—when? Who—who?"

"Those who are based there. . . . That brother from London—"

"For the operation?"

"Ah, ah," Abu Omar affirmed.

"You are certain?"

"Ah, ah!"

"How many people are they?"

"I don't know!"

MAY BROUGHT ANOTHER Egyptian (or perhaps the same), who discussed with Abu Omar, in general terms, how the struggle in Europe was going.

"The work shouldn't be done this way," Abu Omar said. "Above all, the work of the *groups* isn't going well, because it's impossible—because everyone is discovered, and then there are problems."

"And if the work is done by a single person [instead]?"

"It depends if this person isn't arrested. It depends on the results he gets."

"Certainly it must be a job well done. It must be an artist's work."

"If he makes a mistake," Abu Omar said, "he's no longer an artist, and then he becomes a danger to everyone. Even if the work is done by a single person, there is always someone who supports it, and if he falls, the whole group falls."

"The person who carries out this work ought to be aware of not staying alive."

"It depends on what [evidence] he leaves behind him."

"We'll make like the New Yorkers," the visitor said, probably meaning the murderers of September 11, who had struck eight months earlier and had, in one sense, left no evidence.

"It's not an easy thing," Abu Omar said. "You're dreaming. You can't just say, Do like this or like that."

"We have a plan."

"All of you give me pleasure, but say to Abu Albana to stay at his post. To do something, you must have results because at the moment anyone who moves will be immediately arrested, and it's better they stay there."

"And Abu Jalal?" the visitor said. "And his forces?"

"God will see to this. . . . God knows how to eliminate them, and God also knows how to save them."

The visitor returned to fantasies of grandiose violence, and Abu Omar said: "I see you're living the memories of the airplanes. Don't think this way. You must be realistic. You must be reasonable. You must be aware of the moment we're living in. . . . For recruitment, there is nobody. I haven't seen anything like this in a long time."

"Someone is slitting throats somewhere. If I were there, you would see me doing it."

"Listen to me! I will teach you the experience of the jihad with time. Even if you don't make it outside, there are brothers inside prison who make jihad. Everyone who has made jihad in the world is now in prison. This is a strange thing, and it is a dreadful and dangerous moment. If you want to go to prison for nothing, go."

ALI ABDEL AL ALI, known as Ali Sharif, came to Abu Omar in June. An administrator of the mosque, he had been arrested seven years earlier in Operation Sphinx but had been released for want of evidence.

"I fear for you," he told Abu Omar, "because you are certainly inside 'the issue.' "

"We are all inside," Abu Omar said. "Listen, the enemies of God just have terrorism fever."

"It's better that you don't talk like this. Otherwise you'll reach the same end as the imprisoned Tunisians, the Moroccans—ultimately the institute will. But I repeat to you, there are great problems, above all with the means of communication, because all those who were arrested were arrested because of the means of communication. You ought to completely avoid talking on the phone. Even if you call your brother, know that you are already inside the circle. You are already sold. Sold, you are finished."

Abu Omar said he was worried about being betrayed in other ways. "I've noticed several people who run around here who are employed by the consulate, including a Palestinian."

"You shouldn't worry about this person, because you see him. Preoccupy yourself with those who are invisible. You must have your head about you. We don't want you to end up inside. I should explain to you: I agree with you on one part, if there is a wedding or something else. But answer my question: If you end up in prison, how do you serve Islam? How do you serve it? Serving Islam and Muslims and others is good, but if you end up in prison, you cannot do anything."

"I'm not doing anything."

"I'm speaking about the phone. Maybe you are talking of things, like this. Be very careful how you talk on the phone. Maybe you are talking of one thing and they learn about another."

"I'm not talking at all about chemicals," Abu Omar said. The Tunisians whom Ali Sharif mentioned had been arrested for plotting chemical attacks.

They discussed another man, an Israeli, who Ali Sharif believed was helping the Italians translate tapped conversations.

"God curses him," Abu Omar said.

"All that has been translated has been written by his hands, from Arabic to Italian. I'm one hundred percent certain that all the translations were made by a Jew—be careful. I'm not the only one to know this. There are several others who know. Several people have informed me that his name is Sherif."

"He is Israeli and works with the Italians? That Palestinian also seems to me a Jew."

"Listen, I have told you he is a Jew called Sherif."

"I cannot stomach the word 'Sherif,'" Abu Omar said, not minding his guest's honorific.

"Maybe it's a false name. He could be called Muhammad."

"There's also a swine here called Muhammad, and I know where he lives."

"There are many people who will pass themselves off as Palestinian, then they take information. But as I told you earlier, you should worry only about the invisible ones. I have so many memories, even of the group of Sheikh Anwar [Shaaban], peace upon his soul—"

"Peace upon his soul."

"Once he told me that he was coming with his group through Switzerland, but they were all arrested. It's a very dangerous situation. Even if you say the opposite thing or speak in code, they understand you. They know everything."

The listeners of DIGOS must have been flattered.

ON ANOTHER DAY in June, an Algerian arrived from Rome and told Abu Omar that the Roman Carabinieri had taken him to their headquarters and made him look at pictures of Islamists.

"They asked me," the man said, "if I knew these people. I answered that I didn't know them. I've prayed they won't make me go back and ask me everything. They asked me if I know a Syrian, if I know the sheikh Mahmoud, if I know Sheikh Tahar. Later another carabiniere came who told me to be careful because they have recorded everything. They have a conversation in which there was talk of killing a carabiniere because he was a Jew—and do you know who it is [who's to do the killing]? It's me. 'What do you have against the Jews?' And I answered that I had nothing to do with it. They have hundreds of photos, including many of you."

"And you," Abu Omar said, "what did you say to them?"

"I said, what do you want from me? What have I got to do with it?"

"Do they have many photos of me?"

"Yes. There are many of them, particularly of you and of Sheikh Abdurahim, and hundreds of photos that show the brothers in different places. From what I understand from the photos, they have a telecamera in the Great Mosque [of Rome]."

"Oh!!! But my photos—where did they photograph me?"

"In several places. They photographed you close to home, near the mosque, and you were together with Sheikh Nabil."

"And what did they ask you about me?"

"I told them that I don't know you very well, that I know you as imam."

"Is that all?"

The man said he knew nothing more. He did, however, have other news. Brothers in London were going to set up charities across Europe to aid Muslim orphans, and one of the charities (which the Italians believed to be fronts, at least in part) was almost ready to open in Holland.

"But opening offices here," Abu Omar said, "is very delicate, because they've already come under surveillance in Holland. They're seen as offices for recruiting and supporting terrorism."

"We're used to this. It happened this way in Bosnia too. But we must not be weak. It's our duty, especially for we who have survived and know well the situation of the families of the brothers who sacrificed their lives in the name of God—above all for those who knew them. Neither the Christians nor the Jews can thwart this project."

"We're ready to help, but I'm sure they will raise various doubts and problems about these offices because the people here do not understand religion, because they confuse it with politics."

"We will demonstrate the contrary. We cannot forget them. He who has need of bread, we will give bread. He who has need of milk, we will give milk."

Their discussion shifted to a colleague who was to perform an unstated task.

"And how does he go?" Abu Omar said.

"By sea."

"When?"

"Not yet. He needs to study the thing well, because he has been booked. They have taken his fingerprints."

"That's bad."

"He has decided to change his documents—that's the plan. Give me a pen."

There was a shuffling noise, then silence as if the man were writing. At length he said, "The brother already sent me the photos and a catalogue." A "catalogue" was often code for a passport or other documents.

"What?"

"The brother has sent them to me, but for me it's a lot."

"How so?"

"The wax, in my opinion, is too much."

"Who is it that has prepared it for you? Who? Who?"

"One of the Palestinian brothers."

"The Palestinian?"

"Yes."

There followed some talk about using a car for something that was at first inscrutable but whose meaning soon became clear.

"Put a car into a bus," the man suggested, "like that car that exploded against a bus. But inside there was a brother, which I don't like."

"The car sped into the bus with a brother inside?"

"Personally I like to be protected, and I like to protect the youth. Personally I prefer that it be remote-controlled. It's more beautiful this way. You put yourself far off, and this way you're protected. We can say God is with us and with them."

"Amen."

"There is need of an attack. There is need to do what is done to the Jews, to terrorize them that way, to make them like the Jews who are tired even if they don't take the bus."

"Everything at its time," Abu Omar said. "For now we give thanks to God."

ALI SHARIF, the director of the mosque, came to Abu Omar a few hours after the man from Rome did.

"I'm sorry," he said, "but who is that brother running around here?"

"He is a brother."

"Is he from here, or did he come from abroad?"

"No, he's from Rome."

"From Rome?"

"Yes. They have plans to open a school in Rome, and he came to ask my advice. He also asked Mohamed Ali. Anyway, this school has already started. He wanted only some advice."

"I'm sorry, but it's a delicate moment. I must know the brothers who are running around here. You know very well the situation we find ourselves in. It's not that I don't trust you. . . . I don't want to ask you for too much information. You know the brothers come with others and then you discover some strange things. The brothers here have also wondered who he is."

"He is one I've known a long time. He's a good brother."

"This is not a problem."

"He was in prison."

"What do you mean?"

"In the past. He belongs to the family of Djamel Lounici"—an Algerian terrorist who for a time was based in Naples. "He was in prison in '95 or '96 with Djamel's group."

"What's his name?"

"He's Algerian. He's with Djamel Luonici's group. He's of the same family. I don't understand why you're frightened of him."

"We're not afraid," said the imam, sounding more than a little bullied.

"They're good brothers. They're ex-jihad. They're opening some facilities and are asking only for advice."

"Fine. I don't have anything against him. Only prudence. God protect you and peace be with you."

A MAN FROM Germany arrived later that June. DIGOS could not determine his nationality but his Arabic was flavored with idioms of the Maghreb, which suggested he was Algerian, Tunisian, or Moroccan. He had apparently just given a sermon, because Abu Omar said, "Congratulations, you inspired the youth."

"It doesn't end here," said the man. "There are so many things to change to eliminate the enemies of God, the policies of Israel, and those who pursue them."

"It is our hope."

"On the sixteenth of last month, there was a confidential meeting of the sheikhs in Poland. The final decision was to completely change the front of Hizb ut-Tahrir"—a group working to reestablish the medieval caliphate—"and build a new organization that takes care of national and international territory. But we need very educated people at every level."

"It takes time."

"We have time," the man said. "We're going little by little. There are people already on the inside."

"How so?"

"Currently Sheikh Adel and Sheikh Abd al-Wahab have created several groups in which there are various brothers who have returned from Chechnya."

"And Sheikh Adlen?"

"He moved before I came here. I knew him in 1987. But let's return to our subject. Our project has need of people who are intelligent and very educated. As for the jihad part, there is Abu Serrah, who has plans to create a battalion of twenty-five, twenty-six divisions, but the scheme must be well studied."

"Just don't let the devil in your midst," Abu Omar cautioned.

"The first thing I say to you is that we are aware of being under surveillance. We know that half the brothers are in prison, including those who are accused of raising funds. I repeat to you, the plan must be studied in detail, because the thread starts in Saudi Arabia. He who is responsible for this project is Abu Suleiman, who has the same blood as Emir Abdullah, so there is no need for more comments."

They both laughed. "Emir Abdullah" was code for Osama bin Laden.

"The mosques, however," the man continued, "have too high a profile. They must be left alone. We need new structures. We're looking for seven to nine premises. Recently we bought a four-story building."

"And we're not looking after the mosques?"

"Sure, we're looking after them. We finance them too, but money must bring money because the objective is also to form an Islamic army that will have the name of Force 9."

"How are things going in Germany?"

"I can't complain. We are already ten. We are also taking an interest in Belgium, in Spain, in the Netherlands, in Turkey, and in Egypt, Italy, and France. But the headquarters remain in London. Sheikh Adlen has given a lot of money. As I've already told you, this plan doesn't need more comments or words."

"I hope this will inspire the youth."

"This is our objective. Every one of us has a task. For example, if one has at his disposal a force of ten—he becomes their chief—then it is up to him to decide whether to organize them into smaller groups or keep them as they are. The important thing is to use intelligence."

"And if some of them are foreigners?" Abu Omar meant non-Arabs.

"It's not important. We need even foreigners. We have Albanians, Swiss, Englishmen. . . . Just so long as they are of a high cultural level. In Germany we have interpreters and translators who translate books. We also have them in telecommunications, also in Austria. The important thing is that their faith in Islam be true."

"We have never had problems with them," Abu Omar allowed of the foreigners. "To the contrary, we've noticed that they are very enthusiastic and take part readily."

"Besides, it is neither you nor I who decide whether or not to take them. Those who decide are the people with Hizb al-Tawid." He perhaps meant the aforementioned Hizb ut-Tahrir, or perhaps he referred to a new group.

"This plan really excites me," said Abu Omar.

"Never worry about the money, because the money of Saudi Arabia is your money. The important thing is not to run, because it's all new. There are old parts, but the training is completely new. He who wanted to create the plan is near Emir Abdullah, and we are grateful to Emir Abdullah. Prepare yourself."

"I'm ready."

"We're also awaiting the sheikh from Iraq," by whom he may have meant Mullah Krekar, the co-founder of the Kurdish terrorist group Ansar al-Islam.

"Be careful of the Internet," the man warned a little later. "It's frightening. These are the first instructions of Sheikh Adlen: we must ignore the Internet. If you communicate on the Internet, use another language. . . . The main issue is that each group protects the other group without destroying each other. And each group must be far away from the other. Chechnya takes care of training the youth, while another group takes care of information. Even for the air we breathe, another group takes care of it. There is only one condition: at each meeting one or two people from the group participate. They speak of their situation and listen to the others. The important thing is that these people are all of the same rank as the others . . . and everyone must be aware of everything. We are all one, and one is God."

"We fight for the word of God, even by paper."

"Yes, this too is part of our plans. There is a certain amount of information that I can't give until we see each other next time, if God wills. . . . We need businessmen, professors, engineers, doctors, instructors. . . . Dear Abu Omar, it's not the quantity but the quality. Even if they are ten, it's enough, because you can study [the recruits], you can understand them psychologically. You do as at school. There is kindergarten, elementary school, high school, and college. At each stage there is an exam. But the most important things are security, prudence, intelligence, orders, and communication . . . because each group is part of a region. I will give you a small example: Italy is part of Austria, Germany is part of Holland, Holland is part of London. . . . Prudence is what saves you. Take for example the case of Ismail who has been in Holland since 1979 and nobody knows who he is. I repeat to you, the organization must be impeccable where confidentiality is concerned."

"And I, what do I look after?" Abu Omar asked.

"You sell, you buy, you print, you record. Then the person involved will come and talk with you personally. It's enough that things not get mixed. It's enough to avoid the easy arrests. We know perfectly well that you, I, and the others are all under surveillance. I know I am followed by police, but I make fools of them. The important thing is that you find a way of getting the message to the other person. Dear Abu Omar, for combating the enemies of God, we need technology."

"It's true."

"This is why the sheikhs insist that we have many highly educated people."

"Yes, yes."

"We need to have a lot of intelligence. If Sheikh Abu Khalil,
Sheikh Abu Qatada, or Sheikh Aden the Syrian are all under surveillance, there are other people who lead the group in their stead,
who handle the situation. Second, we need to be careful in the way
we speak. One must not throw words about carelessly. The tongue
must always be controlled. Our groups are spread from Algeria
throughout the world. For example, one could lead the group perfectly from Poland, like Sheikh Abdelaziz. He has a group called
the Katilea group. His organization is stunning. It's an impeccable
organization. One may even communicate via a book."

"How? Has he written in a book?"

"Even more. He, in the books—they are books, but they are full
of dollars."

"He sends the dollars via the books?"

"Yes. Also other things."

"How? By mail?"

"Yes, by mail."

"With such ease?"

"Yes, because it's not Europe. Europe is now under surveillance
by air and by land, but in Poland, in Bulgaria, and in countries that
aren't part of the European Community, it's all easy. First of all,
they are corrupt. You can buy them with dollars. I take the sub-
stance over there, and I put it here and here. They are countries less
surveilled, there aren't so many eyes. But the country where everything starts is Austria. There I meet with all the sheikhs, and all our
brothers are there. . . . It has become the country of international
communications, the country of contacts, as I told you earlier. All
the contacts arrive from Austria or from Poland. The most convenient country is Austria and the other countries nearby. If you are
wanted by the law, you have two choices: either you hide there or
in the mountains. Above all, the Sahafi Mosque, the old mosque,

has been a very hot mosque for a long time, very hot. They are very united, particularly after the event that just happened there."

"There is only one God, and Muhammad is his Prophet," said Abu Omar, perhaps in benediction of the unknown event at the hot mosque.

"I will send you the whole explanation with a brother. I only recommend to you the union and Hizb al-Tawid."

"I need only directions."

"If God wills, they will reach you. It's a matter of days, because at this moment the sheikhs are traveling in Algeria, in Morocco, and in Bosnia. Calm and patience: you must never run. . . . One needs only to instruct and study and organize things that may interest us. Study the streets, because war must be studied."

Italian investigators would later say they never learned the identity of the man from Germany.

ALI SHARIF'S WORRIES about Abu Omar continued to grow, as did those of the imam and president of Viale Jenner, respectively Abu Imad and Abdelhamid Shaari, whose combined influence at Via Quaranta was profound. Several times the three men warned Abu Omar to be less flagrant in his pronouncements, but Abu Omar would not be restrained. Toward the end of the summer of 2002, their disagreements reached a climax, not recorded by the police, and afterward Abu Omar limited his time at Via Quaranta to a few hours a week. Later he stopped going entirely. He continued to attend noon prayers at Viale Jenner.

For occupation, he founded the Islamic Media Center, which consisted of himself, a computer, and a printer and through which he aspired to become the voice of righteous Islam in Italy. The center's primary output was an occasional newsletter called *Islamic Truth*, which commented on current affairs in language simple enough for a poorly educated people to understand. He distributed the newsletter to mosques in northern Italy, some of which posted copies in their foyers. They also posted his photo galleries, as he called them, which were printouts of politically themed pictures he had downloaded from the Internet—pictures, for example, of Israeli massacres of Palestinians or American massacres of Afghanis. As a rule his galleries were gorier than the family-friendly violence on offer from most Western newspapers.

He also became an itinerant imam, preaching at radical mosques across northern Italy. Mosques in Parma, Cremona, Como, and possibly elsewhere seem to have asked him to become their regular imam, but he played coy.

"It's very difficult, so difficult," he told a suitor from Cremona. "Three other mosques have called me, but I find myself in a very difficult situation, so very difficult....Very, very."

He described his anguish at some length, like a kid in an ice cream shop.

"I can't relate to you just how awkward it is," he said.

On the phone, he usually said nothing of importance, and DIGOS apparently had no bug in his flat. But investigators followed him in and out of Milan, often fruitfully. On a trip to Parma, for example, he was picked up at the train station by three Kurds whom DIGOS had thentofore known only a little about and had believed to be mostly harmless. Their contact with Abu Omar prompted a more thorough investigation, which revealed them to be part of a pan-European network that, in the run-up to the U.S. invasion of Iraq, was recruiting Islamists to serve the terrorist group Ansar al-Islam in Iraq. American missiles would eventually destroy Ansar 's main camp in Kurdistan, and scores of documents forged in Italy would be found among the ruins. Their bearers had lived mostly in Milan and Cremona. Ansar's recruiters in Italy sent perhaps a hundred men in all to Iraq, and other European recruiters sent perhaps a few hundred more. At least five suicide attacks in Iraq were believed to have been carried out by "Italian" Islamists. After one attack, the martyr's brother in Milan called their mother in Tunisia to tell her the good news. She agreed it was a most wonderful thing and said she had had a vision of her sacrificial son, which was a good omen.

The son in Milan said a rich man was going to give the family €8,000 in reward, and mother and son agreed that half of it might be used to renovate the house. Another Milanese recruit, a young North African named Kamal Morchidi, apparently took part in a rocket attack on Baghdad's Hotel al-Rashid. (*Morchidi* and *al-Rashid*, it happens, are synonyms that can be translated "He who follows the right path.") The target of the strike may have been Paul Wolfowitz, the American undersecretary of defense, who was then in residence and whose unstinting advocacy for the Iraq War helped bring death to a number of innocents that most terrorists can only dream of killing. Wolfowitz survived the strike, but Morchidi died either during it or shortly afterward. His father said he had been a normal, loving son until he started attending the mosque on Viale Jenner, after which he became increasingly dark of mood. Then one day he simply disappeared. The father went to the mosque and demanded its leaders tell him where his son was, but he learned nothing. The next thing he heard, his son was dead. In Milan young Morchidi had lived on Way of the Unknown Martyrs.

The investigators of DIGOS eventually concluded that Abu Omar was an important recruiter for the Ansar network. They drew their conclusion partly from what other terrorists said—one, for example, said he heard Abu Omar sound the call for recruits in Parma, and he thought Abu Omar may have supplied travel papers for their journey to Iraq—and partly from the activities of the people Abu Omar associated with. One of Abu Omar's closer associates was an Egyptian named Radi El Ayashi, known as Merai, who seemed to be the leader of Ansar's efforts in northern Italy. Abu Omar was also involved, although at more of a remove, with one Maxamed Cabdullah Ciise, known as Mohammad the Somali, who apparently raised and laundered funds for Ansar from London. The Italians arrested Merai and Mohammad when the latter came to Italy for forged documents, and, on the slim chance they might talk, put them together in a bugged holding room. It was a ploy Jihad manuals warned about, but the pair were carelessly revelatory.

"We do not know each other," the Somali proposed to his friend.

"You do not even need to say it," Merai said. "They already asked me if I knew you, and I answered that I met you at the mosque."

"Fine, let us stick to that version, because they have nothing on me. . . . But quite honestly here in your place there is something wrong. I am astonished by the business of the bag"—which held potentially incriminating evidence. "How could they know it was there? How did they bring me the bag? Why are they asking me where the training camps in Syria are? I am speechless."

"You know, they try to get you to speak. They try to make you believe that they know everything, but they know nothing."

"When we were arrested and they put me in the car and pointed a pistol at me, they told me they had gathered information on me and they had spoken to the Americans. I told them they were enemies of God, to take their hands off me. After that, they asked me what my true nationality was."

"Take them for a ride," Merai counseled. "Tell them you are Egyptian. Let us thank God they did not find the passports. I have few things at home. I have only money, but the rest is hidden."

"The Moroccan passports?"

"Nothing. When they took us, I had nothing on me. I had given everything to Brahim"—the librarian of the mosque on Via Quaranta.

"How about the Moroccan passport that they prepared for you and that they gave you when we sat down?"

"Brahim has it. He knows what to do. I am not so stupid as to keep it on me. When we get out of here, you disappear at once and I will do the same. If you need support, Brahim knows where the money is hidden too. I have never had anything on me. If you want to take the passports, take them. He knows all my hideouts, and he knows all my movements. Sometimes even we forget where we have hidden things. He is a tomb."

"First let us get out of here, and then I will try to get to Romania because I have support there. I am sorry to put the question to you again, but are you sure that this is the first time you have been brought here? Are you not under surveillance?"

"I would know if I were under surveillance. . . . I do not think I am, because I do not use the telephone very much. I constantly change my phone card, and the phone calls that we made together, we made them from outside."

"I hope that is true, that they do not have any phone calls, because if that were the case it would be a problem for the brothers." And it was: the U.S. National Security Agency had intercepted several calls from pay phones in Italy to satellite phones used by Ansar captains in Syria. The Italians had intercepted similar calls.

"But," the Somali continued, "I think you are under surveillance."

"That may be true. Who is not under surveillance? All they have to do is see you once and they watch your movements."

"No, brother. Now, I remember well Quaranta-Quaranta. I recall a guy who told me it was better to go to Afghanistan or Iran than to go to Via Quaranta. This is the most dangerous place after London because it is known worldwide for the training of terrorists and for logistical and financial support. It is well known for being in the firing line. The whole world knows Quaranta-Quaranta."

"The enemies of God, sons of dogs . . . are terrorized by us. Sooner or later, maybe tomorrow morning, they'll have news because both the Americans and Israelis will pay."

"The enemy of God came to touch my Quran."

"And did you let him?"

"No."

"Tell him to leave and not touch it even with his finger."

"He told me he wanted to check it, and I told him I would open it page by page. He made me open it three times."

"They love life. I want to be a martyr. I live for jihad. In this life, there is nothing. Life is afterward—above all, brother, the indescribable feeling of dying a martyr. God, help me to be Your martyr!"

They recited verses of the Quran together and sang an anthem to jihad. A little later the Somali fretted, "But when they arrest people, do they usually put two of them together?"

"No!"

"So how come they put us together?"

"They conducted a roundup, and all the cells are undoubtedly full."

"Bizarre."

Both men were convicted of crimes related to terrorism.

By February of 2003 the investigators of DIGOS thought they were a couple of months shy of having enough evidence to arrest Abu Omar. They were, however, in no hurry to do so, because they wanted to see where else he might lead them.

On Monday the seventeenth, one month before the United States invaded Iraq, Abu Omar stepped out of his flat and set off down Via Conte Verde under a brilliant sky for the *dhuhr*. The dhuhr is the second of Islam's five daily prayers and must be held neither earlier than midday nor later than when a shadow cast by the sun is twice its midday length. At Viale Jenner the dhuhr was held just after noon. Abu Omar had with him his keys and mobile phone, his passport and residency permit, his social security and health care cards, and, because he intended to pay the rent that afternoon, €450. He never paid the rent.

NABILA GHALI began to worry about her husband when by late afternoon he had not come home and had not returned calls to his mobile phone. She called friends who frequented the mosque, but they hadn't seen him. Then she called friends who might have been in touch with him by phone, but they knew nothing either. She did not call the police. Next day, however, Abu Omar still not having returned, she seems to have contacted a branch of the municipal police, asked to report him missing, and been told that an absence of twenty-four hours did not warrant a missing-person investigation.

Abu Imad, the imam at Viale Jenner, was making his own inquiries. Although he did not have the greatest love for Abu Omar, neither did he like his disappearance. Nobody Abu Imad spoke to, however, knew anything of Abu Omar's whereabouts, and none of the hospitals he called had a patient matching Abu Omar's description. Finally Abu Imad called a lawyer, an Italian who had defended Islamists charged with terrorism, and three days after Abu Omar's disappearance, the lawyer called DIGOS to ask whether the Italian government had detained him. A DIGOS officer said the government had not, and he encouraged the lawyer to send Nabila Ghali to file a missing-person report. Later that day, Ghali went to a police station and did.

The police asked the expected questions: Had Abu Omar ever gone absent before? Where had he gone in the week before his disappearance? Did he travel much? Was there any reason he might want to hide? Ghali told them her husband was a pious man and that in the week before his disappearance, he had left the apartment only on religious errands, some in town, some beyond. When he was in Milan, it was his habit to walk to the mosque to attend the dhuhr. When he left Milan, it was to preach. On the Friday before his disappearance, one of the brothers had picked him up and driven him to Gallarate, an hour from Milan, for the *jumuah*, which is the particular name for the more elaborate dhuhr on Friday. Abu Omar gave a sermon, and the brother drove him home that evening. On Saturday he was picked up by brothers who took him to speak at the mosque in Varese. He stayed overnight after his lecture, and on Sunday a brother took him to Como to speak at the mosque there. He returned to Milan that night. The police told Ghali they would open an investigation.

The next day was Friday, and at the close of the jumuah at Viale Jenner, Abu Imad made an appeal from the pulpit for information about Abu Omar. No one answered during the service, but afterward his wife told him that a sister had told her that another sister had heard from yet another sister that on Monday she had seen an Arab kidnapped. The sisters had not approached Abu Imad during the service because it was forbidden for women to cross from the rear of the mosque, where God had put them, to the front of the mosque, which He had reserved for men. The sister who witnessed the kidnapping had not been at the jumuah, and Abu Imad's wife had not been able to learn her name or the name of the intermediate sister.

Shortly after this discovery, a male parishioner named Sayed Shaban told Abu Imad that a brother at the jumuah had told him the same story—a woman had witnessed a kidnapping. Shaban thought he knew who the woman was, but he would not name her or her husband. He said he did not want to get anyone in trouble. He also declined to tell Abu Imad the name of the brother who told him the story. Abu Imad asked Shaban to ask the witness's husband to come to the mosque and speak with him, it being more correct to invite the man of the family than the witness herself. Shaban said he would try.

SHAWKI BAKRY SALEM came to Milan from Qalubia, a small province on the edge of the Nile Delta where the immense sprawl of Cairo peters out into farmland. The fertile region yields oranges, figs, apricots, and chickens, but there is not enough land for the many would-be farmers and not enough industry to make up for the lack of land, so in 1996 Salem moved to Milan and took a job as a construction laborer. He left behind a young bride, to whom he monthly remitted a share of his paycheck and, when money permitted, himself. A few years after his emigration, the couple were blessed with a daughter, and two years after that Salem had saved enough money to bring his family to Milan. Merfat Rezk was twenty-two years old and nearly parturient with their second daughter when she arrived in September of 2002. Her new home was a second-floor walkup over a tabaccheria near the corner of Via Guerzoni and Via Carlo Cafiero, the latter named for an earlier emigrant who had gone to London, met Marx and Engels, and returned home to spread *L'Internazionale*.

Rezk was the woman Sayed Shaban had heard about. After his talk with Abu Imad, he went to Rezk's husband Salem and said Abu Imad wanted to speak with him about what she had seen. Salem became agitated and said he would rather not. Shaban coaxed, Salem held his ground, Shaban coaxed some more. Just speak to the imam, Shaban said, only to him, nobody else. In the end Salem agreed without enthusiasm.

Abu Imad would later say that when Salem came to his office, he was plainly terrified and would not be calmed. The iman told Salem that the kidnapping his wife had seen was momentous and she must talk to the Italian authorities. Salem would not confirm that his wife had seen a kidnapping—he avoided the mere word. He said only that she had seen something serious, maybe even danger-ous, but he would not let her speak about it. He didn't want to get involved in anything, especially if it was political, which this thing surely was. In fact, he was sending his wife back to Egypt the first chance he got.

Abu Imad told Salem his wife could not remain silent. It was *because* the kidnapping was political, *because* Abu Omar was a mili-tant and had presumably been kidnapped for his militancy, that she must speak. Abu Imad acknowledged that Muslims were not in the habit of trusting the Italian authorities, but in this case the Italians were the only hope.

Salem said he did not care about these things. He cared only for the safety of his wife and daughters. "I do not want to fling open the doors of Hell," he said.

The imam rejoined that if Abu Omar were hurt or killed, Salem would have blood on his soul. Salem was not an overly religious man—Abu Imad couldn't recall ever having seen him in the mosque before—but in the end the argument persuaded him. He said Abu Imad could give the police his wife's name.

Abu Imad did, and on February 26, nine days after Abu Omar vanished, Merfat Rezk was interviewed at the stately yellow palazzo on Via Fatabenefratelli that served as DIGOS's headquarters. She was escorted by her husband, who translated for her, and by Abu Imad and the president of the mosque, Abdelhamid Shaari. She was fearful, and her story came out by bits and pieces. She said that at eleven-thirty on the morning of Monday, February 17, she, her husband, and their two daughters visited a doctor because one of the girls was having trouble hearing. The appointment was brief—they were done before noon—and afterward her husband dropped her and the girls at a bakery on Viale Jenner while he drove on to a doctor's appointment of his own. She bought some bread, then walked with the girls the half block east to Via Guerzoni and there turned north. She had the baby in her arms and was trying to hold the toddler by the hand, but the girl kept wriggling away, running ahead, and forcing Rezk to catch up. They had walked maybe a hundred meters up Via Guerzoni when she saw that a light-colored van was parked crosswise on the sidewalk, its nose nearly pressed against the high border wall so that they could not squeeze by. She caught up with her playful daughter just before reaching the van, took her hand, and crossed to the other side of the street. As they passed the van, she noticed two men standing near its passenger side who until then had been hidden by the vehicle. One of the men was an Arab who had a long beard and wore a galabia. She had never seen him before.

An officer showed her a picture of Abu Omar and asked if this was the man she had seen. She said could not say for sure. The officer asked if she could say more specifically what color the van was, but she could not say that either. He asked if she could say anything else about the van, but she said she had been too occupied wrangling her daughter to notice anything more. He asked about the other man with the Arab, and she said he was a Westerner, dressed in Western clothes and wearing sunglasses. He was looking at a paper in his hand and speaking into a mobile phone wedged between his head and shoulder. She couldn't hear what he was saying or in what language he was saying it, because he was ten or fifteen meters away. By this time, her daughter had again run far ahead of her, and she hurried to catch up. The girl eventually stopped at a break in the wall that opened onto a branch of the Croce Viola, Milan's emergency service. Some of the emergency responders, dressed in their bright orange uniforms, were playing with her. Rezk paused at the entrance just long enough to collect her daughter, then continued up the road. Not too long later, she heard a very loud noise behind her, so loud that she thought there must have been a car crash.

Here she paused in her narrative. Her reticence had been growing steadily, and she asked if she might nurse her baby. The officers said that was fine and recessed for half an hour, leaving her and her husband alone.

When they reconvened, an officer asked her to describe the noise she had heard. She said it was a great blow or thud. It sounded the way a car did when it ran into something, or the way a large object might if it fell from a great height and crashed on the ground. The officer asked what she did when she heard the sound, and she said she turned instinctively to look. The light-colored van that had been on the sidewalk was now in the street and heading her way very quickly. It passed her at the corner of Via Cafiero, just in front of her apartment.

The officer asked if she saw the driver.

She said she did not.

He asked if she could see whether there were passengers.

She could not.

Were there windows in the back of the van?

She couldn't remember.

Were the windows of the cab open or closed?

She couldn't remember.

And where were the Arab and the Westerner who had been on the sidewalk?

They were gone too. She assumed the Arab had left in the van, although willingly or not she could not say. Whatever happened, she didn't see it. She just heard the noise.

And then?

Then she continued to her apartment, terrified, not knowing what to do or whom to tell. After a few days she confided in an Egyptian friend named Hayam, whose last name she did not know. Hayam's husband was named Ayman, and they lived in Vermezzo, outside Milan. She had nothing more to tell.

HAYAM ABDELMONEIM MOHAMED HASSANEIN was a twenty-six-year-old immigrant from the same province in Egypt that Rezk and her husband were from. When the police found her, she was not eager to talk, but over multiple interrogations her story came out. She said that on the Friday after Abu Omar disappeared, she and her husband drove to Merfat Rezk's apartment so Rezk could babysit their daughter while they went to the jumuah at Viale Jenner. While her husband waited in the car, Hassanein took the child inside, and it was then that Rezk told Hassanein what she had seen on Via Guerzoni. Her story to Hassanein was fuller than the one she, Rezk, would later tell police. She said, among other things, that she saw at least two men inside the van, that it was a white cargo van without windows in the back, and that she heard the Westerner on the sidewalk ask in Italian for the Arab's papers. Subsequently she heard not only the loud thud but an accompanying scream—a cry for help in Arabic. When she turned around to look, the Arab was being pulled violently into the van. He struggled, but futilely.

Hassanein returned to the car, and as her husband drove to the mosque, she told him Rezk's story. At the end of the jumuah, when Abu Imad made his plea for information about Abu Omar, she told the story again to one of the sisters. She asked her husband after the service if she had done right, and he said yes—he too had told the story to some brothers. They drove back to Rezk's flat, where Hassanein told her about the imam's plea, and Rezk asked whether Hassanein had divulged her secret. Hassanein said no. She didn't want her friend, who was disturbed enough, to worry further.

After the police asked to interview Rezk, she called Hassanein, nearly in hysterics, and said her husband Salem was irate and she was frightened of what he might do. After the interview, Salem visited Hassanein and said his wife had been very scared at the police station and had not been exact in her recollections. He related the limited story that Rezk had told the police, and he begged Hassanein not to contradict her. Hassanein agreed, and the next week, when the police questioned her, she kept her word. Two years would pass before she told investigators the full story, which meant that in 2003 the police of Milan could not say with certainty that Abu Omar had been forced into the van. It was possible, though unlikely, that he had gotten into it willingly, or he could have left in an altogether different manner.

The police never saw Rezk again. The day after they questioned her, she and her children returned to Egypt.

IN ITALY criminal investigations are conducted by a magistrate, in whose person is combined the roles of prosecutor and chief investigator. This arrangement differs from that of the United States, where the roles are separated: an American prosecutor may advise the police, but he does not direct them. Stefano Dambruoso began his magisterial career in the early 1990s prosecuting Mafiosi in the Sicilian city of Agrigento, which was a bit like running an anti-gang squad in East Los Angeles. After some success, he received a gift box containing half a pig's head. The chief of police got the other half. The Mafia, who do not deal in subtlety, were threatening death. Dambruoso stayed three more years and put more mobsters away. In 1996 he transferred to Milan and became the city's sole prosecutor detailed full-time to Islamic terrorism. Milan was a generally safer posting than Agrigento, although on one occasion police overheard terrorists speaking of "guys from Japan"—meaning kamikazes, suicide bombers—who seemed to be planning to assassinate Dambruoso. Two guards with submachine guns were stationed outside his apartment, and three bodyguards traveled with him until the threat dissipated.

Dambruoso convicted many terrorists, but a frustration of his work was that he rarely convicted them of terrorism per se because in the absence of an attack, conspiracy to commit a specific terrorist act could be hard to prove. Usually he convicted for ancillary crimes like forgery and illegal immigration, which carried lamentably short sentences—two or four or seven years, say. None of the terrorists of Abu Saleh's cell or those arrested in Operation Sphinx was sentenced to more than a decade, and several beat the immigration and forgery raps entirely. Italy would somewhat solve this problem after September 11 by criminalizing witting association with terrorists, which was much easier to prove than terrorism proper. But the sentences for associational terrorism could also have been stiffened, and as a fallback, Italy took to deporting terrorists after their sentences had run. The terrorists about to be deported, men who, given a little more opportunity, would have murdered Italians by the dozen, often made touching pleas to their hosts not to return them to the lash of their native governments.

Dambruoso had directed DIGOS's surveillance of Abu Omar, so the investigation into his disappearance fell to him as well. After Rezk's interview with the police, he sent investigators to question the twelve members of the Croce Viola who had been on duty on February 17, but none had seen or heard a thing. He also sent investigators to ask Abu Omar's associates in Milan, Varese, Como, and Cremona whether he had talked of leaving town, but none had heard him say anything of the kind. One administrator at Via Quaranta reported that Abu Omar's wife had once said that Abu Omar thought he was followed on trips to mosques in Gallarate and Varese. His followers had driven either a car or a white Fiat Fiorino, which is a hybrid between a car and a van. Dambruoso did not know whether Abu Omar had imagined the surveillance, or had spotted the police who sometimes followed him, or had spotted someone else, perhaps his kidnappers. Dambruoso maintained the tap on the phone in Abu Omar's apartment, but the calls Nabila

Ghali made and received revealed nothing of interest, and bugs of Abu Omar's associates revealed nothing either. The tap on Abu Omar's mobile phone, silent since the morning of his disappearance, remained so.

Because Rezk had said that the Westerner standing with Abu Omar on the sidewalk had been using a mobile phone, Dambruoso asked the phone companies with nearby cell towers for logs of the calls routed by the towers between 11:00 A.M. and 1:00 P.M. on February 17. The logs would not contain the actual conversations, but they would show which phones had been used in the area, from which Dambruoso hoped to learn something useful. Italian bureaucracy, however, be it public or private, moves grudgingly, and half a year passed before the logs arrived. When they did, Dambruoso discovered he had erroneously requested them for 17.03.03—March 17—instead of 17.02.03. He corrected the digit, re-requested the logs, and awaited the new ones.

He had only one other clue of note. On March 3, two weeks after Abu Omar disappeared, Italy's Central Directorate for Anti-Terrorism Police, the body that coordinates DIGOS offices around the country, received a brief teletype from the CIA. It was labeled SECRET//RELEASE TO ITALY ONLY and read in full:

> WE HAVE INFORMATION SUGGESTING THAT USAMA MUSTAFA (NASR) AKA (ABU 'UMAR) AKA ABU OMAR AL-(ALBANI) MAY HAVE TRAVELED TO AN UNIDENTIFIED COUNTRY IN THE BALKAN REGION. TO DATE WE HAVE BEEN UNABLE TO VERIFY THESE ACCOUNTS; HOWEVER, WE WILL KEEP YOU INFORM [SIC] SHOULD HIS LOCATION BE FURTHER IDENTIFIED.

The CIA offered nothing more, and Dambruoso's investigation came to a standstill.

Chapter 5

Torment

A **FAST-DRIVING VAN**, or any other machine with a wheel or two, arouses no interest in the Milanesi, who have yet to discover brakes and who regard traffic lights as suggestions. Red is a goad to charge, as with the bull. Stripes down the middle of a road are aids for centering the car, which is useful when passing one vehicle while dodging an oncoming one. A sidewalk may be used by a motorist in a like manner. It is the merest oversight of the law that pedestrians who get in the way are not fined for impeding the flow of traffic.

The van into which Abu Omar disappeared at noon on February 17 sped north on Via Guerzoni in Milanese fashion. It threaded through the diminishing city and its suburbs until, just before reaching the A4 autostrada, a car that had been waiting there for a couple of hours slipped in front of it. Both vehicles got onto the A4 eastbound. Six or seven minutes later, a second van, also having waited for a couple of hours near the on-ramp, followed. The car and the first van passed walled Bergamo, high on its promontory, forty-five minutes after the kidnapping. The other van passed several minutes later. Half an hour after that, in similar formation, they passed Brescia, known as the Lioness for its resistance to Austrian tyrants. Forty minutes later, they passed Verona, fair; then Vicenza, porticoed and proportionate; then Padova, arcaded; then

Venice, subsiding. At four o'clock in the afternoon, two hundred miles beyond Via Guerzoni, the caravan left the A4 at the town of Portogruaro, in Friuli-Venezia Giulia, the northeasternmost of Italy's twenty regioni, and headed north on the A28. Twenty minutes later, they left the A28 to wind along a modest provincial road through pretty hill towns, their narrow buildings framed in timber and rock, their campaniles built with the care, if not the budget, of Piazza San Marco's.

Amid these, Aviano Air Base lay like a pockmark. The barracks and office boxes in which Aviano manifested itself suggested the offspring of a prison that had mated with a dumpster, probably in Lubbock, and the imported commerce in its strip malls ran to Pizza Hut (in the land of pizza) and Bud Lite (in the land of vineyards). The base seemed to betray a wish by its American inhabitants to get back home, though they had hardly left it, and implied a foreign policy both suburban and incurious. Technically Aviano was not solely an American base. Italy owned the land and the airport proper and garrisoned a few hundred airmen and a handful of jets there. But the American complement was the entire Thirty-first Fighter Wing of the U.S. Air Force, with 3,500 airmen, 5,000 staff and dependents, and aircraft by the score.

Shortly before five o'clock on February 17, the three vehicles arrived, still in formation, at a section of the base controlled by the Americans.

It had been a long afternoon for the cargo. From the moment the plain-clothed policeman stepped out of the car and stopped him with a sharp "*Polizia!*" Abu Omar had suspected something was not quite right. It was less the stop itself that aroused his suspicion—document checks were routine enough—than its coming on the heels of several unsettling weeks in which he thought he had noticed people spying on him. When he walked down the street, it had sometimes seemed as if someone were following him, though never the same person twice, and when he traveled out of town, he thought cars tailed the ones he rode in. Sometimes when he answered his phone, nothing but silence greeted him, and, once, a man called from a hidden number and asked for him in Arabic, but when Abu Omar said it was he, the man hung up. Another time, an e-mail attachment made his computer crash, and he wondered (probably without cause) whether someone had sent an electronic worm to upload data from the computer. Another day, he returned to his apartment and thought some of his things had been rearranged, as if someone had gone through them.

The policeman on the street that afternoon had flashed his credentials so quickly that Abu Omar hadn't been able to see which branch of police he was with. His blond hair, pale face, and command of English made Abu Omar think he was not Italian. Later events made him certain the man was an American. He had walked Abu Omar to the sidewalk and stood by a van that Abu Omar had paid no attention to, then looked through Abu Omar's papers and called his dispatcher. As he did, an Egyptian woman and her child walked by on the opposite sidewalk. Abu Omar knew the woman by sight—she lived nearby—but he had never spoken to her. Not long after she passed them, the car that had brought the American began to turn around. While Abu Omar was watching it, the world exploded.

One moment he was waiting on the American, concerned but not alarmed. The next, the side door of the van opened with a thundering tear and he was hauled into the air. He flailed instinctively, and he thought later that he had yelled, but he wasn't sure. It was like in a nightmare, where it is hard to say what screams were in one's head and what came out of one's mouth. At the moment, he understood dimly that his hoisters were two hulks, six feet tall if an inch, which gave them half a foot on him. They were muscled like stallions. As he was pulled inside, he caught the briefest of glimpses of their faces and would later say their owners seemed Italian in complexion and about thirty years old. They threw him against the side of the van, one of them slammed the sliding door shut, and everything went dark. The whole thing could not have taken three seconds.

The hulks hit and kicked him with quick, sharp blows to his head, chest, stomach, and legs, and he fell to the floor on his face. The blows kept coming. He was so at their mercy, which was so obviously small, that he was certain he would be killed. Abruptly, however, the beating stopped, a gag was stuffed roughly in his mouth, something—he thought it was the winter hat he was wearing—was pulled over his eyes, and cords were cinched tightly around his wrists and ankles. He was trussed like a slaughterhouse pig. While all this was happening, he heard the squeal of tires and felt the van moving fast, but his pain and shock were too great for him to think about where they might be going. His mouth was filled with blood and mucus, and he could tell he was bleeding from his nose and knees. Several parts of him felt the way a thumb does when it is smashed by a hammer. He was sure he had several broken bones, and he tried not to shift his position, since even slight movements hurt.

After some minutes he became overwhelmed with the sensation that his body was imploding. He heard strange burbling noises come from his throat and felt foam ooze out of his mouth around the gag. He couldn't breathe, and his muscles became rigid. He wet his pants. It occurred to him that this was what dying must be like. One of the hulks noticed his throes and gave a loud scream. If there was a word in the scream, or a language suggested by it, Abu Omar was too stupefied to notice. Quickly the men tore off his galabia, and one of them massaged his chest while the other lifted the fabric covering Abu Omar's head and pointed a flashlight at one of his eyes. His pupil must have reacted as expected, because the man grunted confidently, pulled the fabric back down, and let Abu Omar be. He could feel himself breathing again, and he knew then that he would not die in the van. They wanted him alive, but the thought did not lessen his terror.

The van drove many hours. It felt like four or more, but it was hard to say, he was so dumb with pain. The hulks stayed in the cargo hold with him the whole time, and two other men, whose

forms he had noticed earlier, stayed in the cab, which was separated from the hold by a metal screen. None of the four said a word
the entire trip. Abu Omar remembered that not long after he left
his apartment that morning, he had walked by a light-colored van
that was parked on the street, and a minute later the same van had
driven by him. He wondered now if that van and this one were
the same. He also wondered whether the Egyptian woman on the
street had seen the kidnapping. For the most part, though, he did
not think. He feared, and the fear crowded out his thoughts and
made him very tired. When he was able, he prayed.

At last the van stopped and the door was opened. Two men—he
wasn't sure if they were the hulks—carried him out like a sack of
sugar and put him inside another kind of vehicle that might have
been an automobile or a small plane. It could not have been a large
plane because they did not carry him up more than a step or two,
if that, when they put him inside. Soon the vehicle began to move.
He did not feel anything like a takeoff or turbulence and did not
notice the changes in breathing that come with flight, but neither
did he feel the hum a car makes when its engine is on or the small
shudders of a car hitting bumps in the road. He did not sense any
people with him. He felt sedated, only half conscious—sixty percent, he would later say. He thought that maybe during the initial beating or maybe when they had given him first aid, they had
jabbed a needle into him or sprayed something in his nose—he
would hardly have noticed. But it could have just been pain and
dread that blunted his senses.

The ride in the second vehicle seemed to last an hour, although
it might have been as much as three. Again he was carried out.
He knew he was at an airport this time because he could hear airplane engines. He was taken inside a cold building and dropped
on the floor and left there a while, maybe ten minutes, before he
heard the footsteps of many people coming toward him. A couple
of them stood him up and cut the restraints from his ankles so
he could stand on his own. Then someone began to cut away his

clothes. It was a skillful job: the cuts were swift but did not nick him, and he never felt the cutter's hands. He was denuded in less than a minute. Without warning, something was shoved roughly up his anus, which hurt terribly, then a diaper was put on him, then he was dressed in what felt like pajamas. To get the pajama top on him, they had to cut his hands free, but as soon as the shirt was on, his hands were again cinched behind his back with plastic cords. Then the covering over his head was yanked off. The light that greeted him, after so many hours in the dark, was blinding. When his eyes adjusted, he could make out a group of eight or ten men outfitted in black balaclavas and khaki uniforms with many pockets on the arms and legs for holding small tools like flashlights and truncheons. Some of the men had knives in sheaths strapped to their thighs. They looked exactly as Special Forces do in movies. One of them photographed him, then they covered his face again, only this time with wide tape, like duct tape, which they wrapped round and round his head, leaving small openings at his nose and mouth. He tried not to think about how much it would hurt when the tape was pulled off. The interval in which his eyes were uncovered lasted only a few seconds, which amazed him. Their speed in everything amazed him. They had obviously planned and rehearsed every detail. They had no need for words and did not use them.

After cinching plastic strips around his ankles, they carried him outside and loaded him into another vehicle of some kind and set him down roughly, although whether on the floor or across a couple of seats, he could not tell. The air was extremely cold, like inside a freezer, and he soon began to lose feeling in his extremities and thought he was becoming hypothermic. He could hear classical music playing lightly, as if far away, which was surreal, but then nothing about his afternoon had been real. The vehicle started to move, and he could tell now that it was an airplane, because he felt a slight pressure on his chest and a rolling in his stomach from the climb to altitude. Just after takeoff, or perhaps just before, someone put headphones on him. The classical music streamed through and drowned out all other sound except the occasional back-and-forth of footsteps. Someone also attached a wire to the big toe of his right foot, he assumed for monitoring his pulse or oxygen. Other wires may have been attached elsewhere, but he could not be sure later if he had only imagined them. After the plane had been aloft a while, it began to warm up, and he deduced that it had been sitting on a frozen runway with its door open when he was loaded. It took a long time for the feeling of being frozen to leave him.

He had not been able to swallow all of the blood and mucus that had pooled in his mouth that afternoon, and at some point in the flight it congealed into a kind of paste that seemed to glue his airway shut. He began gasping for breath, but no one came to his aid, and again he felt as if he might die. When his chest started heaving crazily, someone finally leaned over him, put an oxygen mask to his nose, and stuck a water tube in his mouth. The paste was so thick that he vomited the water back out, which earned him slaps to his face and kicks to his ribs. But the water seemed to have cleared his airway and he could breathe again.

The plane was in the air a long time, he guessed seven or eight hours. Maybe it landed once or even twice, but he was too groggy to say. He wondered if the thing they had shoved up his anus had been a sedative. Thoughts of death overwhelmed him, and he tried to recite the Quran to push them away, but they kept returning. Finally he felt the plane circling, then descending. Someone put more plastic bands around his wrists and ankles, cinching them so tight that they felt like knives cutting through his skin. He screamed, but his caretaker did not loosen the cords. He felt the plane land, then someone removed his headphones and he heard the plane's engines and people moving about. Soon he was heaved to his feet and shoved down the aisle, which felt, to his bruised body, like being battered all over again. A muggy heat greeted him at the door. He was led down a short flight of steps—he had not noticed them on being carried aboard—so he knew now that the plane was small.

"Get in," someone said to him in Egyptian Arabic.

So he knew also that he was home.

He was nudged into a microbus, and a man got in beside him. The man must have seen Abu Omar's bleeding wrists because he severed the plastic handcuffs, replaced them with metal cuffs, then wiped the blood with tissues. Abu Omar wanted to ask him to remove the cuffs from his ankles as well, but he was too scared. The microbus drove quickly through city streets—surely Cairo's, he thought—for half an hour. When it stopped, he was ordered out and led into a building, where his feet were cut free. Someone began to examine his body. It seemed he was checking Abu Omar's wounds, and Abu Omar was relieved to think the examiner might be a doctor. But the man did not linger over the wounds and presently began ripping the tape from Abu Omar's head, every rip bringing with it a piece of skin or a tuft of beard. He screamed as blood trickled down his cheeks and onto his shirt. It took many rips to finish the job. Afterward he would say that of everything that happened to him in captivity, the tape was the thing for which he most hated the CIA.

His eyes, now uncovered, were again struck with the glare of light, and a man at his side ordered him to blink several times to adjust them. The man also shouted that Abu Omar was not to look at anything but the wall in front of him. He did as told but not before seeing three or four Egyptian men standing about the room. One of them removed the cuffs on his wrists, then made him take off his pajama-like clothes. He could see now that they were light gray and that their arms and legs had been cut off to make short pants and a short-sleeved shirt. In his earlier stupor, he hadn't noticed they were cutoffs. His diaper was removed next, and he was given underwear and a blue prison uniform to put on, then his wrists and ankles were re-shackled. A man took many photographs of him—to Abu Omar, it seemed from every possible angle. When the photographer was done, a hood was pulled over Abu Omar's head, and he was led to another room and made to sit in a chair.

He sensed many people present, but only one spoke. The speaker said the interrogation would begin now, and he demanded to know Abu Omar's name, occupation, and address, the names of his family members, how and why he had left Egypt, what he was doing in Italy, what he had done elsewhere. It had the makings of a long interrogation. But soon the man stopped and said, "There are two *bashas* in the room." *Basha* is the Arabic of the Turkish *pasha*, an official of high rank. "One of them would like to talk to you."

The basha stepped forward.

"Osama," he said, "do you hear me well?"

"Yes, I do," Abu Omar replied.

"I'll ask you one question, and I need a short, decisive answer—only yes or no. Will you work for us? If you say yes, we will allow you to go back to Italy this moment."

"No," said Abu Omar, but he was desperate to plead his innocence and began to do so.

"Quiet!" the basha commanded. "Don't say another word."

On later occasions, Abu Omar would sometimes say the basha was an exceedingly senior official, probably Egypt's minister of the interior, Habib El-Adly. But other times he would say he had no idea who the basha was.

The basha left, and Abu Omar was led out of the office through several corridors and into a cell. His blindfold and shackles were removed, and the door was shut behind him. He thought he could hear, very faintly, a muezzin making the *adhan*, the call to the first of Islam's five daily prayers, which is held at dawn and is called *fajr*. The adhan is more song than proclamation—an admission of the power of music by a faith that is, by some interpretations, opposed to it—and it is beautiful even over the tinny loudspeakers that carry it across the great cities of the old caliphate. Cairo is at its quietest during the adhan of fajr, and so it is heard, if only in dreams, by all but a few of its twenty million inhabitants. Hearing it, Abu Omar fell asleep.

FILM AND TELEVISION have dulled brutality. Hardly a person alive has not seen a thousand fists to the jaw, clubs to the knee, boots to the groin. Nearly always the point of view is the beater's, and a beater feels no pain. A pummeled gut is no more than a puff of wind expelled from a surprised mouth, a cracked nose no more than a thin line of blood trickling from a nostril, and in the next scene the expeller of wind and the trickler of blood will walk unbowed.

Reality bows a man. A single hard blow can send a liquid pain searing through a person and make him feel as if he is falling into an abyss. Several blows can brutally define his trunk for him, as if his skeleton has been etched in the medium of pain. A man who is about to be tortured senses as much: when pain is about to be endured, it becomes easier to imagine correctly, which is why awaiting pain is itself an anguish. The anguish will be all the greater if the awaiter lives in a place where torture is common, because he will have heard stories about others' tortures. He may, for example, have heard of *falanga*, which is striking the soles of the feet with a rod and which causes an excruciation so permeating that victims have said it is as if someone stuck a knife in their brain stem. The pain may be minutely lessened by arching the feet, but after several blows the feet swell grotesquely and cannot be arched at all. Or the person awaiting torture may have heard of a prisoner who was made to stand barefoot on the edges of jagged cans so that the cans sliced into the soles of his feet until they bled dry. Or he may know of a victim whose hand was placed on a table and smashed methodically with a hammer, first the back of the hand proper, then the knuckles and bones of one finger, then another finger, and so on until no bone was left unshattered. He may also know of a woman who had her head pounded against the corner of a file cabinet until her skull was split and her brain bared. He may know of another woman whose child was dangled out a sixth-story window until she signed whatever her tormentors wanted her to sign. He may have heard of a man who was forced to watch his daughter raped or his father sodomized. Another man will have had ether injected into his scrotum, which feels like lighting a match inside the testicles. Another's pubic hair will have been set on fire. Another will have had cockroaches inserted in his rectum. Another will have shared a cell with a cobra. Someone else will have been made to sit in a chair and have her upper torso shaken back and forth so quickly that she vomited, urinated, and defecated on herself. Another will have endured the same shaking and will have emerged as if lobotomized. Another will have had his hands cuffed behind his back, then the cuffs will have been connected to chains, which will have been thrown over a pulley and yanked so that he was lifted into the air until his arms were twisted out of their sockets—torture in its truest sense, since the word is derived from the Latin *torquere*, "to twist." Another will have been dragged on her face over unfinished concrete. Another made to swallow large amounts of salt, then denied water for several days until he nearly died of thirst, then finally given a drink that will have turned out to be urine. Another will have had boiling water thrown on his feet. Another's feet will have been submerged for hours in ice cubes. There are prisoners who have been soaked so long in vats, with only their heads sticking out, that when they were removed from the liquid their skin fell off and they died slow, painful deaths. There are places where the cat-o'-nine-tails is still used: the prisoner is stripped of his shirt and tied hand and foot to a post, then whipped with a leather scourge that has seven or nine or a dozen "tails," whose ends are knotted or studded with metal. The first lashes raise horrible welts, and the man will scream ferociously. Subsequent lashes cut through his skin until, slice by slice, his back becomes raw flesh, blood pools at his feet, and his voice fails him. (Thus may have arisen the saying "Cat got your tongue?") If his torture continues, his back will look as if it has been through a meat grinder. If he is lucky, he will pass out.

In Egypt, beatings, falanga, suspension in the air, and whippings enjoy wide currency. The other above tortures have all been used in recent years, some in Egypt, some in countries not far away. The cat-o'-nine-tails, which may have been named for the cat hide that ancient Egyptians used for the tails, was an official tool of the Egyptian state until the twenty-first century, when it was banned because of international censure. The ban is nominal. All such bans are nominal. The prisoner in an Egyptian cell, waking or sleeping, has much to occupy his mind.

THAT A PERSON might say anything under coercion has seldom kept a nation from thinking he might say something worthwhile. In some city-states of ancient Greece, trial judges were permitted to order testimony tortured out of slaves when evidence of a crime was lacking. Aristotle approved. Although he acknowledged that "people under the duress of torture tell lies quite as often as they tell the truth—sometimes persistently refusing to tell the truth, sometimes recklessly making a false charge in order to be let off sooner," he appears to have thought that only free Greeks could be so wily. Slaves and foreigners were simpler, and under torture they would usually tell the truth. The idea that it is bad to torture your own kind but acceptable to torture your lessers is one of the most enduring principles in the history of torture.

The Romans at first differed from the Greeks in that they tortured only as an extra punishment for those condemned to death. Later, however, the Romans adopted the Hellenic practice of torturing slaves for evidence. They initially restricted judicial torture, as the practice was called, to criminal (as opposed to civil) trials. The tortures included flogging, beating with rods, burning with hot irons, piercing with hooks, confining in small boxes, and racking—that is, stretching the limbs of a victim, who lay on a rack, bit by bit until ligaments snapped, bones dislodged, and muscles tore. (The rack has a false reputation as being of medieval origin; it was probably the most common of Rome's tortures.) Under these tortures, slaves testified to all kinds of things, some of which were true, which so pleased the Romans that they eventually permitted the torture of free men and women, although only in trials for very great crimes like treason. Freemen, it turned out, blurted out testimony under torture as eagerly as slaves, which also pleased the Romans, who then reasoned that if someone might be tortured for evidence on the greatest of crimes, why not for evidence on merely great ones? So judicial torture was expanded to these crimes. Later it was expanded to somewhat lesser crimes, then to still lesser ones, so that in time there were a large number of "torturable" offenses.

Torture grew in other ways too. Where at first only witnesses who refused to testify were tortured, now even a witness who testified willingly could be tortured if her testimony seemed suspicious. The means of torture multiplied, and not just for witnesses. Convicts were now mutilated, crucified, or, famously, torn and gutted by wild animals before spectators. Here was another durable theme of torture: once introduced, it was hard to contain. The class of people who required torture, and the ways in which they ought to be tortured, were wont to multiply.

Not all of the ancients tortured. Babylonians, Hebrews, Hindus, many sub-Saharan Africans, Celts, Gauls, and Germans resolved nettlesome questions of proof through ordeals. In an ordeal, a defendant would be given a physical challenge, and her success or failure in overcoming it revealed an Almighty opinion of her guilt or innocence. A mild ordeal might be lifting a heavy weight or eating a potentially poisonous fruit. A more arduous one might require walking across fired ploughshares, plucking a stone from a boiling cauldron, or being thrown into a swift current with a millstone about the neck. Some ordeals were indistinguishable from torture, but generally they were more humane: while torture was prolonged, an ordeal usually was not; while several witnesses might be tortured for a single case, trial by ordeal needed no witnesses—only the accused was tormented. For reasons not entirely clear, most societies that used ordeals seem to have used them only in the way the Greeks and Romans first used judicial torture—that is, only in cases of great crimes where evidence was short or conflicting. Torture was expansive, infectious. Ordeals were not.

Societies that torture have always had reformers who believe the practice is inhumane and ineffective either at extracting more fact than fiction or at extracting fact that can be distinguished from fiction. In the Middle Ages, reformers in Europe came to see ordeals as an alternative to torture, and in 866 Pope Nicholas I banned judicial torture and replaced it with ordeals in those parts of Christendom under his influence. He could do so in part because the lawyers, judges, and legal scholars of western Europe, whose job it had been to administer the torture apparatus, were only too happy to let God decide difficult evidentiary questions. For the next three and a half centuries, God did so. But during these centuries the idea arose that ordeals might not be in keeping with Christ's teachings either. So in 1215 the Church banned trial by ordeal, only this time it offered no replacement. *In absentia dei*, Europe's jurists had to find their own way to evaluate vital questions of evidence, and, what was more, they had to convince people that they, the jurists—mere mortals—could make decisions of life and death that for centuries had been the province of God. Their predicament was no less potentially revolutionary than that of later democrats who sought to replace divinely ordained kings with elected ministers. (The democrats legitimated their decision by giving the vote to the people, or to a narrow subset of the people, but medieval judges did not think to do so. Trial by vote, which is to say trial by jury, would have to wait several centuries.)

In northern Italy jurists resolved the dilemma by brushing aside Nicholas's ban of 866 and reviving the judicial torture of old Rome. Torture, they decided, would bring forth confessions and other compelling testimony, which meant judges would not have to make (as it were) judgment calls about guilt and innocence that God had once made. Like their Roman ancestors, the medieval Italians limited torture to the basest of defendants, the vilest of crimes, and the toughest of evidentiary questions. As a further safeguard, they devised complicated rules about when torture could be used. A judge might be required, for example, to have "half proof" of a crime before he could order someone tortured: an eyewitness to the crime might constitute one-quarter proof; a murder weapon found on the defendant might be another quarter; separately the proofs gave no cause for torture, but together they did. There were endless permutations. The Italians originally forbade the torture of the very old, the very frail, the very young, the pregnant, and witnesses (as opposed to defendants). Nor was torture permitted on red-letter days—Sundays and holy days, which were written in red on calendars. To ensure that only true confessions were tortured out of people, a confessor might be required to repeat his statement in court twenty-four hours after confessing. The idea was that if he had lied just to end the torture, he would recant on reflection. Judges, however, often sent a recanter back to the torture chamber on the theory that if he had lied under torture, he might be lying again in court and only further torture could determine which version of his story was true. It was the kind of logical quagmire that proponents of torture tended to get themselves into, having suspended logic to justify torture in the first place.

The Italian system of torture, which became known as Roman law, eventually spread south to Sicily, north to Scandinavia, west to Spain, and east to Germany. The tortures that spread with it tended to be ones that did not kill accidentally and that could be adjusted quickly in response to a victim's answers. A favorite of Italian torturers was the *strappado*, in which the accused was suspended by ropes in five stages, or degrees, of escalating pain. Hence our phrase for harsh questioning, "the third degree." Thumbscrews and legscrews—hence "to put the screws to"—and the rack were popular elsewhere. Typically governments did not specify what kinds of tortures the torturers should use. Lawmakers thought, as one French bureaucrat was told in 1670 when he tried to standardize which tortures ought to be used across the country, that "the description that would be necessary would be indecent in an ordinance." The belief remains today.

The torturers of the Middle Ages and Renaissance eventually found what the Romans had found: try though they would to restrict torture, it slipped its fetters. If it was alright to torture in the case of a heinous crime, why not in the case of less heinous ones? If a serf could be tortured, why not a landholder? If a defendant, why not a witness? If for trial, why not for punishment? As before, the class of torturables and the kinds of tortures expanded, and when Europeans settled around the world, they took their tortures with them. (Much of the world, of course, knew torture before Europeans arrived.) Thus in colonial America, Connecticut Quakers branded heretics with the letter H, and Virginians pierced the tongues of blasphemers with fired bodkins. Several of the eventual United States flogged criminals even into the twentieth century. Delaware, seized by a fit of reform in 1941, restricted the flogging of thieves to those who had stolen more than twenty-five dollars. In the 1970s, seized again, Dealware abolished the whipping post altogether.

During the seventeenth and eighteenth centuries, several forces conspired to make torture less acceptable in Europe. One was the Enlightenment, which elevated the idea that all men had inherent rights, including the right to be free from cruelty. Another was a growing discomfort among nobles, who had not minded the torture of their inferiors but who began to see in torture a great harm to the nation when it came to be applied to their own caste. Still another was a decline in the number of people being condemned to death or maiming, which made it less essential to convict defendants with absolute certainty, which in turn made it less essential to torture evidence from them or witnesses. (Sentences of death and maiming tapered off largely because states started using condemned men to row their galleys and the condemned of both sexes to work their workhouses.) In this newly humane air, old arguments about the unreliability of tortured testimony drew a heartier breath, and great abolition movements arose. In 1754, Prussia's Frederick the Great became the first sovereign to outlaw torture in all his lands, and most of the rest of Europe followed over the next several decades. Two Swiss cantons held out until 1851. In the West, torture as a matter of policy was dead. It was not forgotten, however. When the civilized world thought it useful, it would reappear.

IN THE EARLY frigidity of the Cold War, not long after the last of the Second World War's fifty million dead had been buried, the United States began studying how best to extract information from its enemies. During the late war, America had resisted the temptation to torture, notwithstanding that Germany and Japan had tortured maniacally. But the fifty million dead seem to have eaten away at American forbearance, and the American elite had come to see in the Soviet Union the greatest threat yet to the nation and the democratic capitalism for which it stood. Dreadful means might be justified in pursuit of self-preservation. Little is known about the government's earliest studies on interrogation, but it is certain the CIA and Department of Defense experimented with "unorthodox" methods on captured spies in Germany, Japan, and the Panama Canal Zone. Some of the captives are believed to have expired.

Since neither the CIA nor the Defense Department knew much about coercive interrogation, they also studied the work of more experienced coercers like the KGB, the Soviet secret police. The Americans learned that sometimes the KGB used the crudest of brutalities, as when they put inverted cups containing rats on the stomachs of victims, then heated the cups with flames, which drove the rats to flee the heat by chewing through their victims. (Orwell used a variant of this torture in the climax of *1984*.) But often the KGB deemed crudity unnecessary. There were subtler ways to break a person.

One way was to make a prisoner sit or stand without moving.

This did not sound grueling, but, as Defense researchers reported, "Any fixed position which is maintained over a long period of time ultimately produces excruciating pain." The researchers found that although some men could withstand the pain of forced standing, "sooner or later all men succumb to the circulatory failure it produces. After 18 to 24 hours of continuous standing, there is an accumulation of fluid in the tissues of the legs.... The ankles and feet of the prisoner swell to twice their normal circumference. The edema may rise up the legs as high as the middle of the thighs. The skin becomes tense and intensely painful. Large blisters develop, which break and exude water serum. The accumulation of the body fluid in the legs produces impairment of the circulation. The heart rate increases, and fainting may occur. Eventually there is renal shutdown, and urine production ceases.... [The victims] usually develop a delirious state, characterized by disorientation, fear, delusions, and visual hallucinations.... [This] is a form of physical torture, in spite of the fact that the prisoners and KGB officers alike do not ordinarily perceive it as such." That an officer might not perceive it as such was a bonus: he was more likely to be willing to inflict a torture that he did not regard as one. The same was true for the willingness of a nation, as the United States would learn after 2001.

The KGB also broke prisoners by denying them sleep. A prisoner would be set to walking in circles, which would keep her awake the first day or two, but eventually she would fall asleep on her feet and would have to be beaten and kicked. In time, blows would fail to keep her awake, and her head would have to be thrust in a bucket of ice water. After some days, reality would recede from her. She might think her captives were her friends and wonder why they would not let her rest. She might have trouble recalling her job or address or the name of her brother or the fact that she was married. If she tried to spell her name or count to ten, she might fail. Her entire being would be reduced to a single desire: "to sleep, to sleep just a little, not to get up, to lie, to rest, to forget," in the words of Israeli prime minister Menachem Begin, a victim of the KGB method. That moment was a good one to ask for a confession.

Seeing promise in such methods, the CIA commissioned its own experiments, one of the more important of which was conducted at Canada's McGill University in 1957 and was disguised as a study to prevent accidents on highways and railroads. The McGill researchers paid twenty-two college students to lie on their backs for a week in featureless cubicles. To minimize visual stimuli, they were made to wear translucent goggles, and the lights were kept on day and night. To minimize auditory stimuli, the cubicles were sound-proofed, a low white noise played continuously, and U-shaped pillows were curved around their heads. The pillows also denied the students the tactile stimulation of moving their heads against their mattresses, and a pair of thick gloves did the same for their hands. The consequences were swift. After only four hours, most of the volunteers could not hold a train of thought. After two or three days, in a few cases, the volunteers' "very identity had begun to disintegrate." The majority quit before the week was up, and all of them hallucinated. One heard a choir, another saw squirrels with bags slung over their shoulders marching in file, and another felt a small spaceship fire pellets at him. Later the CIA would conclude, "Extreme deprivation of sensory stimuli induces unbearable stress and anxiety and is a form of torture."

Encouraged, McGill's researchers devised other tests for the CIA but did away with volunteers who might quit mid-study. Over several years, more than one hundred psychiatric patients were either unwittingly or wittingly but unwillingly experimented on. The special research of D. Ewen Cameron, a past president of the American Psychiatric Association, was "depatterning." To depattern a patient, Dr. Cameron drugged her into a coma, kept her comatose for up to three months, then revived her and gave her electroconvulsive shocks three times a day at charges up to forty times the norm for a month. After that, he strapped onto her head a football helmet equipped with speakers, through which he played a single, looped message—"My mother hates me" was one—up to half a million times over three weeks. His patients became psychotic. In another of Cameron's experiments, captives were kept for up to five weeks in the sensory-deprivation cubes that had broken most of the student volunteers in a few days. Decades later, some of his victims were still "depatterned." Two had a disorder that kept them from recognizing people's faces. In the 1980s the U.S. government compensated the victims modestly, and the American Psychiatric Association claimed "deep regret" over the experiments, but the Canadian Psychiatric Association rejected calls for remorse and extolled McGill's psychiatrists for a tradition of therapeutic excellence.

Further studies taught the CIA and Defense Department about other simple but devastating methods of breaking prisoners. Solitary confinement, for example, could cause damage to a prisoner's brain "much like that which occurs if he is beaten, starved, or deprived of sleep." Disturbing a prisoner's sense of time—retarding and advancing clocks, serving meals at odd hours, shutting out daylight—could also madden a man. Researchers for the Defense Department concluded, "Isolation, anxiety, fatigue, lack of sleep, uncomfortable temperatures, and chronic hunger . . . lead to serious disturbances of many bodily processes; there is no reason to differentiate them from any other form of torture."

The CIA theorized that the onset of such disturbances might be hastened by drugs like LSD, amphetamines, and heroin, and in the 1950s and 1960s its scientists tested the theory on prisoners of war in Korea, partygoers in New York (whose drinks were spiked), johns in San Francisco (drugged by whores in the CIA's pay), convicts in Kentucky (kept on LSD "trips" for eleven weeks), and on its own scientists. One of the scientists, Frank Olson, suffered a nervous breakdown after his encounter with an LSD-spiked cocktail and subsequently hurtled through a window on the tenth floor of a New York hotel. The coroner said Olson committed suicide, but the family's pathologist said he had suffered a blunt-force trauma to his head before crashing through the window. The family believed Olson was murdered because he had soured on the mind-control program. Ultimately, however, the CIA decided that mind-control drugs were unpredictable and usually unnecessary. Simpler methods worked best.

Those methods worked all the better if begun early—if possible, from the moment the victim was captured. He should be taken, the CIA concluded, at a time "when his mental and physical resistance is at its lowest" and in a manner that caused him "the maximum amount of mental discomfort." Complete surprise and a show of overwhelming force were ideal. These precepts probably explained the jarring shout from the man in the van on Via Guerzoni, followed immediately by the terrifying boom of the rear door ripping open, followed in turn by the adamantine grip on Abu Omar, the swift heaving of him into the hold, and the slamming shut of the door. Succeeding acts, the CIA decided, should further disorient the victim and erode his capacity to resist. An immediate beating would do. So would hooding, which was better than blindfolding, because a hood made a person feel more cut off from the world. Stripping and dressing him in something unfamiliar and ill-fitting were good too. "It is very important," the CIA concluded, "that the arresting party behave in such a manner as to impress the subject with their efficiency," which convinced a captive of his impotence. Decades before the CIA carried out its first rendition, it had the science of seizing a man pat.

ALTHOUGH CIA OFFICIALS knew crudity was not needed to break a captive, they did not foreswear it. As throughout history, once one accepted the use of torture, it was hard to limit its forms. The CIA's Phoenix program during the Vietnam War was a vast application of crudity, a "pump and dump—pumping suspects for information by torture and then dumping the bodies," as Alfred McCoy wrote in his indispensable *A Question of Torture*. The pumpers and dumpers were U.S. and South Vietnamese soldiers whom the CIA trained in interrogation. Some of the trainees went on to coil wires around their victims' testicles or stick wires into their vaginas, then send high-voltage current through them. Other interrogators shoved dowels into victims' ears and when their answers proved unsatisfactory tapped the dowels by degrees until they penetrated deep into their brains. It was an agonizing death. Other interrogators, more patient, simply starved prisoners until they talked or died. In another CIA program in Vietnam, a neurosurgeon implanted electrodes in the brains of three POWs and transmitted radio signals to them in hope of stirring them to violence, but the subjects only vomited and shat themselves. Their utility spent, they were shot by Green Berets and their bodies burned. In another experiment, CIA psychiatrists tried to induce Vietcong prisoners to talk by giving them twelve electroconvulsive treatments in a single day. None divulged any secrets, so every day thereafter they were convulsed eight or nine times. One prisoner died after a week, and the rest died over the next few weeks. None talked. Victims of other tortures talked, but unhelpfully, like the man who confessed to being a CIA spy, a hermaphrodite, a Buddhist monk, a Catholic bishop, and the son of the king of Cambodia. He was in fact a mere schoolteacher. Interrogators in the South Vietnamese Army had a slogan: "If they aren't Vietcong, beat them until they are. If they are Vietcong, beat them until they aren't." It was a good prescription for revenge but not for intelligence.

The CIA and Defense Department knew or would soon know that information obtained under torture was unreliable. A few years after the Vietnam War, the CIA instructed its officers, "Intense physical pain is quite likely to produce false confessions, fabricated to avoid additional punishment," and the Army instructed its troops, "Use of torture is not only illegal but also it is a poor technique that yields unreliable results, may damage subsequent collection efforts, and can induce the source to say what he thinks the HUMINT [human intelligence] collector wants to hear." The

CIA and Defense Department also knew there were alternatives to torture. Sherwood Moran, a Marine Corps major, wrote a manual during the Second World War on how to establish "intellectual and spiritual" rapport with supposedly barbaric, unreachable enemies. The manual was based on Moran's success convincing Japanese POWs to reveal their comrades' positions and battle plans. It became a classic in interrogation circles.

The Phoenix program achieved no comparable success. Although its graduates tortured thousands and killed, by the CIA's count, 20,587 (by the count of the South Vietnamese government, 40,994), a CIA commander in Vietnam told Alfred McCoy, "The truth is that never in the history of our work in Vietnam did we get one clear-cut, high-ranking Vietcong agent." President Nixon rewarded the CIA officer who ran Phoenix, William Colby, with the directorship of the CIA.

The United States did not train just the Vietnamese in the American way of torture. It also trained police and soldiers of other countries of the Third World, particularly countries ruled by despots who took a hard line against Communism. If the despots also opposed lesser leftisms, so much the better. Only a few details about the trainings have become known. In Uruguay in the late 1960s a CIA officer was reported to have taught policemen how to electrocute prisoners by demonstrating on four beggars from the streets of Montevideo, all of whom were electrocuted to death. "The special horror of the course was its academic, almost clinical atmosphere," one of the purported witnesses wrote. Another course, taught in Texas by the U.S. Army, was described by a Honduran sergeant: "They taught us psychological methods—to study the fears and weaknesses of a prisoner: make him stand up, don't let him sleep, keep him naked and isolated, put rats and cockroaches in his cell, give him bad food, serve him dead animals, throw cold water on him, change the temperature." The curriculum may have been implemented; a Marxist tortured in Honduras said she was given dead birds and rats for dinner, was kept standing for hours without sleep or the use of a toilet, and had freezing water thrown on her naked body at half-hour intervals.

One of the earliest recipients of the CIA's training was Egypt. The trainers were former Nazi commanders from Germany who were recruited by the CIA not long after the Second World War, probably because the agency was then inexperienced in brutality and wanted men of expertise. One of the Nazis was SS Sturmbannführer (Storm-Trooper Leader) Alois Brunner, whom Adolf Eichmann described as one of his best men and who, during the war, trained Nazi field commanders to liquidate Jewish ghettos across Europe. By one estimate, Brunner personally ordered 128,000 Jews to death camps. Long afterward he said his great regret in life was not having murdered more Jews. Another of the CIA's trainers in Egypt was SS Obersturmbannführer (Senior Storm-Trooper Leader) Otto Skorzeny, who rescued Benito Mussolini in 1943 after his capture by Partisans and who plotted the assassinations, all in vain, of Stalin, Churchill, Roosevelt, and Eisenhower. A Nazi publication once described Skorzeny as "Hitler's favorite commando." The Nazi trainers were supervised in Egypt by a CIA officer on long-term loan to the country's de facto ruler (and eventual president) Nasser, but neither the number of Nazis nor the particulars of their curriculum are known. After they finished their work, some went to Tehran and trained Iran's secret service, the Savak, whose savagery was impressive even by the debased standards of Third World dictatorships. Others may have trained security forces elsewhere. Alois Brunner settled, perhaps suggestively, in Syria, where Israel's Mossad apparently tried to assassinate him by letter bomb, which, however, deprived him only of a few fingers and an eye.

Nasser's relationship with the CIA was complicated, largely because he entertained alliances with both the Soviet Union and the United States. In the early going, in addition to training his security forces, the CIA helped him build and run a radio station, gave him several million dollars, and promised more aid to come. When the White House did not follow through on the aid, Nasser took $3 million of the CIA's original grant and built a latticework minaret as tall as the Washington Monument, a height meant to insult. The CIA dubbed it "Nasser's prick" and planted explosives at its base to (as it were) blow it, but the Egyptians discovered the charges. The Egyptian name for the tower was "Roosevelt's erection," in honor of CIA officer Kermit Roosevelt, grandson of Teddy. Nasser's relations with the West reached their nadir in 1956, when he nationalized the Suez Canal and the dispossessed British proposed to assassinate him. President Eisenhower vetoed the proposal in favor of a campaign of subversion, but the CIA did not handle it deftly. For example, its officers carelessly exposed a newspaper publisher, Mustafa Amin, whom they were paying to print pro-American articles, and Nasser had him imprisoned and tortured. Later there was a détente between the United States and Nasser, and in the last years of his rule the CIA tipped him to a plot by military officers to overthrow him. The purge he undertook was so remorseless that even some CIA officials were alarmed.

The relationship between Egypt and the United States became more stable after Anwar Sadat succeeded Nasser, rejected his socialism, and, eventually, made peace with Israel. Billions of American dollars and other assistance flowed to Cairo in consequence and made Egypt the second-largest recipient of U.S. foreign aid. (Israel was first.) For a time America's embassy in Cairo was its largest in the world. Included in the aid was more training for Egypt's military and security services. In the 1990s, when Gamaa began killing by the dozen, the CIA tutored President Mubarak's special forces in the hunting of terrorists, although the program eventually had to be canceled because, as U.S. ambassador Edward Walker said, "Too many people . . . died while fleeing. It got to be a little too obvious."

When Bill Clinton decided to start extraordinarily rendering suspected terrorists, it was, therefore, natural—indeed almost inevitable—that he turned to Mubarak to receive many of the victims. In addition to the longstanding ties between the United States and Egypt, many of the world's most troublesome terrorists were

Egyptian, and Mubarak had long demanded their repatriation by the countries that had given them refuge. He seems to have been only too pleased to open his dungeons to America. The CIA would later say that before September 11, 2001, it extraordinarily rendered about seventy men. It did not say to which countries, but Egypt almost certainly received the largest number. There could have been little doubt about how the victims were treated. "If you want a serious interrogation," said Robert Baer, who for years was a CIA officer in the Middle East, "you send a prisoner to Jordan. If you want them to be tortured, you send them to Syria. If you want someone to disappear—never to see them again—you send them to Egypt." It was understood that an Egyptian disappearance would be preceded by torture.

A wrinkle in sending men to such places was that it was illegal under American law, the law being the United Nations Convention Against Torture, which Clinton had signed in 1994 after years of stalling by Presidents Reagan and Bush the elder. The law read, in pertinent part, "It shall be the policy of the United States not to expel, extradite, or otherwise effect the involuntary return of any person to a country in which there are substantial grounds for believing the person would be in danger of being subjected to torture, regardless of whether the person is physically present in the United States." After September 11, as Bush the younger rendered men by the hundred, rendition's apologists argued that the extraordinary enemy justified extraordinary measures. But this was a canard the Convention Against Torture had foreseen. "No exceptional circumstances whatsoever," the law read, "whether a state of war or a threat of war, internal political instability, or any other public emergency may be invoked as a justification of torture or other cruel, inhuman or degrading treatment or punishment." The United States, however, was in a cruel, inhuman, and degrading mood.

———

THE STOREHOUSES of men—the keeps, the camps, the slammers, the gulags—have in common spareness, which is economical for the storers and a further punishment for the stored. In Egypt a typical cell reserved for political prisoners is a concrete box furnished with a reed mat or a grain sack or a piece of cardboard to lie on and a vile blanket that has been soiled with the blood and sputum of prior inmates. The latrine, if there is one, will be little more than a reeking hole in the floor, and if there is a window, it is likely to be miniscule, set too high to see out, and admissive more of pests than of light. The door will be of steel or thick wood and will have a sliding slot through which food can be inserted and commands barked. A ventilation duct, if it exists, will not do its job, and the air will be fetid and mildewy. There is sometimes water on the floor, in which case the dankness in the air may approach that of a recently used shower. In some cells, puddles survive for years from the drip of a pipe ten feet overhead. Its plip—plip—plip—plip—plip can derange. Sometimes moisture covers the entire surface of the floor in a thin film, and then the walls will crawl with mold and other spores, the prisoner's bedding will be damp, and there will be no place he can touch, including his own person, that is not clammy. Prisoners have been punished by being held temporarily—days or weeks—in cool water up to their shins. In the South Pacific, where the water is 85 degrees, sailors cast overboard have become hypothermic and died in a few days. Just so, a man may die in the Egyptian desert from standing in what amounts to a wading pool. Other prisoners have been put in sealed cells into which water is poured through a pipe. When the water reaches a man's chest, he will be likely to sign whatever confession is put before him.

Torture through excesses of plumbing is cruelly ironic, because plumbing in its normal form is deficient in Egyptian prisons. If the cell has a sink, it may yield no water or may yield it for only a few minutes a day. The water is apt to be filthy, although it can be improved by filtering through a rag, even though the rag, like everything else in the prison, will be dirty. When prisoners drink, the water may cramp and convulse them, and sometimes it will bring diarrhea that can last months. Cell toilets are apt to clog, and shit and piss can back up into the cell. Warders know the power of shit in annihilating their wards. They may put a man in a cell with no toilet and keep him there a month, so that he is forced to defecate and urinate on the floor. Or they may put him in a cell with shit piled so high in a corner that when he has to add to it, he will barely be able to squat over the pile and breathing will be revolting at any time. Or they may strip him naked and throw him sprawling into a cell whose floor is covered inches deep in excrement and urine.

That a cell is indoors does not imply protection from weather. In the Egyptian summer, the temperature inside a cell may rise to 125 degrees, and in winter it can drop below freezing. If a prisoner has no mat, he must choose in the winter between putting his blanket under him to lessen the cold of the frozen concrete or putting it over him to guard against the frozen air. Either way, one half of him will freeze, and he will pass the night shifting his blanket from one side to the other. He may keep his face warm by wrapping his underwear about his head.

In any weather a penitentiary night is long. It often begins in late afternoon or early evening, when the lights are shut off, and lasts until well past dawn—sixteen hours of darkness or near darkness passed in a silence enforced by cudgel.

In Egypt a man who is walled off from other men is not walled off from life. The lower orders of fauna find their way into cells. Flies, gnats, and mosquitoes mock the swats of confined men and attack with a sandstorm's persistence. Their victim may find partial sanctuary under a blanket, but the blanket is usually so thin that the insects can bite through, and in the Nilotic summer, to be under a blanket may be so stifling that the cure is worse than the cancer. Cockroaches are not put off by blankets and will crawl over a prisoner almost as boldly by light as by dark. After Sadat became president, he took a pickax to a prison where he had once been held, and at each blow of his ax, hundreds of cockroaches poured out of the sodden bricks. He built new prisons that he said would be humane, but the cockroaches overran them too—a metaphor for the Egyptian polity.

Smaller visitors come to the inmate too. One is the mite *Sarcoptes scabiei*, which favors crevices—the valleys between fingers and toes, the crooks of elbows, the cracks of buttocks, the flaps of genitals. With his large family, he burrows under the skin and pushes up little ridges, which turn to pustules that ooze, burst, and release bacteria. His victims develop a savage urge to scratch, but if they do, they will spread the bacteria, which will cause their skin to redden and swell and may bring fever. If they are otherwise weakened, as Egyptian prisoners tend to be, the fever might kill them. Lice scourge similarly, dropping their miniscule eggs across hirsute hills and dales and sometimes bringing typhus, another killer. Such pests are hard to eliminate without medicine and cleanliness, both of which are in short supply in an Egyptian cell. Everything humane is in short supply in an Egyptian cell. Only inhumanity is excessive.

ABU OMAR was awakened by a guard turning a key in the lock of his cell door. He guessed he had slept a few hours. The guard blindfolded him, warned him not to speak, and led him down a hallway to a bathroom, where, standing behind him, he took off Abu Omar's blindfold and said he was not to turn around until the door was closed behind him. After he had used the toilet, he was to knock on the door and turn his back to it, and the guard would come in and blindfold him again. Abu Omar did as told and was returned to his cell and his blindfold was removed. Later he was given food, which he ate without interest.

He had paid little attention to the character of his cell when he had been brought to it that morning. He saw now that it was four and a half feet by six. The floor was mercifully dry. A dim bulb hung from the ceiling, and near it were a very small window that let in almost no light and a very small hole for ventilation, obviously inadequate. The air was rank. There was a thin mat and a blanket, nothing more. It was a box for a man.

Remembering his torture of fifteen years ago and knowing the stories of other victims, he was terrified. He tried to pray and recite the Quran, but he had trouble keeping his thoughts from what might happen to him. His jailers let him sauté in this imaginative broth for some hours, then at last the door opened and guards came in and blindfolded him and bound his hands. They marched him in silence down several corridors until coming to a very low doorway that had to be entered on hands and knees. The guards kicked him through, and on the other side someone removed his handcuffs and ordered him to take off his clothes. When he was naked, they re-shackled his hands behind his back and made him bend one leg so that his foot was pointed back and up toward his hands. Then they shackled the ankle of the leg to his wrists. It is hard to stand on one leg for a long time even when not wearing a blindfold, which removes the visual cues that help a person balance. Eventually Abu Omar fell to the hard floor, with no hands to break his fall. The guards stood him back up, he fell again, and they stood him up again. Each time he fell, he tried to land on a part of his body that would not hurt, but there was no such part. This went on some time, the guards laughing at each fall. In the future this torment would last what seemed like hours, but today it was shorter.

At length, he was held in place, or maybe his foot was unshackled and he was sat down on a chair, and a man asked him questions: Who were his family? Where had he grown up? With what friends? Where did he go to college? Why did he join al-Gamaa al-Islamiyya? Who recruited him? Who were his colleagues? What had he done with them? Why did he preach against the Egyptian government? Why did he conspire to commit terrorism? Wasn't he plotting to kill officials? To overthrow Mubarak? If he was innocent, why did he leave Egypt? Where did he go? What did he do there? Who did he live with? Who else did he know there? What else did he do there? What else? Where did he go next? What did he do there and who did he know? And after that? And that? Which Egyptians did he know in Italy? Which other North Africans? Did he know Abu So-and-so? Did he know the deputy imam at this mosque? How long had he known him? With whom did this deputy imam associate? Abu Imad, the imam of Viale Jenner, was a terrorist—he knew this, of course? Come now, what did he know about Abu Imad's plots? Nothing? Of course he must know something. Who was Abu Imad planning to bomb? Who was Abu Omar planning to bomb? Where? When? What were they planning with their brothers in Egypt? Who recruited the men? Who got the weapons? How were they moved? How were the papers worked out? Come, come, he must know all of this. No? No? Well. They would see about that—and a fist smashed into his head.

It is bad to be struck but worse to be struck when you cannot see the blow coming, because you cannot flinch to soften it. Before Abu Omar could recover, another fist smashed into him. Then another. Then another. The questions continued. It seemed to Abu Omar as if there were hundreds. When his interrogator exhausted one subject, he moved to another, then doubled back and revisited the first—whether to check Abu Omar's answers or wear him out, Abu Omar did not know. When his answers did not satisfy, there were more blows. Hours seemed to pass this way. At some point that day, or perhaps during a later session, the blindfold was removed and someone put a photograph of an Arab before him. Did Abu Omar know this man? What was his name? Where did he live? What did he do for the jihad? Another photo would follow, then another. There were scores of photos, mostly of men who had emigrated to Italy. Abu Omar knew some of them, but whatever he said about them, he would later not tell.

Eventually his questioners pressed to his skin a metal stick that must have been a kind of cattle prod, for electricity shot out of it and into him with horrible effect. Other victims have said such jolts contorted their muscles into grotesque positions, made their jaws clamp shut, and set their teeth grinding together. Some victims felt as if something were exploding inside them or the flesh were being ripped from their bones or their bodies were trying to tear themselves apart only to be held in place by the thin check of their skin. Some felt their eyeballs pushing up from inside, straining to burst from their sockets. Some thought their brains or hearts would rupture. Abu Omar screamed madly. His tormentor paused, gave him a few seconds to recover, then electrocuted him again. Then again. And again. And again. Each time he stopped, Abu Omar cried and pled. He promised to tell them anything, absolutely anything—they had only to name it. But the stick was put back to him. This may have gone on for minutes or hours. He lost all sense of time.

After they stopped, he continued to shake with spasms, and flashes of light darted before his eyes. In his ears the sound of a dentist's drill buzzed. Where the stick had touched him for a prolonged time, his skin was singed. In later sessions he would be electrocuted on his nipples, penis, scrotum, ears, nose, spine, soles – whatever part of his body his torturers fancied. Sometimes he passed out.

On this day or one like it, his tormentors removed his blindfold, gave him pen and paper, and told him to write a statement of his crimes. He could not easily work the pen after the electrocution, but he tried to please them. When he was done, he was given a declaration that said he had not been mistreated, which he signed. Then he was given his clothes and dressed himself in pain, and his guards returned him to his cell. Rather than leave him in relative peace, they chained his hands to an eyelet on the wall that he had not seen before. He was in so much pain that the chaining was at first unworthy of notice, but his hands soon ached miserably, and after several hours they began to swell.

Not knowing when he would be tortured again was its own torture. Each time a door opened in the passageway or footsteps came his way, he became frantic. When the steps continued past his cell, he praised God, but the terror returned almost immediately. Sometimes the steps stopped outside his door, the food slot was slid open, and a pair of eyes looked in at him. Then the slot slid shut, the owner of the eyes walked away, and the unnatural hush that was the jail's usual state returned. Two dozen prisoners may have been within shouting distance, but Abu Omar did not hear them, and they did not hear him. Forbidden to speak, each was alone among many.

THEY CAME for him again after two or three days. He was blindfolded, walked to the torture chamber, and made to strip naked. The questions began, and the photographs were put before him. He was tortured. Sometimes they beat him with fists, sometimes with thick cables. Very often he was electrocuted. At some point they put headphones on him and blared music so loud that he lost most of the hearing in one ear. He was given a document renouncing his asylum in Italy, and he did not hesitate to put his name to it—he would have renounced his children if they had asked. Sometimes his interrogators said they were certain he was a terrorist mastermind, but other times they said they knew he was just a small fish. One interrogator asked him for the passcode to his mobile phone account, which made him think his kidnappers had brought his cell phone to Egypt. Another interrogator claimed to have visited Milan shortly before the kidnapping, and he described the streets between the flat on Via Conte Verde and the mosque on Viale Jenner. Abu Omar thought, without foundation, that this proved Egypt had taken part in the kidnapping. One interrogator said Abu Imad, the imam of Viale Jenner, would be the next person kidnapped. Egypt, the interrogator claimed, had a deal with Italy whereby the latter would export any Egyptian Islamist at the request of the Egyptian government. Abu Omar believed this claim too, also without foundation. During another session, he was told that Egypt had no complaint against him but had to hold him because "the Americans imposed you on us."

"Why, then, do you abuse me so?" Abu Omar said.

"It is our family tradition," the man answered.

During a pause in one session, Abu Omar heard a cassette tape being ejected from a recorder, turned over, and put back in. He wondered who would listen to the recording.

At the end of nearly every session, he was made to sign more statements. Back in his cell, when he was not chained to the wall, he was often made to lie on his rude bed, on pain of beating if he stood up. Sometimes his guards kept him awake for long stretches—he did not know how long. When it was cold, he froze, when it was hot, he burned, and he became rheumatic and arthritic and had pain when he breathed. The insects worked on him, and his skin grew abhorrent. Now and then he fainted. When he slept, it was without rest. His nightmares were peopled by assailants he could not see, and he woke screaming, his body twitching uncontrollably. One morning he found his beard had turned white.

In time his isolation made him desperate enough to risk opening the slot of his door a crack when other prisoners walked by. He wanted only to glimpse someone who was not a demon. He thought he recognized a few Islamist leaders, one of whom, he believed, was Abu Yasser, formally Refai Ahmed Taha Musa, a high leader of Gamaa who had last been seen in Syria in October of 2001 and who was believed to have been rendered to Egypt. It was generally assumed that he had been executed. Seeing Abu Yasser alive gave Abu Omar a brief joy.

Every two or three days the guards came for him—sometimes in the morning, sometimes in the evening, sometimes in the dead of night—and he was tortured. This went on for seven months. It felt like seven years.

But a day came when an officer told Abu Omar he would soon be leaving. He wept. He had often said to himself that the Italian government would not abandon him, and he had even thought the

Italian ambassador himself might visit him and offer his protection. He inferred now that his hope had not been misplaced. He envisioned his return to Milan and his reunion with his wife and the brothers in the mosques. Over and over, he played the scenes in his mind.

The day of his departure arrived, and he was blindfolded and taken to an office, where the blindfold was briefly removed and he was told to sign two documents before him. One said that he had not been abused, the other that he had arrived in prison with no possessions. The papers were dated September 14, 2003, which was how he learned he had been in prison seven months. He signed the papers and was ordered to take off his prison uniform and was given the cut-off pajamas the Americans had dressed him in. He was mildly surprised they had been kept all these months. After he had put them on and was again blindfolded, his hands and feet were shackled and he was led outside the building at a shuffle. It was the first time in seven months he had been out of doors, and the fresh air, notwithstanding that Cairene air tastes of lead and soot, was a miracle to him. He was put aboard a microbus, the preferred transit of the Egyptian torturer, and told to lie on the floor, where he was covered with blankets so he would not be seen.

After the bus had driven for some minutes, one of his chaperons said, "Do you know where you are going?"

"To the airport," Abu Omar said. "Back to Italy. Home."

The chaperon said nothing.

After forty-five minutes, the bus stopped and Abu Omar was ordered out. He did not hear airplanes or other sounds one would associate with airports. He was led into a building and shoved roughly forward to a room, where he was set upon by many fists, boots, and curses. It was his welcome, he soon understood, to the Tora Prison complex, south of Cairo. The prisons of Tora run from a lightly secured farm camp to the most fortified prison in the nation. The latter, run by the State Security Service, is known as al-Aqrab, the Scorpion. It was apparently to the Scorpion that Abu

Omar had been brought. When his hosts were done with their violent greeting, they sat him bleeding in a chair and asked his full name, age, job, and other basic personal information, apparently for the prison's records. Even torture has its bureaucracy. Then he was taken through several hallways and down stairs to a cell well below ground. One of the guards opened the door and said Abu Omar had come to a place where nobody could find him, a place lost to the world.

"Here, the flies don't even come," the guard said.

He told Abu Omar he must never remove his blindfold, even in his cell. If he tried, he would get a "torture party." They would be watching. Abu Omar asked to know the *qiblah*, the direction of Mecca, toward which a Muslim must face during prayer, but the guard would not tell him. He asked where the lavatory was, and the guard took off the blindfold for a moment and said, "You're in the lavatory." Abu Omar saw before him a bowl of dirty water and, for his evacuations, a small hole whose stench he had already smelled. The cell had no light and only the tiniest of ventilation shafts, which accounted for the sodden weight of the air. It was no bigger than his last cell—two steps in any direction exhausted it. There was no bed, only a sheet of cardboard and a thin blanket.

The guard said that whenever Abu Omar heard a key in his door, he must go immediately to the wall opposite and kneel with both hands against it. If he failed to do so before a guard entered, he would be educated with a cattle prod. He also said that Abu Omar's name was now 27, the number of his cell. If Abu Omar failed to answer to 27, he would be educated with the prod. He would also, although the guard did not then say so, learn to answer to Whore, Cunt, and Anus, also on penalty of electrical education.

The guard shut him inside and left him alone. His despair, after his expectation of freedom, was thorough. He tried to console himself with the thought that maybe they would not treat him quite so badly here, but they soon rid him of that idea. At Tora he was to have two interrogations a day, as opposed to the one every few days at the previous prison. The first session ran from late morning until late afternoon, the second from night until nearly dawn. He was introduced to new tortures. In one, he was strapped naked to an iron grate through which electricity was shot, which added to the usual electrical agony a feeling like being seared on a griddle. Sometimes the effect was enhanced by throwing water on him. In another torture, his tormentors lay him on a water-soaked mattress and set a wooden chair over his chest and another chair over his thighs. Two brutes would sit on the chairs to weigh them down, electricity would be sent through the mattress, and Abu Omar's body would leap up and crash into the crossbars of the chairs, which kept him in contact with the current. At other times, he was electrocuted through clamps attached to his nipples or penis or through a kind of wire hat placed on his head, which left his thinking muddled for days. In another torture, he was hung on a door in a crucifix-like position and battered with cables and clubs all over his body, his genitals not excepted. In another, they draped him over a trapeze, hands and ankles bound together, and beat him all over. "Let Italy help you," they said when he cried for mercy. During one session, he was thrown face-first to the floor, naked and with his hands tied behind his back. A guard dropped his pants and mounted him as if for rape. Abu Omar screamed hysterically before passing out and did not know if the rape had been completed. The same thing happened another time.

There was no respite in his cell. Whereas in his previous prison the torture chamber had been far from his closet, here it was nearby, and he could hear the screams of other victims day and night. The impotent listening was as bad as being tortured himself.

After some time, he feared he was going mad—a prospect that frightened him more than death. Death would at least bring peace. In his desperation he opened the slot in his door and asked a guard if he could have a copy of the Quran. He would not have been able to read it, there being no light to read by, but he wanted to hold it and kiss it, if only for a few seconds. He got a beating instead. His tortures grew more severe, he assumed because his keepers were angered that he had the strength to ask for sustenance.

The severity had its effect. Life and pain became inseparable to him. He could not remember what happiness felt like and could not imagine feeling it again. Nor could he imagine his captors would let him go after all they had done to him. He supposed if he were fortunate, he would be killed, but he could also be kept like this for years, maybe decades. He wanted only to die, and resolved to kill himself. It was a sin against God to take one's life for no purpose, but he reasoned that he was already in his coffin and was only helping close the lid. He lacked a tool with which to do the job. After some thought, to the extent his addled brain permitted thought, he settled on hurling himself headlong into a wall. He put his back against one side of the cell and burst toward the opposite side, but there was no ground on which to get up speed and the collision only temporarily deprived him of consciousness. Sometime later he tried again but with the same result. His defeat was now total. He was one of the living dead.

Chapter 6

Inquest

SAFAR, THE SECOND MONTH of the Islamic calendar, is the year's most inauspicious. It is usually translated "the void month," perhaps because early Arabs left their houses void, or *safr*, at that time of year to raid their enemies. Alternatively, Safar may have been so named because an early Safar fell in autumn—Islam's calendar is lunar, and the months migrate from season to season—when leaves turn yellow, or *sufr*, and fall from trees. God cast Adam and Eve from Eden in Safar.

In the late afternoon of 28 Safar 1425 or, Gregorianly, 19 April 2004, Hitham Nasr, a pious chemical engineer, received a call from the State Security Service in Alexandria. The caller said Hitham's elder brother Osama was at the service's local headquarters and Hitham should come get him immediately.

"Just don't ask what happened," the caller said.

Hitham gathered his brother-in-law Magdi and hurried to the office, but Abu Omar was not released to them, and after some time they went home.

In the small hours of the next morning, the security service called again, this time at the home of Magdi and his wife, Abu Omar's sister Rawya.

"If you don't come now," the man on the phone said, "you'll never see him again."

Magdi gathered Hitham and again they hurried to the office. They were shown to a dirty waiting room where sat a bony, disheveled man with a wildly unkempt beard which, as Abu Omar would later say, made him look like Saddam Hussein after his capture. Magdi and Hitham hardly recognized their brother. Safar, however, would not be a void month after all.

AT TEN MINUTES before six on the evening after Abu Omar was released, the counterterrorists of Milan recorded a brief conversation between Mohammed Reda Elbadry, a teacher and lay imam at the mosque on Via Quaranta, and his daughter.

"Hello, Daddy," she said. "Abu Omar is in Egypt."

"Huh? What?"

"Uncle Abu Omar is in Egypt."

"Who?"

"Uncle Abu Omar."

"Who told you?"

"He called Aunt Nabila himself and told her he's staying with his family."

"He did?"

"Yes. She is supposed to call him back any minute."

Half an hour later, from the phone in the flat on Via Conte Verde, Nabila Ghali called her sister-in-law's in Alexandria.

"May peace be with you," a nearly forgotten voice greeted her.

"How *are* you?" she said to her husband.

"I'm fine, praise God."

"You're fine?"

"I'm fine, I'm fine."

"Really?"

"I swear! They brought me food every day."

"Really?"

"Sure. They brought me food from the fanciest restaurant."

"Praise God," she said, not understanding his irony.

He said he had much to tell about his last fourteen months, but he did not want to tell it over the Conte Verde phone. He would tell her another time on another phone. He asked if the police had come to their flat, and she said they had shortly after his kidnapping. They had wanted to see if anything in the apartment might offer a clue to his disappearance.

"Did they touch anything?" he said.

"Everything is in its place!"

"Look, did they take the computer?"

"No. Are you well?"

"Did they take the computer?"

"No."

"So tell me what they took then?!"

"They just took your papers, that's all!"

"They didn't take the computer?"

"No, they took your papers and the lessons you hold over the Internet."

"Is the computer still there? Is it?"

"Yes, it's all in its place!"

She asked if she could join him in Egypt, and he said if she did, the Egyptians might not let her leave. He himself was not allowed to travel beyond Alexandria. He told her he had arranged for one of the brothers in Milan to visit her soon and she should give him two hundred euros, which he would forward to Abu Omar. He also told her to call his first wife and children in Albania and let them know he was alive. She assented and said she was worried he would be imprisoned again.

"Look," he said, "there are no problems for me. There won't be a second kidnapping. . . . They told me, 'We are the ones who lost. You didn't lose. We are the losers!'"

"Alright," she said, although she had no idea what he meant.

"Listen, they warned me that reporters from all Europe will come looking for you. You must meet nobody. I must stress this, no journalists. That is what they said."

"Rest assured, I'll meet no one."

"Neither press nor TV!"

"Sure, sure."

"Do not speak with any channel."

"Nobody, nobody."

HUSBAND AND WIFE spoke again two weeks later, and it was evident that in between the two talks, they had spoken on an untapped phone and Ghali had decided to join him in Egypt. He told her what to do before she left: leave the decorations on the walls of the apartment, ask some of the brothers if they wanted the refrigerator or washing machine, give the furniture to the mosque on Viale Jenner, sell the computer, clean the place. A few days later, they talked again.

"Are you more at peace now?" she asked.

"Yes," he said. "Well, I was very edgy at first, but not anymore. I don't think about death anymore. I was *very close* to dying. Now more than ever I need you by my side to pursue the path that leads me to God. I don't care about anything in this life anymore. I just care to lead an Islamic life. I am deeply saddened because I wasn't able to do what I had planned to do in Italy. I think I did something but not what I hoped to do. If God wills it, I'll do it here."

His choice of words, in Arabic, and other contexts suggested that "what I hoped to do" referred to fulfilling the Islamic duty, more propagandistic than violent, to spread the word of God.

He also spoke during this period with Mohammed Reda Elbadry, the teacher at Via Quaranta, who said during one of their talks, "We are arranging a handsome sum of money for you, if God wills it."

"What's that?" said Abu Omar, perhaps not hearing or perhaps wishing to know the sum with more precision.

"We are arranging a handsome sum of money for you."

"God bless you."

"If God wills it, the price of a house."

"God bless you."

The two men had spoken at other times on untapped phones, and it soon became clear to the listeners of DIGOS that they had discussed the kidnapping. Abu Omar was careful to avoid saying much over Elbadry's present phone, which he evidently thought likely to be tapped, but at one moment he forgot himself and blurted, "They took me straight to a military base, and there they put me on board a military plane." Then he stopped and changed the topic. Few as the words were, they were the first the police had heard about what happened to Abu Omar after Merfat Rezk saw him standing with the Westerner beside the van. That Elbadry might know more details was promising. He did not, however, seem disposed to share them with police.

"Every time we went to report things," Elbadry said to Abu Omar, "they didn't believe it, and they said they know nothing about you and that they started an investigation and that an eyewitness saw you—"

"I saw her. She lives in the next street."

"This woman—they put pressure on her husband, and he changed his statement after ten days."

"Is that right?"

"Yes, they put pressure on her husband. They told him he would have been deported, arrested, and confined to Egypt for the rest of his life." (There is no evidence to substantiate the claim.)

"Right, right."

"I told them"—the police—"these very words: I said, 'This is not your style of kidnapping, this is the way Americans do things.' "

"Yes."

" 'And you are allies of the Americans, and we accuse you because this man had refugee status and was under your protection, and you failed to protect him. So your responsibility is great.' "

Elbadry did not tell the police that he had spoken with the missing man, nor did Nabila Ghali.

A MONTH OR TWO before Abu Omar was released, his tortures at Tora Prison had eased somewhat. It had been a mystery to him why. He could perceive no reason things should have changed. But not long after this easing, he was taken from his cell and led upstairs and outside for the first time in several months and was put aboard a microbus that took him to an office of the State Security Service in central Cairo. There an officer told him he was about to have a hearing before a judge.

Odd though it might seem that a prisoner of his sort should have his day in court, it was not unheard of. Egyptian judges, unlike their counterparts in other Arab nations, had a modicum of autonomy from their autocratic executive—at least in civil, as opposed to military, courts. Civil judges sometimes ordered Egypt's security services to release political prisoners, and sometimes the services obeyed.

The officer told Abu Omar that when he was asked in court about his journey to Egypt, he was to say that he had bought a ticket on EgyptAir, flown from Milan to Cairo of his own will, and surrendered himself to the airport security service on arrival. The officer struck him a few times to impress him with the importance of testifying thus and promised worse to come if he did not do as told. Taken to court, Abu Omar did as told. He had hoped his feral appearance and wounds on his face would prompt the judge or the state's attorney to ask about his treatment—his father had been a state's attorney, after all—but they evidently had seen it all before and asked nothing of the kind. He was returned to Tora.

Some days or weeks passed, then he was driven into town for another hearing and given the same instructions about how to testify. He appeared in court, testified as ordered, and was returned to his cell. Once or twice more, it seems, the routine was repeated. Then came a day in mid-April when he was taken from his cell again but was driven to Alexandria instead of to Cairo. There, to his astonishment, a State Security officer said the court had ruled there were no valid charges against him and he had to be released. If Abu Omar wished to keep his freedom, however, he must follow a set of rules called the "Sacred Don'ts":

Don't visit the mosques of Gamaa.
Don't preach in any mosque.
Don't contact anyone in Europe.
Don't go near the Italian embassy or consulate.
Don't travel beyond Alexandria without the government's
    permission.
Don't contact human rights groups.
Don't tell anyone what happened.

Abu Omar feared a trick. Maybe the officer was only saying he would be released to see if he would betray some sliver of information he hadn't already given a hundred times. But not long after being read the Sacred Don'ts, his brother and brother-in-law stood before him, and that night he slept on a mattress in a bed unmolested by vermin. It was voluptuous.

Why the government let him go rather than bring other charges against him is not clear. Perhaps his release was a result of the latest nonviolence accord that Mubarak and Gamaa had reached only months earlier. More than a thousand Gamaa members had been released from prison, and maybe Abu Omar amounted to just one more. Whatever the case, the government apparently believed he posed little threat.

His liberty did not instantly revivify him. He could walk no more than a few yards without gasping for air, his joints ached even when sitting, he had little control over his bladder, and he was slow to regain even a few of the forty pounds he had lost in prison. Panic seized him throughout the day. During the night, every night, he woke up screaming.

He found a measure of relief in talking, but it was not enough to talk with his family in Egypt, and he continued to call Milan, heedless of the Sacred Don'ts. Two and a half weeks after his release, an officer of the State Security Service called him and said the service had decided to issue him identification papers, till then withheld as a way of restricting his movements. He should come pick them up at the service's local headquarters, the same from which he had been discharged. A disturbed Abu Omar told his wife on the phone that night that he feared he would be re-arrested when he went. On May 13 he went and did not come back. His emancipation had lasted twenty-three days.

INSIDE EVERY MOBILE phone is a microchip no bigger and not much thicker than a postage stamp and that is known as a subscriber identity module, or SIM. The SIM is encoded with what we think of as the phone number but which might be better called, for mobile phones at least, the SIM number. Remove a SIM from one phone, put it in another, and the phone number moves with it. In Italy and most other countries, a SIM can be bought separately from a phone and switched among phones. In the United States, whose mobile system is more authoritarian, a SIM is irremovably encased inside the phone in which it is sold.

When a mobile phone is turned on and detects a signal from a cell tower, the SIM inside the phone initiates a digital *pas de deux* by asking the tower to establish a connection. The tower replies by asking the SIM for information about itself—its SIM number, the carrier that provides its service, and so on—and about its phone —the phone's serial number, its technical capabilities. The SIM in turn might ask the tower to prove that it is in fact a tower and not a piratical device trying to steal the SIM's information (such devices exist), in which case the tower will surrender to the SIM a code that proves its identity. The SIM in turn surrenders its data to the tower, and the tower relays the SIM's information to a small base station called a switch, which forwards the data to a central computer. The computer checks that the SIM's account is current and that neither SIM nor phone has been reported miss-

ing or stolen. If all is well, the computer tells the switch to proceed, the switch tells the tower, the tower tells the SIM, and, if
the SIM wishes to place a call, SIM and tower exchange codes for
encrypting it. All of the communication between SIM and tower
takes place at the speed of microwaves, which is to say of light.
The other processes do not, which is what causes the delays that
mobile phone users know well.

During the call, while humans talk, the SIM and the tower will
continue to chat steadily in the background about whether they
have a good connection. If the phone's receiver senses a stronger
signal from another tower, and if the phone company to which
the SIM is subscribed is privileged to use that tower, and if that
tower has bandwidth for the call (there being a limit to how many
cellular suitors one tower can entertain), the switch, per its name,
will switch the call to the new tower. In a dense city, the phone of a
caller on the go may connect to a new tower every minute, or even
every several seconds. In the ideal mobile world, the caller notices
no interruption. More typically there are lacunae, and sometimes
calls are dropped.

All of which is to say that having a mobile phone turned on in
a dense city can reveal its location to within a few blocks. If the
owner of the phone's SIM is on file with the phone company, her
identity can be revealed too. If she makes or receives a call, the identity of the person on the other end of the call may also be revealed.
For these reasons, the wise criminal uses mobile phones rarely.
She prefers phones and SIMs that have been stolen or bought on
the black market, and she disposes of them rapidly. Police know
as much, and they do not expect to solve many cases by tracking
mobile phones, but they also know crooks make mistakes.

Seven cell towers stood within a quarter mile of where Abu
Omar was kidnapped. The nearest three, owned by separate phone
companies, were clustered atop the Best Western Hotel Blaise &
Francis, one hundred and fifty meters as the microwave flies from
the scene of the crime. It was the call logs for these seven towers

that Magistrate Dambruoso requested for the wrong date and then had to re-request. The phone companies finally gave the new logs to DIGOS in the late spring of 2004, more than a year after the abduction. The logs showed that between 11:00 A.M. and 1:00 P.M. on the abductive day, 10,718 SIMs connected with the seven towers. The investigators had hoped one SIM might stand out as that of the Westerner whom Merfat Rezk had seen talking on a mobile phone— a SIM belonging, say, to a police officer or a known criminal. But none of the SIMs stood out. DIGOS reasoned, however, that the Westerner must have had accomplices, and possibly they had coordinated their work by phone. So DIGOS cross-checked the 10,718 SIMs to see which of them had exchanged calls with each other between 11:00 and 1:00. Some people in the kidnap zone would of course have called each other innocently, but, again, maybe some of the calls would stand out in some way. The results of this and related analyses were months in the making.

ARMANDO SPATARO CHOSE his calling in 1976, in the middle of the epoch known in Italy as the Years of Lead, as in the material of bullets. During those roughly eighteen years, terrorists of the Left and Right murdered hundreds of people in hope of provoking (from the Left) revolution or (from the Right) retrenchment. Magistrates who prosecuted the crimes sometimes became the next victims. The magistracy was not, therefore, the safest field one could have chosen at the time, but Spataro's father had been a magistrate, in Taranto, an arid port lodged like a pebble in the arch of the Italian boot, and had prosecuted many men of violence, including organized criminals. The bedroom of the junior Spataro was the study of the senior, and sometimes at night the son would be awakened by police who came to speak with the father on urgent matters. Young Spataro was not the first, nor even the thousandth, Spataro to grow up in law enforcement, for the family name is descended from the late Latin *spatharius*, or swordsman. When he came of age, he took the trade of his father in much the same way his forebears must have taken theirs. He had an additional reason, perhaps shared by some of his forebears: he felt a duty to serve his country, although he thought it sounded sentimental to say as much. He read law at university and by virtue of a superlative score on the test for incoming magistrates was given a post in Milan, which was coveted.

He was mentored in Milan by a young magistrate named Emilio Alessandrini, one of whose lessons was to treat every offender not only with courtesy but generosity. Spataro once watched him patiently interrogate a madam who styled herself a countess. Alessandrini never addressed her as anything but Contessa nor showed her less than the deference due her imagined station. The defendants Alessandrini convicted at trial sometimes told him as they were led off to prison that they would never forget his humanity. Years later, when Spataro prosecuted Islamic terrorists, he would remember these lessons. When a suspect asked to interrupt his interrogation so he could pray toward Mecca at the time required by his faith, Spataro would accede and find him a newspaper to kneel on to satisfy the injunction against praying on the ground. When Muslims asked him to refer to Islamic terrorism as "so-called Islamic terrorism" because terrorists practice a perverted Islam, Spataro changed his habitual speech.

One of his first assignments was to prosecute several members of the leftist Brigate Rosse, the Red Brigades. The defendants had nearly stood trial on related crimes in Turin, but the trial had been canceled after their colleagues assassinated their court-appointed defender, whom they regarded as an abettor of the oppressor state. The terrorists also held jurors in low esteem, and it had been impossible to seat a Turinese jury. The Brigades thought even less of prosecutors. Spataro's boss appointed him to the case in Milan because he was unknown and thus, perhaps, less prized as a target for assassination than his more senior colleagues. Early in the proceedings, Spataro angered lawyers who were affiliated with the Brigades (but who, in protest of the system, were not representing the defendants) by denying their request to see their jailed comrades. Before one hearing, one of the lawyers told Spataro that if he persisted in his opposition, they would have to report the young prosecutor's obstinacy to Renato Curcio, the leader of the Brigades. It was a raw threat.

"In that case," Spataro replied, "it would be preferable to tell him the prosecutor's name as well," and he wrote his name on a piece of paper, handed it to the lawyer, and turned his back. The lawyer left without another word.

"Ah," said his mentor Alessandrini, who had been sitting discreetly behind him on the assumption he would need instruction, "I see you have played prosecutor before, no?"

Spataro confessed he had learned a few tricks from his father. Alessandrini patted him on the back and, smiling, left the courtroom. The show of faith that Spataro could do the job alone sprang reflexively to Spataro's mind a year and a half later when he saw his mentor slumped over a steering wheel and streaming blood. Alessandrini had just dropped his son at elementary school and was driving to work when assassins from the leftist Prima Linea, Front Line, opened fire on him at a stoplight. Called by the police, Spataro ran to the intersection, which was not far from the Palazzo di Giustizia, but his friend was already dead. Front Line had chosen Alessandrini because as a man of integrity he made the Italian state more palatable to its subjects, thereby postponing the hour of revolution. On the day of his funeral, it seemed to Spataro that all Milan turned out, the streets and piazzas full of people applauding and crying.

Spataro had another mentor, Guido Galli, with whom he worked on one of Italy's most important terrorism cases. The case arose from the kidnapping by the Red Brigades, in 1978, of Aldo Moro, a recent prime minister and continuing leader of the ruling Christian Democratic Party. The Brigades held Moro for fifty-four days, throughout which they released pathetic photos of him and still more-pathetic letters from him that sent the nation into something approaching shock. Ultimately his kidnappers executed him. One of the conspirators was later caught in Milan, and his arrest led investigators to other Brigadiers, some of whom Spataro and Galli were assigned to prosecute. As they traveled across northern Italy building their case, they were appalled to find that many police officers had collected strong evidence against terrorists but could do nothing with it because magistrates were too frightened to prosecute. Spataro and Galli offered to take the cases, and their craven colleagues were only too glad to get rid of them. Other magistrates, leftist in their politics, denounced Galli and Spataro for prosecuting terrorists of the Left. Galli responded that prosecutors prosecuted criminals, whatever their ideology. Conversely, another magistrate, a man of some seniority, warned Spataro that the leftist Galli would betray him to the Brigades. Spataro never saw evidence that Galli was a leftist—or a rightist or a centrist. He was professionally nonpolitical and did not tell Spataro, even as an aside, how he voted in elections. Galli's was a model Spataro tried to hold himself to, not always with success. The two magistrates consolidated the many cases they had gathered into a mass trial, the first maxi-trial, as Italians call such affairs, of terrorists in Italy. During the proceedings, Galli honored Spataro by putting forward his argument, then novel, that the leader of a terrorist cell could be held responsible for a murder executed by the cell, even if there was no proof that the leader had ordered the specific murder. The argument carried, and Galli and Spataro convicted their terrorists. In future trials, many more terrorists would fall to Spataro's argument.

The danger of their work notwithstanding, Galli had no police escort, partly because he was not a full-time magistrate (he also lectured in law at the University of Milan) but also because he was out of favor with his superiors. Spataro, who had an escort, sometimes accompanied his mentor home to give him its protection. Fourteen months after Alessandrini was assassinated, Galli walked out of a university lecture hall and was shot three times in the back, fatally, by an assassin from Front Line. He had been targeted for the same reason Alessandrini had. Shortly before his death, Galli had invited Spataro to speak to his class, and Spataro could not help thinking that if only he had given his lecture on the day of the murder, his escort would have been there and his friend would not have been killed. (Front Line, in all likelihood, would only have killed him another day.) On a leaf of his address book, Galli had written, "If anything happens to me, call Armando Spataro." Spataro kept a copy of the page for decades, as if to remind himself that he had been called on. Although he would not have put it in precisely these words, he believed the assassinations had invested him with a sacred trust.

A captured member of Front Line would later tell Spataro that the group thought he was nothing more than a tool of his mentors, that with Galli in particular gone, he would do little. But Spataro became the leading prosecutor of Front Line, the Red Brigades, and other leftist terrorists in northern Italy, and among those he convicted were conspirators to his friends' murders. Years later, after some of them repented, he was able to feel something like forgiveness toward them. But the memory of one witness in Galli's case stirred anger in him decades on. The witness was a law student who worked in his father's bicycle shop, from which the assassins had bought the bicycles on which they fled through the warren of streets. Spataro had solved most of the case and needed the student only to confirm the identity of the buyers, but the student refused. He said he did not want to be *tirato in ballo*—dragged to the dance—and that anyway if Galli had been murdered, there must have been a reason. Salt to Spataro's wound, the young man had been a student of Galli's. Spataro jailed him and his father, who also refused to testify—an example to his son no less than Spataro's father had been to him—but eventually had to release them. Long after the student's name disappeared from his memory, Spataro remained offended that such a specimen had probably become his colleague at the bar, maybe even in the magistracy. Bystanders to justice disgusted him, particularly those who had a special obligation to uphold it.

By the end of the 1980s, Spataro and other magistrates had prosecuted the terrorists of the Years of Lead nearly out of existence. He switched to prosecuting the Calabrian and Sicilian Mafias, whose drug trafficking, extortion, money laundering, and attendant violent crime had crept north to Lombardy. In 1998, after a decade convicting mafiosi, his fellow magistrates and select members of the bar elected him to Italy's governing council of the magistracy. He served a four-year term in Rome, then returned to Milan to prosecute the new terrorism that had blown into Italy like a sirocco. Hardly had he begun this work when he learned he would have to fight not only terrorists but the fighters of terrorists as well.

SPATARO HAD a Roman nose, not in the classical iteration—long and tall—but in the sense of the old vaudeville line "It's roamin' all over his face." Congenitally curvilinear, it had been further improved by a car wreck. In mid-life the face from which it looked out was blotched like an old leather recliner, and during summertime liver spots emerged from under his hair of thinning, patriarchal white like an archipelago in the Tyrrhenian Sea at low tide. His thick mustache waffled, uncharacteristically for him, between the ivory of his hair and the ebony of his strong eyebrows. He was handsome, but atypically.

In the spring of 2004, Magistrate Dambruoso left for a posting abroad, and the Abu Omar case fell to Spataro. Weeks later Abu Omar emerged from prison, began calling people in Italy, then was re-arrested. After a few more weeks it became clear from phone taps that Nabila Ghali planned imminently to return to Alexandria in case her husband should be released again. Spataro, not wanting her to leave unquestioned, summoned her and Abu Omar's other colloquist in Milan, Mohammed Elbadry, to the Palazzo di Giustizia. He also had the apartment on Via Conte Verde searched.

The chief item of interest in the apartment was Abu Omar's

computer, on which, it turned out, were stored several documents testifying to his fanaticism. In one, titled "Italian Terrorism," he condemned Italians for their intolerance of Islamists and promised their "Satanic prejudice" would be "neither forgiven by history nor forgotten by the children of Islam." Islam's children, he said, were "of a breed that does not forget to avenge itself. Vengeance will stay in our hearts until God allows us to return to our homeland." He had apparently distributed "Italian Terrorism" at a mosque in Como the day before he disappeared, and after his release from prison, he said (either naively or disingenuously) that he thought he had been kidnapped in retaliation for the tract. Another document on the computer, apparently written by someone else, was a three-pager called "Military Jihad." Under headings like "Preparation of the Mujahidin" and "The Jihad, Men and Money: Creating Jihadist Factories," the author said that holy warriors who wished to make their exile useful must study everything about the enemy: his streets, his bridges, his banks, his police stations, his culture, his desires, his habits. Anything might be needed for jihad. For the same reason, the jihadi should be versed in science and medicine, business and the humanities, geography and mathematics. The memo's audience, it was clear, was less the obeisant suicide bomber than the man who would lead him. Perhaps because of the audience, the memo was surprisingly bland of diction and lacking in rhetorical flourishes, its inflammatory subject notwithstanding. With the substitution of a few terms, it could have been a précis of how to assemble a mid-tier sales force.

When Nabila Ghali and Mohammed Elbadry met with Spataro, they were not at first forthcoming. Over the course of their interviews, however, they seemed to understand that he was an ally of sorts, and they told him what Abu Omar had said in his calls from Alexandria: that an American-looking policeman had stopped him on the street, that while the American was inspecting his papers, other men opened the door of a van and dragged him inside, that he had been beaten and bundled and driven for what seemed like four or five hours, that he had been transferred to another vehicle, possibly a plane, which had traveled for a short time, that he had been taken out of the vehicle and into a building where commandos had stripped and repackaged him, that he had been loaded onto another vehicle, definitely a plane this time, and flown for several hours, that he had been unloaded at last in Cairo, and that for the next fourteen months the Egyptians had abused him in ways almost to horrific to describe.

The story resembled those of other kidnappings, just emerging, that the CIA had carried out elsewhere since September 11, and it seemed to Spataro that the CIA was probably behind Abu Omar's disappearance too. If so, the drive of four or five hours from Milan must have been needed to get him to an American or NATO air base, since it would have been too risky to fly him out of the country from a civilian airport. As it happened, only one international air base lay within four or five hours of Milan—Aviano. Spataro asked DIGOS to learn what flights had left Aviano on the evening of the kidnapping and the following day.

BRUNO MEGALE, the young director of DIGOS's counterterrorism squad in Milan, was so somber that when he testified at trials, reporters had been known to lay bets on whether a full hour or only a portion thereof would elapse before he smiled. A Deep Southerner like Spataro, he seemed to have raised himself from the Calabrian toe of the Italian boot to his position on the Lombard calf by means of the severity with which he invested his work. Since he was not given to causeless excitement, when he told Spataro in almost a flutter, in the fall of 2004, that the analysis of the 10,718 SIMs in the kidnap zone had revealed something fascinating, Spataro was sure it had.

Between 11:00 A.M. and 1:00 P.M. on February 17, 2003, about three hundred of the 10,718 SIMs had exchanged calls with one another. Most of the calls seemed innocuous. But eleven of the SIMs had called one another more than once during the two hours, each call had lasted only a few seconds, and the calls had increased in frequency with the approach of the kidnapping, had peaked immediately afterward, then had fallen off drastically. The phones of nearly all of the callers had been connected to the cell towers atop the Best Western Blaise & Francis, the closest towers to the spot of the kidnapping. The picture the callers presented was about what one would expect of a group coordinating the stakeout and capture of a man.

Moreover, the users of the eleven SIMs had not acted alone. They were in frequent contact with six SIMs that had been connected to cell towers in the suburb of Cormano, on the northern edge of Milan. The most logical route from the site of the kidnapping to Aviano was via the A4 autostrada, and its nearest entrance was at Cormano. It was likely that the six SIMs in Cormano were some kind of support group for the drive to Aviano. Even allowing that some of Abu Omar's kidnappers might have had more than one phone, seventeen SIMs suggested a large group. Later the investigators would find another SIM that had been in Cormano and two more SIMs in Abu Omar's neighborhood of Dergano, bringing the total to twenty.

Spataro asked Megale to learn everything he could about the SIMs: Where did they go the rest of the day? Where had they been on other days? When, where, and by whom had they been bought? Were they still in use now (more than a year after the crime)? To and from whom had they made or received calls throughout their period of activation? Could the phones the SIMs were in be identified? If so, who were their owners? Were any of the SIMs, by chance, among the thousands tapped by Italian police in other investigations? If so, did recordings or transcripts of the conversations exist?

The answers trickled in. Megale's investigators were not so lucky as to find that any of the phones had been tapped, but they had other luck. To start with, they found that in the months before the kidnapping, the twenty SIMs in Dergano and Cormano had often called and been called by thirty-four other SIMs. No one of the fifty-four total SIMs had called every other SIM, but their calls so overlapped and criss-crossed as to create an obvious web that tied them all together. While none of the newly discovered thirty-four SIMs had been in Dergano or Cormano on the day of the crime, nearly all of them had been to Dergano in the several weeks before. One had connected to cell towers in Dergano ninety-five times. After the day of the kidnapping, however, none of the SIMs ever went there again, which strongly suggested they did not belong to residents of the quarter. Almost certainly the newly-discovered thirty-four belonged to conspirators who had gone to Dergano to plan the kidnapping.

Megale's investigators were also enlightened by the SIMs' movements on the day of the kidnapping. Of the twenty that had been in Dergano or Cormano that day, one had started the morning in Cormano, then moved at driving speed toward Dergano—connecting to cell towers along the way—and met up with the Dergano group twenty or thirty minutes before the kidnapping. The investigators thought the user of this SIM was a liaison between the two groups. Nearly all of the SIMs in Dergano were located on or within a few blocks of the route Abu Omar would walk, and they remained there during his walk. After the kidnapping, almost all of the Dergano SIMs dispersed or were shut off, but the liaison moved back toward Cormano, again at driving speed. Probably he or she was in the van that held Abu Omar. The liaison's SIM then entered the A4 autostrada eastbound, and as it did, it was immediately preceded or followed (it was hard to say which) by about half of the SIMs in Cormano. To judge from their movements, these Cormano SIMs were in their own vehicle. Six or seven minutes later, the remaining SIMs from Cormano followed in another vehicle. Spataro theorized that the first group from Cormano was traveling with the kidnappers in case they needed immediate, minor help, while the second Cormano group was to be available for bigger trouble, like a blown tire or an intrusive traffic cop. Spataro guessed that the trailing group was in another cargo van to which Abu Omar could be moved if needed.

As the caravan made its way to Aviano, the people in the three vehicles called one another and, in a few cases, called kidnappers who had stayed in Milan. Two and half hours after the kidnapping, one of the SIMs in the lead vehicle called a SIM that was connected to a cell tower at Aviano Air Base. The call lasted thirty-five seconds. An hour and a half later, shortly after the caravan exited the A4 at Portogruaro, the same SIM called the same phone at Aviano, this time for nineteen seconds. Twenty minutes later, there was a third call, of fourteen seconds. A few minutes later, just before five o'clock, the SIMs in the caravan connected to the cell tower at Aviano. Evidently the caller in the caravan had been coordinating the kidnappers' arrival at the base. Moments later one of the SIMs back in Milan made two short calls to a mobile phone in the Virginia suburbs of Washington, D.C. Spataro theorized that the caller was passing the happy news to headquarters that Abu Omar had been delivered.

SIMs were not the only means by which the kidnappers revealed their route. The A4 was a tollway, which meant the kidnappers had to pass through toll plazas on entry at Cormano, en route past Venice, and on exit at Portogruaro. They could have paid their tolls with coins, which would have left no trace of their passage, but instead, as Megale's team found when they checked the records of the tollway company, they had paid with scannable farecards, whose use the company logged. Possibly the kidnappers had used the cards because it took less time to pay with them than with coins. Farecards might also have lessened the chance of encountering a human toll collector. In any case, the company's logs showed that three and only three vehicles entered the A4 at Cormano and exited at Portogruaro at times corresponding to the movements of the kidnappers' SIMs: at Cormano at 12:46, 12:47, and 12:54 and at Portogruaro at 4:00, 4:00, and 4:07 respectively. Because tolls on the A4 varied with the size of the vehicle tolled, the first vehicle was proven to be a car, the second a van, and the third, as Spataro had guessed, another van. (The toll company did not keep videos from its plazas or record license-plate numbers, so no more could be learned of the vehicles. Two of the kidnappers' three farecards had never been used before, but one had been used a few weeks earlier on a reverse trip from Portogruaro to Milan. All three of the cards turned out to have been bought at convenience stores in Milan, but since sellers were not required to keep information on buyers, the investigators could not discover who the buyers were. None of the farecards was ever used again, notwithstanding that each card had a credit of ten or more euros remaining. CIA officers, it seemed, might risk betraying their travels by reusing a farecard once, but no more.

The kidnappers stayed at Aviano a few hours. Probably they were debriefed. Possibly they had a celebratory round at the California Beer Parlor. Some of them drove back to Milan that night. Others drove part of the way back and spent the night in Padua, from which some of them probably returned to Milan the next morning. Others simply disappeared.

MEGALE'S INVESTIGATORS were not long in discovering that one of the fifty-four suspect SIMs was owned by the chief of the CIA office in Milan, whose name was Bob Lady. The discovery was distasteful to Megale. Lady had been a great collaborator with DIGOS, a generous sharer of tips and reports and technology. By some accounts, it was Lady who gave DIGOS the bug that was installed in Abu Omar's office. It was also Lady who gave DIGOS the software to analyze terrorists' phone calls—the same software, it seemed, that was now being used to investigate him. Megale had found Lady a pleasure to work with. He had none of the crabbed guardedness that some spies, particularly spies for larger countries, had about them, and the two men had celebrated their victories over terrorists with convivial dinners. Several times they had discussed Abu Omar, but never had Lady hinted the CIA might snatch him. Megale was blindsided.

Lady's SIM had not been in Dergano or Cormano on the day of the abduction. Indeed, it had never been to Dergano at all and seemed to have been in Cormano only in passing. But both his SIM and the landline in his apartment had made and received several calls from the SIMs of conspirators who had been in Dergano, and thirty or forty minutes after Abu Omar was kidnapped, one of the kidnappers called Lady, presumably to tell him the job had come off. The same kidnapper called again several times that afternoon, presumably to apprise Lady of the team's progress from Milan to Aviano. Lady, in brief, was a conspirator.

Another of the fifty-four suspect SIMs also belonged to a U.S. official. She, Sabrina De Sousa, worked from both the U.S. embassy in Rome and, like Lady, the U.S. consulate in Milan. She was accredited as a second secretary but was known to DIGOS as a CIA officer (she later maintained she was not). She too had collaborated on counterterror investigations with Megale's squad, some of whose members found her haughty and brusque, the antithesis of Lady. Her SIM, like Lady's, was implicated in the conspiracy rather than the kidnapping proper.

A third suspect SIM was registered to an administrative technician at the U.S. consulate named Barbara Suddath. At first, Suddath's SIM was a riddle to investigators because they had no information suggesting she worked for the CIA. But after they studied the movements of the SIM during the years of its activation, they saw that at night and earliest morning—the hours a person would normally be in bed—it was usually connected to a cell tower near Bob Lady's flat. Later, after Lady and his wife Martha bought an estate in the Asti wine country, the SIM began connecting to a tower there. Clearly Suddath had given the SIM to Lady. She seemed to have had nothing to do with the kidnapping, and DIGOS never learned to what extent, if any, she worked with the CIA.

A final SIM registered to a U.S. official was the one at Aviano that the kidnappers called three times from the highway. It was owned by the U.S. Air Force and assigned to Lieutenant Colonel Joseph Romano III, who was the chief of security for U.S. forces at the base. Among other duties, Romano oversaw who came and went from the base's American-controlled gates. A few weeks before the kidnapping, Romano's SIM exchanged calls with another of the suspect SIMs—probably, Spataro thought, as part of the logistical planning for Abu Omar's transport.

The SIMs of the four officials had been used long before the kidnapping and would be used long after it. But the other fifty suspect SIMs were activated only a few weeks or, in a handful of cases, a few months before the kidnapping. Some of the SIMs were used only briefly, for a week in December, say, or two weeks in January, while others were used, incautiously, for six or eight weeks. None was used more than a few days after the kidnapping. The pattern was that of a group that came from afar for a temporary job, did it, and left.

Italian law did not require the sellers of SIMs to record who bought them, although sellers could do so if they wanted. When they did, they usually forwarded the information to the phone companies to which the SIMs were subscribed. Many of the fifty SIMs had been sold without being registered. Others were registered, but unhelpfully. Ten of the SIMs, for example, were registered to one Mihai Timofte, who turned out to be a thirty-one-year-old Rumanian mason living outside Milan. Timofte had never had anything to do with the SIMs registered in his name, but he had once bought a SIM from a shop in Milan, and that shop was listed with the phone company as the seller of "his" ten SIMs. In the past, the same shop had also "sold" other SIMs to Timofte that were used by criminals in other cases. Those cases had already prompted the Carabinieri to investigate Timofte, whom they adjudged "of normal moral and civic behavior"—just an unfortunate victim of identity theft. DIGOS never learned whether the shop stole Timofte's identity or someone else did—someone, say, working for the phone company. Other shops "sold" SIMs used in the kidnapping to other innocents:

a jeweler, an octogenarian pensioner, a mother who bought a similar SIM for her son.

The great majority of the fifty suspect SIMs were either registered in this manner or not registered at all. Some, however, were registered to people with American names and addresses, and some of the Americans had even shown passports or international driver's licenses when they bought their SIMs. One seller had made a photocopy of one of these licenses. It had been issued by the American Automobile Association to a Monica Courtney Adler, who, so the license claimed, was born in Seattle in 1973 and lived in Arlington, Virginia. The grainy copy of the license showed a cheerful, bigtoothed woman, full of cheek and long of dark hair, which she had either drawn back over her high forehead or had closely banged. Her attire was conservative but not too, and she had signed her first name with a magnificent lasso that flew off the *a* and doubled back over the rest of the letters, as if to capture them. On the whole, she could have been a young Xerox manager delighted to be leaving Stamford to run the Milan accounts. It was doubtful her real name was Monica Courtney Adler or that the other data on her license were strictly correct, but since she had bought the SIM in person, her photo was probably genuine, and the year of her birth could not have been far off 1973. Her SIM had been in Dergano at the moment Abu Omar was kidnapped.

The other shops that sold SIMs to Americans only transcribed the data from their IDs rather than photocopying them. But Megale's investigators, by means presently to be described, ferreted out copies of several of the SIM-holders' passports and driver's licenses, all of which were presumably falsified in one degree or another. Thus:

Ben Amar Harty, whose SIM had been in Dergano at the moment of the kidnapping, was forty-nine and claimed nativity in Iowa Falls and residence in Washington, D.C. His heritage seemed Arab or similar, but large glasses, darkened by photocopying, obscured his staid, round face.

Cynthia Dame Logan and Drew Carlyle Channing had both been in the Cormano-to-Aviano group. Logan, forty-two, had a smile as be-cheeked as Adler's, dark hair that ran in two streams down her chest, and no fear of lipstick. She alleged Maryland for her birthplace. Channing was thirty-seven and a New Yorker by birth, but photocopying had turned him into a silhouette, and about all one could say of his person was that it was thick of neck.

John Kevin Duffin had not been in either Dergano or Cormano on the day of the kidnapping but in a distant part of Milan. After the kidnapping, he had traveled separately from the caravan to Aviano, perhaps in some unknown supervisory or supporting role. He lived in King of Prussia, outside Philadelphia, and if his fifty years had brought him wrinkles, not many survived the photocopier. He was perky and a touch doughy, styled his hair *alla* coconut—short and bristly—and wore a striped knit shirt with a wilted collar that would have been at home on a King of Prussian fairway.

James Robert Kirkland, Anne Linda Jenkins, and James Thomas Harbison had not been in Dergano or Cormano during the kidnapping but had visited one or both many times before. Kirkland, sixty, was trim as a colonel and had a face as poker—mouth zipped, eyes narrowed. He claimed a Milanese address, Via Washington 39, which turned out to be a park. Maybe he was homeless. More likely he was uninventive: DIGOS eventually learned that he had stayed at the Milan Marriott, at Via Washington 66, which suggested he could concoct no better cover address than one down the block. "Washington" was also easy for an American to remember and, perhaps, patriotically satisfying. Anne Jenkins, a fit fifty-six, had good teeth, the practical short hair of a gym teacher, an equally sensible mock turtleneck, and an air of efficient friendliness. Her passport originated in Washington. She had originated in Florida. Harbison was two years her junior, native to New Jersey, and had also been passported in Washington. His face was another silhouette, although his natty striped Oxford and impeccably knotted tie survived the copying. Like Kirkland, he claimed a Milanese address,

Via Mac Mahon 109, which was a block of flats not far from Dergano that yielded no sign of his residency.

Six other SIMs were registered to Americans for whom DIGOS could find only transcribed data, no photocopies. None of these SIMs was in Dergano or Cormano on the day of the kidnapping. Their owners were Raymond Harbaugh, a sixty-three-year-old native of Alaska; Joseph Sofin, fifty and born in Moldova; Brenda Liliana Ibanez, a native New Yorker of forty-three years; Pilar Maria Rueda, a native Californian of forty-one; Victor Castellano, Texan and thirty-four; and Eliana Isabella Castaldo, Floridian and thirty-three. Castaldo said she lived or worked in Norristown, Pennsylvania, not far from Duffin in King of Prussia. The others claimed residency in greater Washington.

MONICA COURTNEY ADLER first arrived in Milan on January 9, 2003. She spent three nights in room 1027 of the Westin Palace, then decamped to the Principe di Savoia, room 704. The Savoia occupies the pinnacle of the Milanese hostelry and is perhaps best known for its presidential suite, in whose pool have dipped Frank Sinatra and Madonna (separately), to say nothing of mere presidents. The establishment's other rooms, a touch less luxurious, still qualify as opulent. By day Adler scouted Dergano and its environs, and by night she repaired to the Savoia, in whose glass-domed, crystal-suffused, winter-gardened bar she perhaps refreshed herself. After three weeks, she was apparently permitted a break from this taxing regimen, because on the morning of February 1 she checked out of the Savoia, drove to the coastal resort of La Spezia, and checked in to the Hotel del Golfo. The next day, she went to Florence and put up at the Grand Hotel Baglioni, in which she meant to stay two nights, but she returned to Milan the following day and checked in to the Hilton, room 869, where she remained until February 18, the day after the kidnapping. Then she vanished. She had not been easy on the American taxpayer. Her nightly rate at the Savoia was €344, about $400, for a total bill of nearly $8,000.

The Hilton's rate was €300, about $350, for a total of nearly $5,000. The going rate for a good room in Milan was about half that.

Megale's investigators were able to discover Adler's lodgings by examining where her SIM stopped for the night, the same technique they had used to learn that Bob Lady was using Barbara Suddath's SIM. Lady's case had been much simpler, however, because DIGOS already knew where Lady lived and had only to see that Suddath's SIM was connecting to cell towers near his homes. In Adler's case, though, the DIGOS investigators had no idea where she was sleeping. But they assumed she was staying in hotels, so each time they found a tower to which her SIM connected overnight, an officer visited the hotels within the tower's range and looked at their guest registries. Invariably, one hotel within the range contained Adler's name. She could have made DIGOS's work harder by changing her name from hotel to hotel, but she never did. DIGOS found the hotels of several of the other Americans in the same manner; they did not change their names either. Nearly all of their hotels were as immoderately priced as Adler's.

DIGOS also put names to some of the dozens of SIMs that either had not been registered to anyone or had been registered to stolen identities. These cases were more complicated than Adler's because although the nameless SIMs connected to cell towers overnight, their namelessness meant that the investigators could not simply match them to hotel registries. DIGOS overcame the problem by tracing the SIMs' movements more minutely and comparing those movements with the precise check-in and check-out times of hotel guests. In a relatively simple case, a SIM might have connected to a cell tower at 9:00 p.m. on a certain night, then disconnected at 8:00 a.m. the next morning. On checking the hotel records, DIGOS would find only a few guests—Tim Davis, Lena Kohl, and Stefania Ragusa, say—who had arrived around 9:00 and left around 8:00. DIGOS would follow the SIM to its next hotel, and when Davis turned up there but Kohl and Ragusa did not, the investigators could be sure Davis was the user of the nameless SIM. A few of the

users of nameless SIMs made some of this detective work unnecessary by giving their phone numbers (i.e., their SIM numbers)
to their hotels when they gave their names at check-in, thereby
making their anonymous SIMs onymous—which rather undid the
trouble someone had gone to to get them a nameless SIM in the
first place.

Seven Americans were newly unmasked by DIGOS's hotel work.
Four of them—Lorenzo Gabriel Carrera, a thirty-two-year-old from
Texas; Vincent Faldo, fifty-two and from Massachusetts; Michalis
Vasiliou, forty and born in Greece; and Betnie Medero-Navedo,
thirty-five and of unknown nativity—had traveled in the escorting
caravan to Aviano on the day of the kidnapping. Medero-Navedo,
like Sabrina De Sousa, was a second secretary at the U.S. embassy
and was the only diplomat accused of a hands-on role in the kidnapping proper. (She was eventually exonerated, in a manner to be
discussed.) Two more of the seven newly discovered Americans—
Gregory Asherleigh, a forty-seven-year-old Marylander, and George
Purvis, forty-three and born in China—had been in Dergano during the kidnapping. Purvis, it seemed, was a leader. He had arrived
in Milan in September of 2002, months before most of the other
spies, presumably to plan the kidnapping. He had also exchanged
calls with Bob Lady, who kept his distance (at least telephonically)
from most of the spies. The last of the seven Americans newly discovered, John Thomas Gurley, a thirty-two-year-old claiming residency in Orlando, seemed to have been a lesser planner and was
not in Dergano or Cormano on the day of the kidnapping.

As the investigators studied the SIMs, they also noticed that
some of them traveled always and exactly in pairs, from which
they deduced that each pair belonged to one spy. Often one of the
paired SIMs was registered in the spy's name, or at any rate in his
American alias, while the other was unregistered or falsely registered to an Italian. Possibly the spy had used the unregistered SIM
for more-sensitive calls and the registered SIM for less-sensitive
calls. If so, he was unaware that the SIMs' joint movements would

tie the pair together. Some of the spies were more foolish still, using both SIMs in the same phone. Perhaps they thought only a SIM, not the phone it was in, could be traced. But the serial number of the phone showed up in the call logs with both SIMs and betrayed their user. By these means, DIGOS learned that four spies—Harbaugh, Harbison, Rueda, and Sofin—who till that point had been implicated only by their named SIMs and only in the planning stages had in fact been in Dergano with their nameless SIMs when Abu Omar was kidnapped. The discovery was particularly damaging for the sixty-four-year-old Harbaugh, who was revealed as a probable co-leader of the kidnapping with Purvis. Harbaugh had arrived in Milan in August, a month before Purvis, and to judge from his calls was a frequent go-between between Lady and the rest of the kidnapping team. None of the other spies had more than two SIMs, but Harbaugh had a prodigious five, one of which was the SIM that called Lady several times on the afternoon of the kidnapping, presumably to update him on its progress.

In all, DIGOS tied thirty-four of the fifty-four conspiratorial SIMs to twenty-five Americans.

This, however, was not all that DIGOS learned. Several of the Americans, when checking into hotels, gave out addresses, almost all of which were post office boxes not far from the CIA's headquarters. Evidently the CIA could not be bothered to rent a box or two in Wichita and have the contents forwarded. A few of the spies also listed employers, which, with very little investigation, were discovered to be fronts. One was Coachmen Enterprises—aptly named for the rendering trade. When the spies settled their hotel bills, many paid with Visa, Master-Card, and Diners Club accounts whose numbers were so unsubtly similar—sharing the first eight, eleven, or fourteen (of sixteen) digits—as to betray a common origin.

The spies did not bare themselves only to DIGOS. They also bared themselves to each other. When Monica Courtney Adler took her break by the sea at La Spezia, John Kevin Duffin shared her room. Ben Amar Harty and Eliana Castaldo shared another room in the same hotel. Two nights later Raymond Harbaugh and Pilar Rueda recreated together in a chamber in the Alpine resort of Chiesa di Valmalenco. After the kidnapping, many of the spies passed a few nights (not necessarily in the same room) in Venice's more exquisite hotels, like the fourteenth-century Danieli, off Piazza San Marco, and the Europa and Regina, on the Grand Canal. The frolics and the regal bills were manna to headline writers, the best of whom wrote, "The Spies Who Came in From the Hot Tub" and "Be All That You Can Charge" and "Ask Not What Your Country Can Bill to You, But What You Can Bill to Your Country."

Then there were the frequent-flyer numbers. On checking in to hotels or renting cars (which DIGOS also identified and which, after the splendor of the lodgings, were an anti-climax: gray Fiat compacts and such), several of the Americans gave account numbers for United Mileage Plus, Delta Sky Miles, Northwest World-Perks, Hilton HHonors, and the Starwood Special Preferred Guest Program. They perhaps thought Abu Omar should not be the only one to get a free trip out of the job. When investigators looked into the accounts, they learned that two months after the kidnapping, Gregory Asherleigh flew from New York to Oslo, stayed a month, then returned. He banked the miles from his flights on his North-west WorldPerks account. Two weeks after he came back, Cynthia Dame Logan flew from Washington to Oslo, stayed two months, and banked her miles on her United Mileage Plus account.

Almost certainly, Asherleigh and Logan had been scouting another rendition. Their target, almost as certainly, was Mullah Krekar, the co-founder of an Iraqi group that evolved into Ansar al-Islam—the same group for which Abu Omar had allegedly recruited suicide bombers. Krekar had fled Iraq for Norway in 1991 and been granted asylum on grounds of persecution under Saddam Hussein. Later he was suspected of traveling back to Iraq to help Ansar al-Islam, and his asylum was revoked. Norway did not expel him, however, because he might have been put to death if sent home. As the Iraq War drew near in 2003 and the United States worried increasingly about Ansar al-Islam, the CIA weighed whether to render Krekar. Asherleigh and Logan, it seems, were sent to Oslo to scout the possibility. But the rendition did not come to pass, partly because someone in Norway's intelligence services tipped Krekar's lawyer to the plan. "A lot of people with integrity in the government didn't like the situation," the lawyer, Brynjar Meling, later explained, "and therefore there were quite a lot of leaks." Meling begged the police to protect his client, but they apparently declined. When Krekar took to denouncing the CIA's plan in public, he was generally dismissed as paranoid. He was vindicated a few years later when Norway's main intelligence service admitted it had known that CIA officers had come to Norway with illicit intentions.

DIGOS could not trace the rest of Abu Omar's kidnappers beyond a day or two of the kidnapping. (The exceptions were the accused kidnappers in the diplomatic corps, but their movements after the kidnapping proved uninteresting.) A few of the kidnappers returned their rental cars in Munich or Frankfurt, but DIGOS could not learn why. Sometimes CIA officers traveled to and from covert jobs through irrelevant countries where they changed and then changed back their identities. Perhaps Abu Omar's kidnappers had been muddying their trail.

All of the non-diplomats' SIMs were abandoned (or at least disused) after the kidnapping, but the same could not be said of their phones, four of which had an afterlife. Each of the four was used more than a year after the kidnapping for a week or two in Rome with a new SIM, each bought by a different American. Each connected multiple times to a cell tower a few blocks from the U.S. embassy. Spataro theorized the phones were office phones, the office being the CIA, and that the officers were in Italy on short assignments. It was uncharacteristically frugal of the CIA to have recycled the phones.

Chapter 7

Flight

AVIANO AIR BASE has a history of renditions, although before the kidnapping of Abu Omar they seem to have been only of a leporine kind. On the lands around Aviano, rabbits have bred like, well, rabbits and have become aeronautical hazards, chiefly by turning the air-intake valves of jets into rabbit-intake valves. The rabbits are also terrestrial hazards. Pilots of F-16s have returned to Aviano from dropping five-hundred-pound bombs on an al-Qaeda safehouse or a Baghdad hospital, gotten in their cars, and headed home, whereupon bunnies have hopped in front of them. Warriors have been known to swerve off the road to save the innocents. Consequently, the air base instituted an annual rabbit round-up in which hundreds of volunteers form a line on a runway and march as a wall on the adjoining fields, driving the rabbits before them into a long net. The detainees are then transferred to vehicles and rendered to the forests and mountains beyond U.S. jurisdiction, where they are set free—a testimony to American mercy. An Italian would have turned the captives into *coniglio fritto dorato*, which is rabbit that has been chopped, marinated in olive oil and lemon, slathered with egg and flour, and dropped in a pan of boiling oil, the result of which is a convincing argument against animal rights.

After Magistrate Spataro and DIGOS followed the trail of Abu Omar to the hermetic American enclave at Aviano, there were fewer ways to trace him. The trail did not vanish entirely, however. All planes that take off in Italy must follow either a civilian or a military protocol. Under the civilian protocol, a pilot files a flight plan with her originating air-traffic control tower, the tower in turn guides the flight through takeoff, then, once the plane reaches a certain altitude, a regional control center takes responsibility for guiding and monitoring it. If the plane leaves one region of Italy for another, the responsibility passes to another control center, and if it leaves Italy altogether, the responsibility passes to the new country. At the same time that the regional centers are tracking the flight, an international aviation authority in Brussels called Eurocontrol does the same. All civilian flights and some military flights fly under civilian protocol. Other military flights may be declared "on mission" and exempted from the civilian protocol. In those cases, the pilot files no flight plan with Italian authorities, and military rather than civilian air-control centers guide the plane. The flight still shows up on civilian radar, but civil authorities essentially ignore it.

Spataro asked all of the civilian and military monitoring agencies for records of flights that left Aviano between 5:00 P.M. on February 17, 2003, and midnight on February 18. He hoped the agencies would have flight plans and radar traces, maybe even recordings of conversations with the pilots, but he learned that such data were purged every few months unless there was a reason, like a crash, to keep them. There had been no reason to keep the data on flights from Aviano on February 17 and 18. Several of the authorities did, however, have scaled-down flight plans known as departure logs, and these showed that in the period of Spataro's request, six flights left Aviano under civilian protocol and thirteen under military protocol. All of the militarily protocoled flights were made by F-16s, which had room only for their pilots, so Spataro ruled those out. Of the civilian flights, only one had an itinerary that matched what Abu Omar had described to his wife and his friend Elbadry.

That flight was made by a Learjet 35 that left Aviano at 6:20 P.M.

and landed at Ramstein Air Base in Germany at about 7:40 P.M. Ramstein, which Hitler had carved from his southern forests to aid in the annihilation of Western Europe and from which the United States, having carved it from him, had meant to annihilate the Soviet Union if things came to that, was the headquarters of the U.S. Air Force in Europe. The Learjet had a capacity of ten passengers and used as its call sign SPAR 92. "SPAR" was short for Special Air Resources, which meant a military flight carrying senior officers or other VIPs. A call sign is the name air-traffic controllers call a plane by, and it is sometimes identical to the plane's tail number. SPAR 92, however, was not the Learjet's tail number, and Spataro never learned what it was. Earlier on February 17, while the kidnappers were en route to Aviano with Abu Omar, SPAR 92 flew from Ramstein to Aviano, arriving at 5:14, just a few minutes after the kidnappers. The timing suggested the coordinators of the rendition did not want their torture taxi idling on an Italian runway should the kidnappers get stuck in traffic or run into other trouble. SPAR 92 left Aviano for Ramstein an hour after it had arrived. Six minutes later, the SIM of Lieutenant Colonel Joseph Romano, the security chief at Aviano, called a mobile phone registered to the U.S. Air Force at Ramstein. Presumably he was letting someone know the plane was on its way.

Spataro asked Eurocontrol for the logs of flights that departed Ramstein in the following twenty-four hours. There were several, but only one had been bound for Egypt: a Gulfstream IV, tail number N85VM. It departed at 8:31 P.M., less than an hour after Abu Omar arrived, again neatly matching the account he had given his wife and Elbadry, and landed in Cairo at 12:32 A.M. Spataro could learn no more about N85VM, but other investigators did.

A MAN RICH enough to own a jet hates to think of it hangared. Hangared, it is an investment earning no dividends, like money under a mattress. Many men of means will therefore lease their planes. There are companies that will make the arrangements—finding the clients, handling the money, maintaining the plane, providing the crew. The owner of the plane may place limits on the clientele, for example by disallowing flights from the Colombian highlands to private airstrips along the Rio Grande. On the other hand, he may not scruple over the details, like an investor in Liggett or Blackwater. The interests of the less preoccupied man align with those of the CIA, which needs secret jets for its secret work with few questions asked. The CIA owns jets of its own, but with ownership comes maintenance of plane and crew, and if a plane is exposed as the CIA's, it will have to be sold and another will have to be bought, which is onerous. The CIA can change a plane's tail number, and sometimes does, but the change will be registered with the Federal Aviation Administration and linked to the old tail number, which may defeat the change. By contrast, if a leased plane is exposed as a spy craft, the CIA can walk away from it and lease another. Then too after September 11, 2001, the White House demanded far more missions from the CIA than its small in-house fleet could handle. So the agency leased planes.

Phillip H. Morse was a rich man, an ex-insurance salesman who had founded a business that invented a device that catheterized blood vessels serving the heart. The Morse manifold, as the device is known, made Morse flush—the catheter king, some called him. He summered in Lake George and wintered in Palm Beach, where he built a golf course with his friend Jack Nicklaus. He liked to play the links of Scotland. He bought himself a vice-chairmanship in the Boston Red Sox (having grown up in Danvers) and traveled to and from Sox games in season. He also collected coins around the world, including two hundred and forty Double Eagles, which were magnificent twenty-dollar gold pieces in Beaux Arts style that President Theodore Roosevelt commissioned of the artist Augustus Saint-Gaudens. The sale in 2005 of the Morse Double Eagle Collection, as the coins are known in collecting circles, set several price records; one of the Eagles fetched $3 million. A lifestyle such as Morse's is insupportable without a private craft, so he bought a Gulfstream IV from El Paso Gas and Electric. The jet could seat eleven in leathered comfort, and a six-foot-tall man could stand in its aisle without stooping. The catheter king put Red Sox logos on its fuselage.

For accounting purposes, Morse created a company called Assembly Pointe Aviation, which owned the plane and little or nothing else and whose terminal *e* in "Pointe" carried a faint odor of new money. Assembly Pointe leased the plane to intermediary companies that covered the Red Sox logos and leased it in turn to clients. One of the intermediary companies was Richmor Aviation of Hudson, New York, which advertised the plane at $5,365 an hour, which was to say $129,000 a day (if not discounted), or just under $900,000 a week. Richmor middlemanned for the CIA.

For two and half years starting in June of 2002, the CIA used Morse's plane for dozens of flights around the globe: to Afghanistan and Azerbaijan, Morocco and the United Arab Emirates, Jordan and Japan, the Czech Republic and Romania, Switzerland and Guantánamo. The plane often landed on Spain's Majorca and Canary Islands, both of which were eventually recognized as rest-and-refueling stops for rendition flights. It also called eighty-two times on Dulles International Airport, just down the road from CIA headquarters. When the CIA was not using the plane, Morse or the Red Sox usually were. Once, Morse lent it to the Sox's manager so he could fly to his son's high school graduation. More than once, Morse flew on it with his friend the first President Bush. One of their trips was to the Baseball Hall of Fame in Cooperstown. Torture, one might conclude from the Gulfstream's overlapping uses, was as American as baseball and apple pie.

When it was reported in 2005 that the Gulfstream was a torture taxi, the president of Richmor Aviation, Mahlon Richards, said he knew nothing about the transport of "detainees," as the kidnapped and tortured are tepidly called by U.S. reporters. He knew only that the Gulfstream was flying federal workers. As to their purpose, he said, "I don't ask my customers why they go anywhere, whether it's

West Palm Beach or the moon." In his youth, Richards had been a recipient of his church's God and Country Award for a Boy Scout. His fidelity to Country, at least, had remained true.

Morse rather undermined Richards's disavowals by saying, "It just so happens, one of our customers is the CIA. I was glad to have the business, actually. I hope it was all for a real good purpose." Told by a reporter that the plane might have been used for kidnappings, he said he was stunned.

It was Morse's Gulfstream that flew Abu Omar from Ramstein to Cairo. The jet did not tarry in Egypt. A few hours after landing, it left for Shannon, Ireland, another way station for torture taxis, and from Shannon it continued to Dulles, then returned home to Hudson.

It is unclear why Abu Omar was flown first to Ramstein, then to Cairo. Maybe his conveyors preferred to launder him rather than fly him directly from Italy to Egypt. Or maybe he needed to be photographed and re-packaged in Ramstein for some reason. It was a mystery.

TO BE CHIEF of the CIA in Milan is to have done well for oneself. It is to have escaped Dili and Guatemala City, dysentery and uncertain electricity, and to have landed among ossobuco and opera and the Pinacoteca di Brera. Bob Lady got to Milan in 2000. He was born Robert Seldon Lady in Tegucigalpa in 1954, the son of a Honduran mother and an American father. The latter, William Lady, was an Arkansan who seems to have been a mining engineer, although he may also have worked in some capacity with the U.S. military. Bob Lady considered himself a Southerner, notwithstanding that his first language was Spanish. In high school in Honduras, when a group of students with wild Che Guevara beards taunted him with cries of *Gringo! Imperialista! Yanqui!*, he replied that he might well be a gringo, and he might well be an imperialist, but he wasn't no goddamned Yankee. His self-assessment would prove accurate on all counts.

After high school, he settled in New Orleans, where he may have joined the New Orleans Police Department (by another account, he headed north and joined the New York Police Department) and where he married Martha Coello, late of Redemptorist Boys and Girls High. They raised two children. In the late 1970s or earliest 1980s, Lady joined the CIA, where his fluency in Spanish and ease among Latin Americans must have been appreciated. For the next two decades, he served in the region of his birth, the gringo imperialist.

In Milan the Ladys lived on Via Cimarosa, a wide boulevard that was planted in atypically neat hedges. Their small apartment building was detached from the rest of the conjoined city and surrounded by high walls—a suburban privacy for Milan. Bob Lady's employer of record was the U.S. State Department, and his official title was deputy consul, but all of the Italian counterterror police knew Mr. Bob, as they called him, for the CIA officer he was. He liked his Italian counterparts as much as they did him, and he understood that the hundred small considerations he extended them were as important as the dozen big ones. He was liberal, for example, with mugs and pens from the CIA, whose cachet was considerable. Only rarely did the Italians refuse his overtures, as when he offered to pay for a hotel room from which the Carabinieri were staking out an apartment. The Carabinieri, not wanting to be unnecessarily dependent on the CIA, gently declined.

Lady was fond of his work, but by the time he had come to Italy, he had given half his life to the CIA, and he did not mean to give the rest of it. Nearly a quarter century of service had endowed him with a substantial pension, which, if supplemented with private consulting, could provide him a comfortable income indeed. He had encouraging leads on a contract to help protect celebrities at the 2006 Winter Olympics in Turin, and he was confident that other lucrative, if not quite Olympic, consultancies would follow. He and Martha looked for a place to pass their seniority and found it in the gentle hills of the Asti wine country, just outside the hamlet of Penango. It was an old farmhouse with walls in a shade of terra cotta, a roof of red tile, and ten acres of orchards. Via Don Bosco, on which the farmhouse fronted, honored a priest who espoused the theory, perhaps novel to a CIA man, that love was a better educator than punishment. No matter. From the fruits of an antithetical career, Bob and Martha would bottle their Barbera and live in graceful repose. They left Milan for Penango in late 2003, a few months before Bob turned fifty. Their peace did not last long.

Spataro completed his investigation in April of 2005 and asked a judge to indict nineteen Americans for kidnapping Abu Omar. Two months later, the judge issued arrest warrants for thirteen of the Americans: Lady, Adler, Asherleigh, Carrera, Channing, Duffin, Harbaugh, Harty, Logan, Purvis, Rueda, Sofin, and Vasiliou. Spataro appealed the six he had been denied—Castaldo, Castellano, Gurley, Ibanez, Jenkins, and Kirkland—and won indictments and warrants for them too. A little later, he won indictments and warrants for three more: Faldo, Harbison, and Medero-Navedo. Spataro had argued, and the judge agreed, that neither Lady nor Medero-Navedo was immunized from arrest by their consular (in the case of Lady) or diplomatic (in the case of Medero-Navedo) employment. For lesser alleged crimes, Spataro allowed, they might have been; for a crime as serious as kidnapping, no.

The day after the first batch of warrants was issued, Spataro sent officers from DIGOS to Via Don Bosco. Martha Lady was home, and was displeased by her visitors' arrival. Her husband was not in the country. DIGOS's search of the farmhouse turned up several documents of interest, most of which were on Lady's computer. One pair of documents showed that a few days after the February 17 kidnapping, Lady booked a room at a hotel in Zurich for February 23, then booked a ticket to fly from Zurich to Cairo on February 24, returning March 7. This itinerary matched what DIGOS had already learned from one of Lady's SIMs, which had traveled east from Milan on February 21, stopped for the night in Vicenza, then continued the next day past Venice to Gorizia. The SIM then went silent, apparently upon crossing the Slovenian border. When it was next heard from, on March 3, it was in Egypt, where it received two phone calls. Probably Lady attended to (though not necessarily attended) some part of Abu Omar's interrogation.

The police also found on Lady's computer three black-and-white photos of Abu Omar walking along a street bordered by a high wall. The photos had been taken from inside a vehicle, a little of whose dashboard crept into the bottom of the pictures. A caption read 12:25 HOURS 14 JAN 2003 VIA GIUSEPPE GUERZONI NEAR MEDICAL PARK—the place and hour of Abu Omar's kidnapping, one month before it occurred.

Other files of interest on the computer had been deleted, but DIGOS was able to resurrect them. They included maps and directions from Via Guerzoni to Aviano downloaded from the Web site Expedia on January 23 and 24. (January 27 was the first day Lady sent Maresciallo Luciano Pironi, a.k.a. Ludwig, to Piazza Dergano to intercept Abu Omar.) Also deleted was an e-mail sent to Lady (rslady01@hotmail.com) from a Susan Czaska (ciaobellasue@hotmail.com) on Christmas Eve of 2004.

"I am so glad to hear from you," Czaska wrote. "Since I got your last note, I suddenly got an e-mail through work which was entitled 'Italy, don't go there.' It was from Maura, giving a short run-down regarding the Milan Magistrate's intentions. I was a bit taken aback by all this since this was the first I had heard. Then when I didn't hear back from you, I was truly concerned that you were sitting in some Italian holding cell. I sent a note to Torya, trying to get some more information (since everyone seems to be so tight-lipped), and she said she had gotten a note from Sabrina, telling her that could [sic] not visit Italy and that you were in Geneva until this all blew over. I was extremely relieved to get your note—do be careful, and let me know if I help [sic] in any way."

Czaska, Spataro learned, was a U.S. citizen of fifty-odd years who clerked at the consulate in Milan—or did until three days before the raid at Penango, when she left Italy for good. Spataro suspected her of more than mere clerking for the State Department but could learn nothing more. He was not entirely surprised to discover from her e-mail that the CIA, with its informers burrowed inside Italy's government, like Massimo of Chapter 1, had learned of his investigation long before it was made public. (Reporters for *La Repubblica* also got wind of it and published some details a couple of months after Czaska's e-mail.) But the discovery was still disappointing.

The Sabrina whom Czaska mentioned, Spataro assumed, was Sabrina De Sousa, the CIA officer from Rome and Milan whose SIM was among the suspect ones. The other women Czaska mentioned, Maura and Torya, were unknown to the Italians. Probably they were CIA hands elsewhere, Langley maybe.

Also in Lady's study were compact discs that had been intended for old-fashioned deletion, but the trash can in which they had been tossed had yet to be emptied. One of the CDs had a list of hotels in Milan, including hotels that gave discounted rates to employees of the U.S. government. The kidnappers had stayed in some of the hotels. This discovery cast the CIA's seeming extravagance in a more favorable light: the $400 a night that Adler and others spent at the Savoia had perhaps been a steal. (There were no records to say for sure.) If so, the CIA apparently did not mind having its officers identified as federal employees in pursuit of a bargain.

After Spataro's raiders left Penango, Bob called Martha from a mobile phone in Honduras. His Italian SIM had been deactivated some time earlier, but Spataro had tapped the phone in Penango.

"Hear me out and don't say anything," Martha told her husband. "They came to the house today, the Milan police, and they seized stuff. They looked everywhere—outside, inside—and they took off with everything they found—your PC and the hard drives in your study. They took all your documents and floppy disks. They showed me the judge's warrant. Megale was also there and others I'd never seen, but they knew you. It's bound to become public tomorrow in the press."

"And they found nothing?" Lady asked.

"What are they supposed to find if there's nothing to find?"

Afterward, theories abounded about why the CIA had been so reckless from start to finish—why, for example, the spies had not used satellite phones, which the Italians could not have traced, why they had used their phones like teenagers, why they had not paid in cash, why Lady had brought work home. One theory focused primarily on mechanics: satellite phones had larger antennae and might have seemed more conspicuous on the street; paying $8,000 hotel bills in cash would have seemed suspicious. But this theory was unsatisfying because the mechanical problems were easily solved: satellite phones would not have been conspicuous if used sparingly; the team could have stayed in less expensive hotels and changed them every few nights. And no mechanical dilemma explained Lady's domestic carelessness, the frequent-flyer accounts, and other Keystone Kommando-isms.

A second, somewhat more satisfying theory was that after September 11, American covert operations grew so rapidly that the CIA could not properly run them all. Jobs that would once have been closely managed and scrutinized by headquarters were now put together in haste, and the chiefs of station who should have provided local oversight were, in cases, ill trained to manage operations like a rendition. It may also have been relevant that after September 11 the CIA increasingly outsourced parts of its covert operations. Several of Abu Omar's kidnappers were almost certainly contractors—the spies who billed me, as they were known in the trade. Perhaps they were properly trained, perhaps not.

A third, also satisfying theory focused on idiocy, of which the CIA has a long history—as, for example, the case of the CIA's forty agents in Iran who were imprisoned or executed in 1989 after the CIA mailed all of them letters at the same time, in the same handwriting, at the same address, from the same German mailbox; or the case in 1994 of the U.S. ambassador to Guatemala whom the CIA tried to smear as a lesbian (because of her support for human rights) by leaking transcripts of her cooing in bed to her female lover, who turned out to be a poodle; or the case of CIA analyst Aldrich Ames, who over many years betrayed dozens of American agents to the Soviets without arousing the CIA's suspicion, even though he bought his $500,000 house with cash, drove a Jaguar, and regularly paid credit card bills of $20,000 a month on a salary of $70,000. Nathan Hale predated the CIA, but it is apt that the agency honors him with a statue in its headquarters, since in his week as one of the nation's first spies, he gave General Washington not a jot of intelligence before the British discovered and hanged him. Had he had more than one life to give for his country, he might have given it a couple of centuries later with a frequent-flyer number.

A fourth and still more satisfying theory was that the kidnappers believed they would not be caught or that, if caught, they would be immune. This theory too had a pedigree, one specific to Italy.

Chapter 8

Gladiators

IN 1972 near the village of Peteano, in Italy's northeast, an anonymous caller lured several Carabinieri officers to an abandoned car
with bullet holes in its windshield. As they examined the car, a
bomb inside it exploded, killing three of the officers and badly
wounding a fourth. In the investigation that followed, the Carabinieri first concluded that leftist terrorists were to blame, but the
leftists were eventually exonerated. The Carabinieri then concluded
that other, non-political culprits were behind the crime, but they
were not convicted either. The case fell dormant.

Ten years after the bombing, a young magistrate named Felice
Casson, dissatisfied that the case had never been solved, reopened
it and discovered several oddities. For example, a junior Carabinieri
officer who had examined the crime scene had found two .22-cali-
ber shells, presumably from the bullets that had been fired through
the windshield of the car, but he had been told by his seniors that
the shells were irrelevant to the investigation and he should ignore
them. The shells then disappeared. The Carabinieri said the shells
had been given to a lab technician, but this proved untrue. A report
in which the young officer mentioned the shells also disappeared,
and a new report that did not mention them was put in its place.
Magistrate Casson also found that a small group of senior Carabinieri had tightly controlled the investigation, which was unusual,

and that this group had steered the blame, without cause, first to the leftists and then to the other innocents.

Casson's case might have gone no further but for a related mystery. Around the time of the bombing, police in Aurisina, not far from Peteano, found a buried cache of guns, ammunition, and explosives. From the way the cache was packed, it seemed that it had once held more explosives than it did when the police found it, but there was no sign of when the missing explosives might have been removed. At the time, the authorities concluded that the cache's explosives were not similar to the ones used at Peteano, but Casson discovered that their conclusion was without foundation. No one knew who had put the cache there.

Casson was curious about why the Carabinieri might cover up, as it seemed they had, the murder of their own officers. He was also curious about whether there was a tie between the cover-up and the arms cache. It took him years to find answers, and he did not find them all, but what he found was incendiary enough: the caches belonged to a secret stay-behind army that the CIA had created to fight Communists, and some of the officers who papered over the Peteano bombing were linked to the army. The army was called Gladio, after the short sword favored by the gladiators of ancient Rome.

IN THE YEAR of its founding, 1947, the CIA honored Italy with the agency's first campaign of political subversion anywhere in the world. The campaign was aimed at the national elections of 1948, which Italy's Communist Party, the strongest in Western Europe, stood a chance of winning, at least in coalition with the smaller Italian Socialist Party. This prospect struck dread in the breasts of American Cold Warriors, who disapproved of Communism whether it ascended by bullet or ballot. It did not matter that in Italy an elected Communist government would have been constrained by the republican constitution. A country that "went Communist" might allow the Soviet Union to quarter its forces there or forbid

Dow and Exxon to quarter *their* forces there. The first possibility was a threat to global peace, the second to American prosperity.

Congress had not authorized the CIA to interfere in foreign elections, which meant the CIA's plans for Italy were illegal. It also meant the CIA had no budget for propagandizing and other campaigning. But the agency's senior ranks were filled with Ivy Leaguers and erstwhile corporate lawyers who were able to beg money of anti-Communist industrialists and bankers of their acquaintance. The CIA also convinced the secretary of the treasury to shunt funds that were meant for rebuilding Europe to the Italian campaign. The recipients were mostly leaders of Italy's Christian Democratic Party, which had been founded at the end of the Second World War as a conservative counterweight to the Communists, and leaders of Catholic Action, the political arm of the rigidly anti-Communist Church. (Pope Pius XII, who had been careful not to condemn Hitler's Final Solution, excommunicated Italy's Communists en masse in 1949.) Sometimes the CIA laundered the money before giving it to the Italians, but other times CIA officers just handed it over in suitcases full of cash at the Hotel Hassler above the Spanish Steps in Rome. "We would have liked to have done this in a more sophisticated manner," CIA officer F. Mark Wyatt said many years later. "Passing black bags to affect a political election is not really a terribly attractive thing."

There is no reliable record of how much money the CIA funneled into the campaign or, for the most part, what it was spent on, although CIA-funded pamphlets that depicted Communist candidates as sexually depraved are known to have been distributed. The agency would later tell Congress it spent $1 million. James Jesus Angleton, the CIA's then chief of station in Italy (later its megalomaniacal director of counterintelligence), once said the figure was $10 million, which would have gone far in poor Italy of the immediate post-war. Others have estimated $30 million, which today would be roughly equivalent to $300 million. Whatever the case, the Christian Democrats won the elections by a wide margin. The portion of the margin attributable to the CIA is unknowable, but the success helped resolve a debate then taking place in Congress and the White House about whether the CIA should be a mere collector of intelligence or a subverter as well. The advocates of subversion won, and over the next few decades, the CIA ran dozens of covert campaigns in other countries based on the Italian job.

To undermine the Italian Communists for the longer term, the CIA turned after 1948 from ad hoc electioneering to systemic subversion of the Italian polity. The CIA gave money to anti-Communist labor unions and strike-breaking gangsters, founded publishing houses that excreted anti-Communist tracts and books, paid reporters to write and editors to approve anti-Communist articles, threatened other reporters and editors who would not be bought, and held membership drives and rallies for the Christian Democrats. The Soviet Union was doing some of the same for the Communists but, to judge from evidence revealed since the end of the Cold War, with fewer resources.

The Italian Left grew anyway. In the elections of 1953 the Communists and Socialists won a combined thirty-five percent of the seats in Italy's parliament, against the Christian Democrats' forty percent. A rattled CIA responded with so vigorous a campaign of "political action" that William Colby, who ran the station in Rome (years before he ran the Phoenix program in Vietnam, then ran the entire CIA), could say twenty years later that the agency had yet to run a bigger campaign. But in the elections of 1958 the Communist-Socialist bloc again lost by only a few percent, and in 1963 the bloc finally won a narrow plurality. The Christian Democrats could maintain their power only by giving the Socialists a few shelves in the national cabinet, a development that, in the CIA's view, portended the fall of Western Europe. Money continued to flow from Langley to Rome. The CIA would later claim that in the twenty years after the 1948 elections, it gave politicians of the Italian Right $65 million. That sum did not appear to include the money the CIA gave reporters, labor bosses, and the like. Victor

Marchetti, a former senior CIA officer in Italy, estimated that a truer and more inclusive figure for the 1950s was $20 million to $30 million per year. Other students of the topic have concluded that every Christian Democrat who held a ministerial post between 1948 and 1968 took money from the CIA, although the money was apparently well-enough laundered that not all of the ministers knew its source. Italy was an extreme but not unique case. German chancellor Willy Brandt and French prime minister Guy Mollet were both beneficiaries of the CIA's political fund.

Concerned that these comparatively genteel efforts to influence Italy's electorate might fail, the CIA, in or around 1951, created Gladio. The precise date, like many other details about Gladio, remains shrouded. Gladio had for a co-founder the Italian military secret service, the Servizio Informazioni Forze Armate, SIFAR, which was much the lesser partner. (SIFAR was a precursor of the Servizio Informazioni Difesa, SID, which was a precursor of SISMI.) Since the close of the Second World War, the CIA had exerted its considerable influence to ensure that SIFAR was run by ardent anti-Communists, including Fascists and members of a secret paramilitary wing of the Christian Democrats who were to have seized power if the Communists had won the elections of 1948. For years, whenever SIFAR gathered important intelligence, it sent it to "the boys at Via Veneto," as the CIA officers at the U.S. embassy in Rome were known. The CIA and SIFAR hid Gladio's birth from the rest of the Italian government. While some Italian prime ministers and presidents would be told of Gladio's existence over the next four decades, many seem not to have been. Nor, as a body, was Parliament. Under Italy's Constitution and laws, Gladio was as illegal as the Mafia.

To man the army, SIFAR quietly recruited zealots from Italy's military and police forces and trained them in guerrilla warfare and specialized arts like espionage, electronics, and propaganda. The trained men in turn kept an eye out for other zealots to recruit, some of whom were trained as well but others of whom were kept as untrained reserves available for muster by the regular Gladiators when the great clash with Communism came. Apparently Gladio grew briskly, because by the late 1950s or early 1960s the CIA and SIFAR built a training center for the army on the island of Sardinia. The site was chosen because it could be defended should Communists take mainland Italy and because its remoteness helped maintain Gladio's secrecy. At about the time the center was built, the CIA and SIFAR began sharing the management of Gladio with NATO. Probably NATO helped pay for the training center, which was no rude camp. A runway was laid, a firing range cleared, a small harbor dug, underwater structures for training frogmen built, and buildings erected for training in explosives and house-to-house fighting. Trainees were flown to Sardinia in planes with blacked-out windows, then driven in blacked-out vans from the airfield to their barracks. In the early years, the trainees seem to have had little idea where they were.

The CIA supplied the Gladiators with an arsenal, which was scattered about the country in caches that were to be opened when the war came. Most of the caches, like the one found near Peteano, were buried under fields or churchyards or mountainsides, but others were more brazenly stored in police barracks. Some may have held gold, whose worth, unlike the lira, was assured over time. When Gladio was exposed in 1990, Prime Minister Giulio Andreotti said there had been 139 caches, a number that might have been true or might have been gross understatement. Even 139, with dozens or scores of weapons per cache, suggested a sizeable army. Estimates vary widely, but regular Gladiators over the four decades of the army's existence numbered at least several hundred, more probably several thousand, and possibly ten thousand. Irregular recruits were probably several thousand more. After Gladio's exposure, a few Italian generals and prime ministers who had been complicit in Gladio's operation said the army was to have been used only against Communists who invaded or mounted an insurrection, not against Communists the electorate might empower by vote. It was a highly improbable claim.

A PROBLEM with preparing men to seize a country is that they may grow dissatisfied when not allowed to do so. If they have been encouraged in the belief that the enemy is not merely objectionable but diabolic, they may become more dissatisfied still. This may help explain how Italy came to be threatened with a coup d'état after the Socialists and Communists won their narrow plurality in 1963. A year and a half before the election, some senior CIA and military officers at the U.S. embassy argued that if the Socialists won a share of the government, the United States should encourage its proxies to intervene militarily. Their argument did not carry, and the Socialists were given their small share of the cabinet without violence. But the governing coalition of Christian Democrats and Socialists was shaky and soon collapsed. As negotiations got underway between the two parties for a new government, the head of the Carabinieri, General Giovanni de Lorenzo, publicly rattled his saber (and his armored brigade) and privately, it seems, threatened a coup. De Lorenzo took a dim view of Socialists, and his rattles were understood as a suggestion that the Socialists should have a diminished role, or none at all, in the new government. De Lorenzo had until recently been the longtime director of SIFAR and thus Gladio, a post in which he had been installed largely because the United States thought him more unyieldingly anti-Communist than other candidates and demanded he be put there. After he moved to the Carabinieri, he maintained influence over SIFAR and Gladio through men he had appointed during his tenure. The blueprint for his coup called for seven or eight hundred opposition leaders to be arrested and flown to the Gladio base on Sardinia for internment. It is conceivable that De Lorenzo would have planned a concentration camp at a base funded by the CIA and NATO without first getting their approval, but just. As it happened, the coup was not needed. The Socialists concluded from De Lorenzo's threat that they would be annihilated if they did not restrict their ambitions, and they quickly accepted a minimal role in the new government and muted their calls for leftward change. The government listed rightward and stayed in that position for quite some time.

A few years after his gambit, De Lorenzo was discovered to have illegally compiled dossiers on tens of thousands of innocent Italians. His particular focus was the sexual and financial peccadilloes of the elite, although he was not averse to gathering whatever else might be used for blackmail. The file on former and future prime minister Amintore Fanfani ran to four fat volumes. When the dossiers were exposed, De Lorenzo said the United States and NATO had suggested he create them, a claim that has never been proven nor disproven.

Six years after De Lorenzo's averted coup came another. Its leader was Prince Junio Valerio Borghese, who had commanded a Fascist corps of saboteurs under Mussolini and, after the war, had founded the Fronte Nazionale, with which he hoped to return Italy to Fascism. He recruited his putschists from current and former military men, and on December 7, 1970, the anniversary of Japan's attack on Pearl Harbor, they struck. The signal Borghese passed to begin the coup was "Tora, Tora," after the code name Japan's Fascists used for their attack. In the first hours of the coup, fifty of Borghese's men penetrated the Ministry of the Interior and stole hundreds of submachine guns while two hundred other troops, already armed, advanced on Rome. Other conspirators prepared to seize parts of other cities. But before the insurrection matured, Borghese received a call—from whom is still debated—telling him that the support of the Italian Army, which he had expected, had not materialized. He had little choice but to recall his men and quietly return the stolen weapons. For years it was rumored that the coup had been backed by the United States, but the principal source of the rumor was a co-conspirator of Borghese's who was of doubtful reliability. Decades later, however, a more reliable conspirator stepped forward and said that before the coup he had asked a CIA officer for a guarantee that the United States would not oppose it. The CIA man supposedly spoke with his superiors and reported back to the conspirator that his government would support the coup so long as Giulio Andreotti, already a rajah of the Right, were installed as prime minister. Years later the United States released archived documents showing that the U.S. ambassador to Italy, Graham Martin, had indeed been told of Borghese's coup months in advance. Martin in turn cabled Nixon's secretary of state, William Rogers, to ask if he should warn the Italian president or prime minister. What Rogers told Martin is not known, but there is no sign the Americans alerted the Italians. (If they had, it is unlikely the coup would have progressed as far as it did.)

One of Borghese's co-conspirators was General Vito Miceli, who at the time ran SID (the successor to SIFAR) and thus Gladio. Not long after the aborted coup, Ambassador Martin gave Miceli $800,000 in cash, despite warnings from subordinates that Miceli was "linked to antidemocratic elements of the Right." By some accounts, Miceli spent the American money "merely" on anti-Communist propaganda, but around the time he received the cash, he illegally created a secret intelligence organization whose funding has never been fully accounted for. The Super SID, as it came to be called, was patterned on the Gladio model—a force that was run by the uppermost officials of SID but hidden from the rest of the government. After the Super SID was exposed, Miceli was asked at an inquest whether it was he who had founded it.

"A Super SID on my orders?" he replied. "Of course! But I have not organized it myself to make a coup d'état. This was the United States and NATO who asked me to do it!"

Prince Borghese's threat was followed by one from Count Edgardo Sogno. (Italy's nobility tended to Neanderthalic politics.) In the early Cold War, Sogno had founded a group that ostensibly propagandized against Communism but in fact gathered dirt on labor organizers and other leftists, with funding from the auto giant FIAT. "When FIAT stopped financing us," Sogno later said, "I decided to go to the United States and ask for help from my old friend Allen Dulles," the director of the CIA. Dulles apparently gave Sogno the money he needed. As the years passed, the electoral gains of the Communist Party increasingly angered Sogno, and in the 1970s he became irretrievably outraged by suggestions from some Christian Democrats that for the stability of Italy the Communists should finally be given a piece of the government. Sogno began plotting a coup, and in the summer of 1974 he shared his plans with the CIA chief of station in Rome, Rocky Stone. "I told him," Sogno later wrote, "that I was informing him as an ally in the struggle for the freedom of the West and asked him what the attitude of the American government would be. He answered what I already knew: the United States would have supported any initiative tending to keep the Communists out of government." Sogno moved forward with his preparations, but before their culmination the Italian government discovered and quashed them. If the United States betrayed Sogno, he never suspected it.

THE YEARS OF LEAD, Italy's grisly era of domestic terrorism, were inaugurated on December 12, 1969, by a bomb that destroyed seventeen people and disfigured eighty-six others at a bank in Milan's Piazza Fontana. As with the bombing near Peteano, which followed three years later, police rushed to blame leftists, hundreds of whom were eventually arrested around the country and thousands of whom were harried. Newspapers followed the government's lead with McCarthyite assaults in print, and the Left, which had been in a strong position after the global protests of 1968 (which had been particularly potent in Italy and had essentially continued through 1969) found itself suddenly on the defensive.

There were signs early on, however, that something was amiss in the haste to accuse the Left. To start with, only a few days after the bombing, the police's leading suspect, an anarchist named

Giuseppe Pinelli, tumbled out a fourth-floor window at Milan's police headquarters. The police said Pinelli leapt to his death when his alibi began to crumble under interrogation. It was an unconvincing explanation. It was the more so after investigating magistrates showed that Pinelli was not behind Piazza Fontana. Rightists were. Which rightists has never been irrefutably proven because for the next four decades police and intelligence officers covered up for them, and sympathetic judges dismissed cases against both them and their coverers on the thinnest of legal grounds. One of the first magistrates to expose pieces of the truth was Spataro's mentor Emilio Alessandrini.

Terrorists of the Right followed Piazza Fontana with scores of lethal attacks that achieved their apotheosis in the slaughter of eighty-five and the mangling of two hundred others at Bologna's main train station in 1980. It remains the deadliest attack by terrorists in Italian history. The Right's assaults were part of a "strategy of tension" whose goal, as several terrorists eventually said, was "to destabilize in order to stabilize"—that is, to create such fear in Italians that they would call for or tolerate the re-imposition of Fascism. Short of that, Italians might at least call for or tolerate what might now be called the Cheney agenda: an erosion of civil liberties, a fettering of the legislature's power to check the executive, and, as a kind of a garnish, largesse for corporations and attacks on the rights of workers. No single body coordinated the strategy of tension. Rather, a common tune circulated along the rightist underground and was picked up and passed along by groups large and small, much as would happen among Islamic terrorists twenty years later.

The Left, as noted, had its savages too. They had not been of much consequence before Piazza Fontana, but afterward their ranks swelled and they murdered scores of officials like Spataro's mentors. The leftists did not see that their efforts to spark revolution only played into the strategy of tension. As the number of dead and dismembered grew, Italians, though not so terrorized as to call for Fascism's return, punished the Left at the polls, particularly after the Red Brigades murdered former prime minister Moro in 1978. The prospects of the Communist Party became crepuscular, then went out altogether.

By the end of the Years of Lead in the late 1980s, political attacks had, by one count, killed 491 people and wounded 1,181. Perhaps three-fifths or two-thirds were the victims of rightists, the balance of leftists.

It was against this background that Magistrate Casson investigated the bombing at Peteano. In time, he found and convicted the bomber, who was a leader of a cell of the rightist Ordine Nuovo, New Order, named Vincenzo Vinciguerra. Vinciguerra's family name means "a victor in war"; his redundant given name means "conqueror." He explained to Casson that right-wing terrorists had not carried out the strategy of tension entirely autonomously. "There exists in Italy," he said, "a secret force parallel to the armed forces, composed of civilians and military men in an anti-Soviet capacity—that is, to organize a resistance on Italian soil in case of a military invasion on the part of the Red Army. . . . [It is] comprised of soldiers and civilians entrusted with military and political tasks and possessing its own network of communications, arms, and explosives and men trained to use them." The men of the secret force, Vinciguerra said, did not limit their work to preparing a defense against the Red Army. Instead, "in the absence of a Soviet military invasion, [they] took up the task, on NATO's behalf, of preventing a slip to the Left in the political balance of the country. This they did, with the assistance of the official secret services and the political and military forces." In short, Gladio, which Vinciguerra did not name (but which could have been no other), had played more than a passing role in the strategy of tension.

Casson subsequently discovered documents in military archives that proved Gladio's existence, then he discovered that Gladiators were among the whitewashers of the Peteano bombing. He also discovered a list of probable Gladiators, some of whom were tied in varying degree to other rightist attacks. But he could not learn with certainty whether Gladiators carried out or gave direct support for the attacks, nor could he learn whether Gladio as an organization had sanctioned or supported them.

After Casson exposed Gladio in 1990, the man who ran it from 1971 to 1974, General Gerardo Serravalle, said that during his tenure the CIA's Rocky Stone told him the United States did not much care whether the Gladiators could fight a stay-behind war against an invading Red Army. The United States was far more interested in "the subject of internal control—that is, our level of readiness to counter street disturbances, handling nationwide strikes, and above all any eventual rise of the Communist Party. Mr. Stone stated quite clearly that the financial support of the CIA was wholly dependent on our willingness to put into action, to program and plan these other—how shall we call them?—internal measures." Serravalle did not specify what, if anything, Gladio did to counter "any eventual rise of the Communist Party"—whether, say, Gladio merely drilled in riot control or, say again, gave aid to the strategists of tension. (Other Gladiators and Gladio documents suggested that Gladio had been tasked as early as the 1950s with combating internal rather than external threats.) Serravalle also said that on taking command of Gladio, he discovered it was full of hotheads who wanted to attack the Left and that he was so appalled by the discovery (evidently he thought he would be running a kind of anti-Communist Junior League) that he ordered Gladio's arms caches dug up and flown to the Gladio base in Sardinia. Since he seems to have had them dug up only after the cache near Peteano was found, the truth may be that he feared other caches would be unearthed and Gladio with them. He may also have feared that explosives from the cache near Peteano had been used in the bombing and that other caches might be put to similar use.

In 1998, several years after Serravalle offered his revelations, a terrorist from New Order named Carlo Digilio said that he and others in his Venetian cell regularly discussed their plans for the strategy of tension with a certain U.S. Navy captain. Digilio and his cellmates assumed the captain was either a CIA or military intelligence officer, but they had no evidence of either possibility. Digilio said he told the captain in advance of a plan that he had heard, at second or third hand, to bomb Piazza Fontana, but although the captain seemed concerned, he did nothing Digilio could see to deter the bombing. After the attack, Digilio told the captain what he knew of how it had been carried out, and again the American seemed to do nothing with the information. A magistrate thought enough of Digilio's claims to ask a judge to indict the mysterious captain, which would have allowed the magistrate to put questions to the U.S. government, but since it was impossible to prove even the captain's existence, the judge declined to indict.

In 2000 came another testifier. Paolo Emilio Taviani, minister of defense in the 1950s and of the interior in the 1960s and 1970s, said that senior officers of SID had not only been aware of the plot to bomb Piazza Fontana but had even been on the verge of stopping it. However, they decided not to, and later they tried to protect the bombers by framing leftists in Padua with the attack. Taviani said he did not believe, as some did, that the CIA had organized the bombing. But he added, "It seems to me certain, however, that agents of the CIA were among those who supplied the materials and who muddied the waters of the investigation." He offered no proof.

Taviani's testimony was followed by that of General Giandelio Maletti, who ran SID's counterintelligence section in the early 1970s. Maletti said that the materials for several rightist bombs, probably including the bomb at Piazza Fontana, had been brought to Italy from military bases in Germany, and he thought it likely the CIA had been the courier. He did not elaborate why he thought so. He also said that the CIA routinely worked with right-wing groups it knew to be violent, because "the CIA, following the directives of its government, wanted to create an Italian nationalism capable of halting what it saw as a slide to the left . . ."

Other witnesses of lesser rank and varying reliability also came forward. Some claimed that U.S. intelligence officers were told in advance of a bombing in Brescia in 1974 that killed eight and wounded nearly a hundred, and others claimed that the makings of the bomb at Bologna's railway station in 1980 came from a Gladio arsenal. Some of the claimants might merely have been trying to share the blame for their sins with the CIA.

After Gladio's exposure in 1990, Prime Minister Andreotti admitted that the army had existed but said it had long ago been disbanded. When documents emerged that proved his claim untrue, he owned up to the army's continued existence but shrewdly deflected attention from himself by saying NATO was running Gladios all over Europe. A NATO spokesman said in reply, "An organization of this kind does not and never has existed within the framework of the NATO military structure." The next day, however, NATO said its spokesman had erred, then refused to say more. NATO's supreme power, the United States, said nothing. Investigators were not long in learning that NATO had run, and was still running, Gladios all over the continent—in Germany, France, Great Britain, Belgium, Holland, Luxembourg, Denmark, Norway, Sweden, Switzerland, Portugal, Spain, Greece, and Turkey. The CIA seems to have had a hand in setting up some of the secret armies, but the details are far from clear. The revelations were a great scandal in Europe, and the Gladios were supposedly shut down. In the United States that begat them, the story was hardly a blip.

The CIA and Gladio may or may not have directly helped terrorists in the Years of Lead. But there is an abettor's guilt in training and arming fanatical saboteurs in a politically volatile country, in encouraging them and their fellow travelers to believe themselves beyond the law. That such men go on to murder and maim can be of no surprise, nor would it be surprising if the CIA had intended that outcome. The CIA has never been held to account for its work in Italy, and it seems to have thought it never would.

Chapter 9

In Absentia

THE INDICTMENTS and arrest warrants that Armando Spataro won in June of 2005 were valid throughout the European Union, which was to say that if any of the spies set foot in any of the twenty-five EU nations, he was to be arrested and sent to Milan. Never before had an ally of the United States indicted CIA agents for doing their jobs, so the indictments and warrants would have been big news in any era. But their press was the wider still because nearly four years into America's "War on Terror," few governments had challenged the American warriors. For millions of people, Spataro's charges were, if not the stone with which David struck Goliath, at least one of those he picked up from the brook to give it a try.

Reporters came from every point of the compass to interview Spataro and found an Amerophile. The magistrate, it happened, had long believed that the Constitution of the United States was one of the world's most beautiful pieces of literature, and he thought no less of America's ongoing effort to perfect its union. In his office hung a print of Norman Rockwell's *The Problem We All Live With*, 1964, the moving (if heavy-handedly Rockwellian) painting of Ruby Bridges in a dress of unsullied white entering kindergarten in New Orleans under the escort of four faceless U.S. Marshals. Spataro kept the print to remind himself and his guests of the power of the law, impersonally enforced, to do good. Also on his walls were Edward Hopper's *Nighthawks*, a Warhol, and commendations from the FBI and DEA for his successful collaborations on Mafia and drug cases. Some years earlier the U.S. State Department had hosted him for a comparative study of the American and Italian justice systems, and on other occasions he had traveled extensively in the United States. In his young adulthood he had journeyed from coast to coast over forty-five days on only a few hundred dollars; he had detoured to Albuquerque because he liked its name. In his middle age he wrote essays on American culture, among them an appreciation of Sam Peckinpah's film *Pat Garrett and Billy the Kid*, and he had lectured, also appreciatively, on the music of Bob Dylan. He thought Philip Roth's *American Pastoral* surpassing brilliant. Like many Italians, he was fond of New York, but as befit one who must make do with Milan instead of Rome, he thought Chicago one of the most beautiful cities in the world. He was under the impression that Chicago was fronted by a lake pure as a mountain stream (perhaps the comparative mountain was Milan's Monte Stella, built from the rubble of the Second World War), that it was free of trash, graffiti, and traffic jams (further understandable confusions for a Milanese), and that it was graced by the most perfect skyline in America (he had seen Seattle only in the fog). The photos on his computer's screen saver were of Chicago's waterfront and of a German shepherd he had named Bill because of the dog's democratic approach, like that of the recent American president, to the females of his species. The screen saver also had photos of the Twin Towers.

Reporters inevitably asked him why he had brought the case, and just as inevitably he answered that he fought not the United States but lawlessness. A kidnapping was a kidnapping, no matter its perpetrators or victim. A country in which a person could be stripped of liberty without due process was a country in which nobody was truly free. He liked to quote Supreme Court Justice Sandra Day O'Connor on the principle—"we cannot fight tyranny with the instruments of the tyrants"—and also Aharon Barak, president of the Supreme Court of Israel—"A democracy must sometimes fight with one arm tied behind her back. Even so, a democracy has the upper hand." On his own authority he would add, "We in Italy have lived under Mussolini. We have known the way of Fascism. We do not wish to repeat our mistakes." To those who said Islamic terrorists were a new kind of foe—warriors rather than criminals, defeatable only with violence, not law—he replied that the same had been said of Front Line and the Red Brigades, but they had both been broken in court. Moreover, Italy was already succeeding against so-called Islamic terrorists, scores of whom he and his colleagues had imprisoned. He allowed that the lawlessness of George W. Bush had probably stopped some terrorists, but he doubted it had stopped more than it had created. "We make a big gift to the terrorists," he said, "when we behave contrary to our democratic principles. We give to those fish other water to swim." A two- or three-hour soliloquy on such topics refreshed rather than fatigued him. Most reporters, after reviving themselves, returned to their laptops and made him the esteemed protagonist of their dispatches.

Those who did not tended to be rightists. The *Wall Street Journal* editorial page, a proponent of law and order when it came to, say, welfare cheats or dope pushers, said Spataro's prosecution of the U.S. kidnappers branded him "a rogue." Other detractors more explicitly decried him a leftist saboteur of America's fight against al-Qaeda, but his years prosecuting leftist terrorists made this line a hard sell, as did his having charged Abu Omar with terrorism on the same day he charged his kidnappers.

When the indictments and warrants were made public, Prime Minister Silvio Berlusconi summoned the U.S. ambassador to Palazzo Chigi for what aides described as a stern lecture on Italian sovereignty. But it soon became plain that Berlusconi had no enthusiasm for Spataro's work. When Spataro sent Berlusconi's minister of justice requests to extradite the spies (the United States having ignored Spataro's requests to question them more gently), the minister refused to forward them to the United States. He also refused to forward the warrants to Interpol, which is to say to the rest of the world. After Berlusconi's government fell in the spring of 2006, Spataro re-submitted his requests to the center-left government of Romano Prodi, but Prodi's minister of justice refused him too. After Prodi fell in 2008 and Berlusconi rose again, Spataro submitted the requests again and was again denied.

Had the papers been forwarded to Washington, they would have been coolly received. The Bush administration said publicly it would not extradite the accused and privately that were it asked to do so, there would be repercussions. Italy's governors knew their place. They also had their own reasons not to push extradition.

LUCIANO PIRONI, nom de guerre Ludwig, the maresciallo whose dream of leaving the Carabinieri for SISMI impelled him to help Bob Lady with the kidnapping, had not, at first, been disappointed in Lady. Even before the kidnapping, the head of SISMI's office in Milan, Major Stefano D'Ambrosio, told Ludwig at a chance encounter that "a mutual friend" had spoken highly of him. Major D'Ambrosio had himself risen from the Carabinieri to SISMI and so was in a position to understand the plight of talent trapped in the Carabinieri. Not long after Lady's commendation, D'Ambrosio asked Ludwig to collaborate on anti-terror investigations, and Ludwig gratefully accepted. A month or two later, Ludwig gave D'Ambrosio his résumé, and D'Ambrosio said he would pass it straight to Marco Mancini, director of SISMI's operations in northern Italy. D'Ambrosio thought it likely SISMI would hire Ludwig sometime in the next year.

Then events took a difficult turn. Shortly before Christmas of 2002, D'Ambrosio called Ludwig to say that SISMI was relieving him of his command in Milan and moving him to Rome. He did not say why and did not sound happy. Later he told Ludwig he would be transferring back to the Carabinieri, an indignity Ludwig felt as his own. D'Ambrosio said, however, that Ludwig should not worry about his application to SISMI. He had given Ludwig's résumé to Mancini as promised, and although Mancini had been mildly annoyed that it had not gone through regular channels, D'Ambrosio still thought Ludwig would be hired. It would be best, though, not to invoke D'Ambrosio's name.

The next time Ludwig saw Lady, the maresciallo said he feared his application was sunk. Lady told him to relax, everything would be OK. Mancini was in line to become SISMI's next director (he was soon promoted to SISMI's number-two position), and the CIA had great "feedback" with him. Ludwig's application, Lady said, was in good hands. As for why D'Ambrosio had been so abruptly dismissed, Lady could offer no insight.

MAJOR D'AMBROSIO FIRST learned that Bob Lady was interested in Abu Omar in the late spring or early summer of 2002. Lady had asked D'Ambrosio what he knew of the Egyptian, and D'Ambrosio had said he knew only that DIGOS was investigating him. Lady told him some of the fruits of DIGOS's inquiry and said he had intelligence of his own that Abu Omar was planning to hijack an American school bus. (Spataro would later say the plans did not exist.) From time to time, as DIGOS learned more, Lady added a few details. He said he thought the investigation was going well.

But in October Lady announced unexpectedly that the CIA was planning to seize Abu Omar. He explained, as D'Ambrosio later told the story, that the CIA's chief of station in Italy, Jeff Castelli, had proposed the rendition and that he, Lady, had objected. Lady supposedly argued that a rendition would bring to an abrupt halt all that DIGOS was learning about Abu Omar's network, and unnecessarily because DIGOS had Abu Omar well enough surveyed to know if he was planning an attack. The rendition would also badly damage the CIA's vital relationship with DIGOS, whose officers were not to be forewarned. Castelli, Lady said, had ignored him and lobbied headquarters for approval, which had been granted. A Special Ops team was in Milan scouting the kidnapping as they spoke, and SISMI, whose collusion Castelli had also obtained, was helping with the scouting. Lady asked D'Ambrosio what he knew of the operation.

D'Ambrosio had been listening appalled. He said his superiors at SISMI had told him nothing, perhaps because they had suspected he would object. He was offended both by the plot itself and by its execution in his territory without his knowledge.

Lady continued. After Abu Omar was "collected," he was to be driven to the Italian air base near Ghedi, ninety minutes east of Milan, where the U.S. Air Force had a small contingent. While he and his collectors were en route, the CIA would send a plane from Ramstein to fetch him. SISMI had already sent a team to Ghedi to study where to hold him in case the plane were delayed. Where Abu Omar would be taken from Ghedi, Lady did not say. Nor did he say, as he would to Ludwig, that the CIA hoped to turn Abu Omar into an informer, or even to get information from him. The only objective seemed to be to get him off the streets.

D'Ambrosio said he found it impossible to believe that the Italian commandant of Ghedi, Colonel Gianmarco Bellini, would cooperate. Bellini had been shot down over Iraq in the Gulf War and tortured by the Iraqis. He would never let his base become a way station for a torture taxi.

Lady spread his arms wide to indicate the imbecility of it all.

"Why," D'Ambrosio asked, "was Castelli set on the rendition?"

Lady didn't have an answer. He got along terribly with his boss and said only, "What do you expect a Buddhist who burns incense in his office and listens to the music of Bob Marley to know about terrorism?"

D'Ambrosio had met Castelli twice before, once when he and his wife had come to Milan for an opera at La Scala and once when he had come alone for a routine check of the Milan station. He was a bit under fifty, wore glasses, seemed level-headed, and was said to keep a shrine to Jimi Hendrix in his office. D'Ambrosio would later theorize that Castelli had pushed the rendition with an eye to promotion. Other CIA chiefs were collecting scalps in the War on Terror, and he did not want to be left out.

Lady also said that Castelli had sent an aide, Sabrina De Sousa, from Rome to Milan, ostensibly to help manage the kidnapping but in truth to keep an eye on him. D'Ambrosio knew De Sousa: a dark-haired, dark-eyed, khaki-skinned woman of forty-some years who had sometimes treated him, he would later say, like a junior officer in a Third World militia.

D'Ambrosio assumed Lady was telling him about the plot at least in part because he hoped D'Ambrosio could stop it, but if so Lady was too circumspect to say so outright.

"Talk to your people," he only said.

It was just what D'Ambrosio meant to do.

A FEW DAYS later, D'Ambrosio traveled to the SISMI office in Bologna to meet with Marco Mancini. Given the igneous nature of his subject, he asked Mancini to go for a walk, and on the city's colonnaded streets he related what Lady had said. When he had finished, he said he hoped there had been some misunderstanding, that either no kidnapping was in the works or, if one were, that SISMI was not involved. But he urged Mancini whatever the case to speak to General Gustavo Pignero, SISMI's chief of counter-terrorism, to make sure the CIA did not try anything so foolish. He also asked Mancini not to tell anyone, not even Pignero, that Lady was his informer. He feared Castelli would punish Lady if he learned he was D'Ambrosio's source. Mancini, as D'Ambrosio later told the story, listened mostly in silence. He did not seem surprised by the plot, but neither did he seem to approve of it. He was also disturbed by D'Ambrosio's informer.

"But was it really Lady himself who told you?" he said.

"Yes."

Mancini turned this over wordlessly.

D'Ambrosio asked if he should make a report of his conversation with Lady, but Mancini replied, a bit irritatedly, that that would not be necessary. He would speak with General Pignero personally. D'Ambrosio went back to Milan.

Some weeks later the general called D'Ambrosio and told him to come to Rome immediately for an urgent discussion whose topic he did not disclose. D'Ambrosio arrived at Fort Braschi, SISMI's headquarters, the day after next. In the hallway outside Pignero's office, he ran into one of Pignero's aides, an acquaintance of D'Ambrosio's, who asked what he had done to Mancini. D'Ambrosio, not understanding, asked what the aide meant. The aide replied that Mancini was furious with D'Ambrosio.

"He has done you in," the aide said.

D'Ambrosio was not certain that Mancini's furor stemmed from their talk in Bologna. He suspected another, equally inflammatory cause, also with Lady at its root. Some weeks before Lady told him about the rendition, he had told D'Ambrosio (again, according to D'Ambrosio) that Mancini had offered to become the CIA's mole. The CIA apparently considered the offer but in the end declined it, partly because the agency feared a trap: maybe SISMI was only testing how brazenly the CIA would try to infiltrate its upper ranks. Also, according to Lady, the CIA thought Mancini was too willing to auction himself to the highest bidder. He was a bad risk. D'Ambrosio asked Lady for evidence of Mancini's offer, but Lady said that while the affair was recorded in the CIA's computers, any copy of the files that he made could be traced back to him. D'Ambrosio was not sure whether Lady's tip was real or was manufactured for a reason he could not divine. (The motives of spies are often inscrutable even to their allies.) Lacking proof, he had let the matter lie. Now, outside Pignero's office at Fort Braschi, he wondered if Mancini had learned of his talk with Lady—maybe even from Lady himself—and was angry that D'Ambrosio hadn't reported it to him. (Mancini later denied that he had offered to spy for the CIA, and Lady denied that he had said Mancini had. Either man, subsequent events would show, would have had difficulty winning a reliability contest against D'Ambrosio.)

D'Ambrosio entered Pignero's office, and the general did not waste words. He said he was transferring D'Ambrosio to Fort Braschi and assigning him different duties. His tone made clear this was not a promotion.

D'Ambrosio said he did not see why he should be relieved of his command. His work in Milan had never been called into question. Indeed, he had had several important successes, including the recent arrest of an arms trafficker that had earned the praise of Prime Minister Berlusconi himself. What, he asked, had he done wrong?

Pignero answered metaphorically. Imagine, he said, that a soccer coach had a player on the field who was playing at eighty percent, which, Pignero allowed, was pretty good, but on the bench sat a player who could play at one hundred percent. Was it not the coach's duty to make a substitution?

"When will I have to move?" D'Ambrosio said.

"Immediately."

D'Ambrosio returned to Milan and surrendered his post the following morning to Mancini, who—rather officiously, D'Ambrosio thought—demanded his service phone on the spot. D'Ambrosio asked Mancini who the hundred-percent player was who would replace him, and Mancini said he would run the station himself. D'Ambrosio thought this odd in light of Mancini's many other duties supervising SISMI chiefs across northern Italy. Understanding his career at SISMI was over, D'Ambrosio requested the transfer back to the Carabinieri himself. A colleague at Fort Braschi would later tell him that his ruin had been effected less by Mancini than by Jeff Castelli, who had wanted his head.

The next time D'Ambrosio saw Lady, Lady asked whether he had spoken to anyone about the "confidential information" they had earlier discussed.

D'Ambrosio lied that he had not.

Lady said that was interesting, because he too had received a summons to Rome, where Jeff Castelli had chewed his ass for fraternizing too closely with the natives. Castelli had mentioned D'Ambrosio by name. No matter, though, Lady said. Water under the bridge. He was only sorry for D'Ambrosio. His fate was another sign, of which Lady had seen many, that the era of the honorable intelligence professional was over. The show was now being run by men like Mancini and Castelli, bastards out for their own interests. Men like D'Ambrosio and Lady, servants devoted to their countries, got shat on for thanks.

AFTER THE KIDNAPPING, Ludwig expected Lady to call, but he did not hear from him on the evening of February 17, nor on the next day, nor the next. Eventually he called Lady's two mobile phones, but there was no answer. Weeks passed, during which Ludwig also heard nothing from SISMI about his hoped-for transfer. Then one day, maybe a month after the kidnapping, he was watching TV and saw a news report about the disappearance of a Muslim cleric. The newscaster said the police suspected he had been kidnapped and that a woman on the street may have witnessed some of it. The cleric's name was Abu Omar.

Ludwig was dismayed—he hadn't noticed a woman on the street. He would later understand that his preoccupation with Abu Omar had been total and that the woman must have been the reason the men in the van had waited so long before seizing Abu Omar: they had been letting her pass, but, as it happened, incompletely. Maybe another pedestrian had been approaching, or maybe they were just incompetent. Ludwig was also disturbed by the news report because he thought of what he had done on Via Guerzoni as an intelligence job, not a crime, but here the newscaster was discussing it as a run-of-the-mill felony, prosecutable like any other. It put the thing in a new light.

Ludwig finally saw Lady about six weeks after the kidnapping. He came by the Carabinieri office, looking a touch less ebullient than usual, and Ludwig managed a few private minutes with him to say that his superiors in the Carabinieri suspected the CIA was behind the kidnapping. He asked what had become of Abu Omar. Lady told him not to worry. Abu Omar was now in the Balkans with his first wife. The operation had gone well, in fact was still going well, still reaping benefits, by which Ludwig understood that Abu Omar had talked and the CIA was fruitfully pursuing leads he had given.

Ludwig also asked what had come of his application to SISMI. Lady, by way of reply, asked whether Ludwig had considered the private sector. He said he himself was about to retire from the CIA and do security work for the Olympics, and he was entertaining offers or near offers from the manufacturing giant Pirelli and a company of former CIA officers that negotiated the ransom of hostages. He did not remark the irony of a kidnapper working to free the kidnapped. A man of Ludwig's talents, Lady said, could do well in the private sector. A cynic might have thought he had cared less about Ludwig's career all along than about securing his help in the rendition. Ludwig was desolated.

Apparently sensing his desolation, Lady eventually offered, as a kind of consolation prize, to fly Ludwig and his wife to Washington when they vacationed in New York later that year. They were going to New York partly because Ludwig wanted to pay homage at Ground Zero. Lady would arrange a tour of the CIA's headquarters for Ludwig while Mrs. Ludwig shopped or saw the sites in Washington. His offer had the intended effect, and the maresciallo accepted with the awe, as he later said, of "the little priest going to the Vatican." On the appointed day, Ludwig was given his tour, and when it was done, Lady surprised him with a small ceremony honoring his service to the CIA. Some of the CIA's lesser counterterror nobility were in attendance and drank his health. The toastmaster apologized for serving Bordeaux to an Italian, but Ludwig took of it as if it were communion. After the ceremony, Lady asked if there was anything else Ludwig particularly wanted to do, and Ludwig replied that he would like to visit the CIA's gift shop and buy souvenirs. The shop, however, was closed. Lady promised to send him a cigarette lighter.

Over the next year or so, Ludwig tried several other routes to SISMI, all without success. In the end he gave up and accepted a post with the Carabinieri at the Italian embassy in Belgrade. In November of 2004, before he left for Serbia, he and his wife went on a trip that took them near the Ladys' villa in Penango. They stopped to visit, and while the women were elsewhere Ludwig said he was still concerned about the Abu Omar affair. Could he be prosecuted? Could they all be prosecuted?

Lady told him to relax, there was nothing to worry about. Ludwig had seen his magnificent villa among the vineyards, yes? He had invested all his savings in it. His entire future lay in Italy. Would he have made it so if he weren't certain that there was not now and never would be an inquiry against him?

BRUNO MEGALE'S INVESTIGATORS at DIGOS had tracked the SIMs of the conspirators who had called one another, and they had tracked the SIMs of those who had stayed in hotels, but they had not tracked the SIMs of those who had made no calls and stayed in no hotels. If any such conspirators existed, they would be all but impossible to find—unless, perhaps, they had staked out Abu Omar's neighborhood of Dergano at the same times the other kidnappers had and, also, they had had mobile phones with them that, although neither making nor receiving calls, had been powered on. With other demands on their time, the investigators did not look, or did not think to look, for these hypothetical conspirators in the first phase of the investigation. But in the spring of 2006, nearly a year after Spataro had won the arrest warrants for Lady and the other spies, DIGOS analyzed the many thousands of SIMs that had been in Dergano when the spies had been there. They found one suspicious SIM. It had been in Dergano around noon on each of January 27, February 2, February 9, and the day of the kidnapping,

February 17, after which it never returned to the quarter. The SIM was registered to one Luciano Pironi, who on investigation turned out to be a maresciallo of the ROS Carabinieri with the nom de guerre Ludwig.

In April Spataro invited Ludwig to a dialogue at the Palazzo di Giustizia. He arrived and said he knew nothing about a kidnapping on Via Guerzoni, nor did he know how his mobile phone—the one that had rung just as he and Stocky were approaching Abu Omar—might have connected to cell towers near there. Spataro said he found Ludwig's ignorance unconvincing. The maresciallo left with a scent of indictment trailing him. Eight days later, however, he came back and admitted that he had not been truthful. He proceeded to relate, with only a few evasions, all that he had been involved in, from his recruitment by Lady to his abandonment by same. He acknowledged having his personal phone with him on the day of the kidnapping and on his other outings to Dergano. Had he left it at home or simply powered it off, he would never have been discovered.

His confession led Spataro to Major D'Ambrosio, who willingly told what he knew and who impressed Spataro as a moral soldier who had refused to acquiesce in immoral orders. His testimony about being removed from his post by Mancini and Pignero prompted Spataro to tap their phones. The taps were fructiferous, for the two men called each other often.

"At the end of 2002," Pignero said in one of the calls, "I often met with Castelli."

"Of course," Mancini said.

"One of the things we talked about was that the CIA was planning to start up the American public project of—"

"Of renditions."

"I didn't talk about 'renditions.' I said exactly this: of search, localization, and capture—"

"Ah, perfect."

"—of people they believed were—"

"—involved—"

"—anywhere they might be in the world, even in Europe and Italy—who were involved in the attack on the Twin Towers or with al-Qaeda activities."

"Exactly."

"In this context," Pignero said, "informally and only orally, he gave me a series of names, a series of characters."

"Americans?"

"No, Arabs."

"Arabs, ah, yes."

"To look for, to look for."

"Yes."

"They were in Europe . . . Holland, Belgium, Austria."

"You didn't tell me this, this thing here."

"Also in Italy. He gave me some names of people in Italy, but I can't remember the names now. . . . But Abu Omar was one of these names, only in the sense that—he wasn't referring to him as 'Abu Omar,' but with his proper name."

"Yes."

"In addition to this, he also told me about this guy working in Vercelli."

"Hey," Mancini said, "you didn't tell me about that guy."

"In Vercelli, Naples, Turin—"

"Yeah, but you didn't tell me about this part."

"Yes, but there was a list of—"

"I understand, I understand."

"Turin, et cetera, et cetera."

In all, at least ten candidates for rendition were on the list. Pignero said he didn't tell SISMI's director, General Nicolò Pollari, about his conversation with Castelli, apparently because he wanted to protect Pollari. He later learned his protectiveness was unnecessary. Pollari and Castelli had also talked about renditions, and according to Pignero, Pollari had offered SISMI's help. Pignero told Mancini that eventually Pollari ordered him to help the CIA plan Abu Omar's rendition.

"How was that request made?" Mancini said. "Was it protocol?"—meaning written in a formal memo, signed, dated, and filed.

"Which request?"

"The one for the rendition, the one the director gave you. Was it protocol or not?"

"Noooo! No, no."

"Then what was it?"

"It was an anonymous note," Pignero said. "Just a note I kept until one year ago when—I kept it in my office. Then one fine day I read this thing—" by which he seemed to mean a news report of the Abu Omar affair.

Mancini laughed.

"Ah, go fuck yourself!" Pignero said.

Mancini laughed again.

"I destroyed it," Pignero continued, "and it was the only copy."

"The one the director gave you?"

"Yeah."

"The fucking director," said Mancini, who, it became apparent, thought Pollari a coward for not publicly taking responsibility for SISMI's part in the rendition. Mancini and Pignero then discussed whether Pollari had written the anonymous note himself, and Pignero said, "I remember that it was written in English."

"Shit," Mancini said. "The director doesn't speak English, so it's difficult to believe he wrote it himself."

"There wasn't even a remote chance of tracing anything in any fucking direction. And even if the Americans did make a copy and by some absurd, crazy chance somebody drags out that copy, it was still a piece of paper with no date, no protocol. It could have been written today."

"As long as the Americans don't say, 'Yes, the Italians knew about it.' "

"They do say that. But I say no."

AS EVIDENCE of SISMI's involvement in the kidnapping mounted, an editor from the right-wing newspaper *Libero* asked to interview Spataro and his colleague Ferdinando Pomarici, who was helping with the investigation. Spataro granted the request, and the editor, Renato Farina, arrived with a young reporter in tow and said they too had been investigating whether Italy's government had been involved in the kidnapping. He and his reporter then asked a series of questions that seemed to the magistrates designed chiefly to learn how much they knew of SISMI's role. Next Farina told the magistrates he had quite a scoop, which he would generously share: Italian officials had indeed been involved in the kidnapping, but they were not the officials Spataro and Pomarici might have expected. The ringleader was Magistrate Stefano Dambruoso, the first prosecutor on the case, and his co-conspirators were officers in DIGOS. Together they had covered up for the CIA and had possibly done worse. This astounding news explained why the case had not advanced before Spataro took it over from Dambruoso. Spataro and Pomarici said they would study the matter, and Farina and his protégé left.

Farina was not quite the editor he seemed. A few days before the interview, a SISMI officer named Pio Pompa had called Farina and asked him to set up the interview. After Farina had done so, Pompa and Farina exchanged further calls to discuss what questions Farina should ask. Pompa then called General Pollari, SISMI's director, to keep him abreast of the developments. Unfortunately for all three men, DIGOS had already suspected Farina of colluding with SISMI and had tapped his phone. What the investigators heard led them to tap Pompa's phone too, and when Farina interviewed Spataro and Pomarici, his interesting but false claims about Dambruoso and DIGOS were recorded by a bug that Spataro had had DIGOS install in his table. Hardly had Farina walked out of Spataro's office than he called Pompa to report on the interview, and Pompa in turn reported to Director Pollari. Pompa and Pollari then deliberated whether they might be able to get the investigation taken from Spataro and given to friendlier jurists in Brescia. (Ultimately they couldn't.) Throughout, the men of SISMI exhibited a remarkable oblivion to the fact that they did not have a monopoly on phone-tapping in Italy.

Pollari and Farina were well known to Spataro, but until this episode Spataro had never heard of Pompa. When he looked into him, he found that although Pompa worked in Rome, he did so not from SISMI's headquarters at Fort Braschi but from a large, off-the-books aerie atop a splendid commercial building. Spataro ordered the suite raided in the summer of 2006, and the raiders found, among other documents, a memo saying that not long after Abu Omar was kidnapped, the CIA told SISMI that he had been taken to Cairo for interrogation—notwithstanding that the CIA had told DIGOS he was probably in the Balkans. Other damning papers, unrelated to the kidnapping, showed that someone working from the suite had had phones tapped, subjects tailed, and informers paid, all for the purpose of gathering dirt on politicians, magistrates, and reporters. The snoopers seem to have been particularly interested in antagonists of SISMI and Prime Minister Berlusconi. One might say that their outfit was a successor to the bygone Super SID of General Vito Miceli and the blackmailing dossier shop of General Giovanni De Lorenzo, although the men of the aerie had improved on the tradition by propagandizing more extensively. One of their specialties was drafting half-true and baldly false newspaper articles that were favorable to the government, which they gave to reporters for publication under the reporters' bylines. Some of the journalistic shills, like Farina, published the compositions verbatim. Farina, it would turn out, fronted for SISMI not just in the Abu Omar case but also in the notorious Yellowcake Affair. In that episode SISMI gave the CIA fake documents purporting to show that Saddam Hussein was buying weapons-grade uranium from Niger. The documents gave George W. Bush one of his crowning justifications to war on Iraq, and when they were exposed as SISMI frauds, Farina tried unsuccessfully to pin their creation on France.

Spataro had Farina and Pompa indicted and Mancini and Pignero indicted and arrested. Farina confessed everything. He said General Pollari, SISMI's director, had recruited him to sham for SISMI, notwithstanding that Italian law forbade Italy's spy agencies from employing reporters, and he said that over two years SISMI had paid him between €20,000 and €30,000 and given him other tokens of gratitude, like World Cup tickets. He had, however, given most of the money to the Catholic Church and other charities, for he was no mere mercenary. He was, rather, a patriot who in his estimation had been "fighting the fourth world war—against Islam." In return for his confession, he was given a light sentence, eventually converted to a fine, then he stood for Parliament with the party of Silvio Berlusconi, who hailed him "a guerrilla fighter for liberty." He was elected.

Pio Pompa, whose name can be translated "Pius Pump" or, by a more colloquial rendering, "Pius Blow Job," refused to tell Spataro much of anything and said he would see him at trial.

General Pignero at first lied wantonly to Spataro but eventually confessed to ordering subordinates to help the CIA plan the kidnapping. He said that when Jeff Castelli first asked SISMI to help with renditions, he, Castelli, had offered in return to have the CIA kidnap a fugitive leader of the Red Brigades who was living in South America. The CIA would have handed the fugitive to the Italians (apparently in South America), who could have brought him to trial in Italy or done what they wanted with him. SISMI declined, probably because on the one hand its officers would have had a hard time explaining to an Italian judge how the fugitive had been brought to Italy in violation of an extradition treaty and because on the other hand they did not care to summarily dispatch their own justice to the fugitive. Pignero may have been moved to confess to Spataro by a cancer that was killing him. The counterterror chief died two months later, on the fifth anniversary of the September 11 attacks.

As for Marco Mancini, Spataro showed him the transcripts of calls in which he and Pignero had agreed on lies he would tell Spataro. Several of Mancini's subordinates also came forward, or soon would, to say that Mancini had ordered them, in preparation for the kidnapping, to stake out places Abu Omar frequented. (None of the SISMI men, it seems, was involved in the kidnapping proper, although it is possible that other Italians, like the double-agent Massimo, were. There were, after all, twenty SIMs whose users Spataro never identified.) At roughly the same time, allegations emerged that Mancini and two other men had run an illegal wire-tapping shop similar to Pio Pompa's, although more as an append-age of Telecom, the state telephone company, than of SISMI. The shop allegedly sold its intelligence for large sums to businessmen and politicians who wanted compromising information on their rivals. The buyers included a clique of right-wingers who squelched an electoral bid by Alessandra Mussolini, a rightist parliamentar-ian herself, though on the outs with her squelchers, who was best known as the granddaughter of Benito who had sometimes omit-ted to clothe her torso when appearing before cameras. Another client was an executive of the soccer club Inter Milan who paid to have his star player spied on because he feared the star's off-field play was vigorous enough to disrupt his on-field play. These logs burning beneath him, Mancini yielded a few words to Spataro, the essence of which was that he had only been following Director Pol-lari's orders. It was a *sua culpa*.

By the end of 2006, Spataro had enough evidence to charge Pol-lari with conspiracy to kidnap Abu Omar. The director had repeat-edly denied that he or SISMI had been involved in the rendition, and he said now that he had documents proving his innocence but that they had been classified secret. Much later Pollari suggested that the decision to kidnap Abu Omar had not been his to make. His lawyer, asked by a reporter whether someone higher up in the

Italian government had ordered the abduction, replied, "Evidently. It wasn't the doorman."

Spataro questioned Pollari's predecessor at SISMI, Admiral Gianfranco Battelli, about who might have ordered the kidnapping, and Battelli also suggested it hadn't been the doorman. He said that days after the attacks of September 11, Jeff Castelli had proposed to him that the CIA render men from Italy, and he had replied that if the project moved forward, he would need to tell Prime Minister Berlusconi. But Battelli had retired a few weeks later and, the project not having advanced, he only referred the matter to Pollari.

Of the rendition Silvio Berlusconi had once said, "There has not been, I repeat for the umpteenth time, any involvement by the government in those events. Neither I, nor my ministers, nor my undersecretaries, nor any Italian institution has been advised or informed by anyone. I deny in the most absolute way every false reconstruction, and I reject with disdain every attempt to distort the truth." After Spataro indicted the whole top drawer of SISMI, Berlusconi's denials were slightly tamer, but he maintained his claim of personal ignorance.

"Are you kidding?" said Vincent Cannistraro, a past director (long before Abu Omar's kidnapping) of the CIA's Counterterrorist Center, when an Italian reporter asked him about the plausibility of Berlusconi's ignorance. "The CIA wouldn't send a single man into Italy for a covert operation without first informing your premier and SISMI."

SPATARO WAS EGALITARIAN. When he charged Italy's top spy and aides with conspiracy, he charged America's too. A judge found merit in his charges and issued arrest warrants for diplomats Jeff Castelli, Sabrina De Sousa, and Ralph Russomando and for Lieutenant Colonel Joseph Romano of the U.S. Air Force. Russomando had only recently come to Spataro's attention. Officially he was a first secretary at the U.S. embassy, but his indictment claimed he was a CIA officer who had sent DIGOS the mendacious note after the kidnapping that said Abu Omar was probably in the Balkans. All four indictees had long since left Italy. (The charges against Castelli, Russomando, Pollari, and Mancini were later dismissed, for reasons to be discussed.)

AT THE END of 2006, as Spataro was putting together the last of his indictments, the newspaper *Corriere della Sera* published a document that began:

> My name is Osama Mustafa Hassan Nasr, known as Abu Omar, the Islamist kidnapped from the streets of Milan on February 17, 2003, by intelligence agents of the U.S. and other states. I am currently an inmate at Cairo's Tora Reception Prison.
>
> I write this testimony from inside my grave and burial place. My body has been weakened, my mind has been distorted, I am ill and diseased, and I can sense the signs of my death.
>
> I write this testimony from inside my grave and burial place. The screams of the tortured, the whips of the torturers, the living hell inside this cell have changed the very features of my face.
>
> I write this testimony from inside my grave and burial place. I give thanks to all those who are trying to shed the light of hope on the mystery of my kidnapping from Italy and my imprisonment and torture in Egypt.

Two and a half years had passed since Abu Omar had been summoned by the State Security Service to pick up his identification papers. When he had not returned home, his family had asked first the State Security Service and then other entities of the state where he had been taken, but all were dumb to their questions. Months went by, and they feared the worst. But in late summer or early fall of 2004 the police of Alexandria called and said they were holding Abu Omar and he could receive an occasional visitor. Nabila Ghali flew from Milan to see him. On arriving at the police station, she was shaken to find in place of her portly husband of a year and a half ago a near skeleton who hobbled more than walked and wheezed when he breathed and whose beard of rich black had gone almost completely white. He told her that a State Security officer had told him he had been re-arrested for not abiding by the Sacred Don'ts, particularly "Don't contact anyone in Europe." He had been sent back to Tora and held there some weeks or months when a judge ordered him released. The State Security Service had complied by "releasing" him to police custody in Alexandria. New charges were then brought against him, and he was given back to State Security, which returned him to Tora. Later, however, a judge ordered his release again, so State Security had brought him to the police in Alexandria once more. Now here he was, uncertain whether the release would be made real this time. He said nothing about how he was being treated.

Ghali visited him on one or two other occasions, but when next she came back, he was gone. She was not told where he had been taken. More months went by, then suddenly he was in Alexandria again on "release" and permitted visitors, but he disappeared just as suddenly. Months later he reappeared. This happened several times in 2005 and 2006. At some point in the sequence, he smuggled the testimony he had written in Tora to his wife, and she sent it to Milan. That he could write it—that is, that he had pen, paper, light, and the privacy to use them—were indications that his current imprisonment was not as severe as his previous one.

In his testimony he described his kidnapping and transport to Egypt, his first imprisonment and torture, and his miraculous release and re-arrest. The second arrest had been followed by beatings and electrocutions like those of his first imprisonment, but eventually, he would later say, the torture tapered off and he was abused irregularly—more remindfully than habitually. He would also say that after he wrote the declaration but before it was published, two Egyptian officials visited him in prison and said if he would agree to tell reporters that he had come to Egypt freely, a foreign intelligence service would give him $2 million. The claim was perhaps not as far-fetched as it might sound. The CIA had wanted to make a similar offer to Khaled El-Masri, a German the CIA had mistakenly rendered and brutalized. The agency had abandoned the idea only after the White House decided that El-Masri's case could not be hushed up. Abu Omar said he spurned the offer on principle, but he also suspected that had he accepted, the money would have been taken back after he spoke to reporters.

After his testimony was published, he was tortured with renewed vigor, but again the abuse eventually fell off. A few months later, in February of 2007, four years after his capture and nearly three after his re-arrest, a court again ordered him freed, only this time on being returned to Alexandria, he was freed not just in theory but in fact. The State Security officer who discharged him said if he wished to keep his freedom, he should have nothing more to do with journalists. Abu Omar shuffled out into Alexandria, at large again.

JUDGE OSCAR MAGI of the Tribunal of Milan set trial for the American defendants in absentia and the Italians in praesentia for June of 2007. (In the United States, indictees who abscond before trial generally cannot be tried, but Italy believes in trying even those who would as soon skip the process.) Twenty-five of the Americans ignored the trial and were appointed counsel by Magi. The twenty-sixth, Bob Lady, hired his own lawyer. After several months, however, Lady acceded to the government line of ignoring the proceedings, dismissed his lawyer, and was appointed a replacement by Magi.

The governments of Italy—Silvio Berlusconi's until 2006, Romano Prodi's from 2006 to 2008, and Berlusconi's thereafter—moved repeatedly to stop the trial. The essence of their several arguments was that SISMI and its collaborators needed secrecy to defend the nation and that the few trespasses they might from time to time commit in its defense were trifles compared to the threat posed by investigating them. In the governments' reading of the Constitution and relevant statutes, Spataro's investigation had illegally ruptured this vital secrecy and Judge Magi's trial would further rupture it.

Spataro argued in reply that while spies must of course be able to act in secret, their actions had to be legal. If spies became their own law, there was no law. If today they could kidnap Abu Omar, tomorrow they could kidnap any of us. He maintained that his investigation had revealed nothing that hurt Italy or the United States in their fight against terrorists, and he found nothing in Italy's Constitution or other law that permitted felons to hide behind the scrim of national security.

The competing arguments went to the Constitutional Court, Italy's highest for constitutional questions. The court was not known for celerity.

When the date for trial arrived in June of 2007, the Constitutional Court's decision had not, so Judge Magi, a dapper man with a judicious Vandyke, opened trial just long enough to suspend it until October, by which time he hoped the high court would have ruled. But October arrived without a ruling, so Magi convened and suspended again, until March of 2008. Come March, the status was much the same, but Spataro urged Magi to proceed, and Magi agreed. Then he adjourned for a month. When he reconvened, he heard motions for a day and adjourned for another month. When finally he began trial in earnest, in mid-May, he convened once every two weeks, until mid-July, then recessed until September. (No sensible Italian would testify in August, or, if he would, his character would be presumed suspect. August, in the eyes of the Italian judiciary, is a period of eight weeks.) In September, Magi quickened the pace to a hearing a week, but the schedule was understood to be like a New Year's resolution and there was slippage.

Magi was not lazy. Like other Italian judges, he worked long hours, just not on one case consecutively, which Italians evidently believe would overtax judicial interest. An Italian judge will have several trials lurching along at once, which helps explain why the average Italian lawsuit over a mere broken contract lasts three and a half years (the average in Britain is seven months) and why the average defaulted mortgage in Italy takes eight years to foreclose on (the Danish average is six months). A trial of a major crime can take an age.

When Magi finally permitted Spataro to call his first witness, in the spring of 2008, he led with Nabila Ghali, whom Egypt had allowed to leave the country. Her husband was given no such license. She arrived draped entirely in cloth, her black hood with its narrow eye slits making her look, unfortunately in this context, a little like a medieval executioner. To identify her, Judge Magi asked her to lift her hood behind a changing-room screen that he interposed between her and the rest of court. She testified to her husband's abuse. She wept.

The scores of witnesses who followed over the many succeeding months were so much anti-climax. They said what they were expected to say, which was whatever they had said in their pre-trial depositions. When drama occasionally threatened, as when SISMI's General Pollari sought to compel Berlusconi and Prodi to testify, it was smothered under a mound of appeals and delays. (Pollari's bid was eventually disallowed by an appellate court.) In the fullness of time the Constitutional Court issued its ruling, which said that Spataro and Judge Magi had trespassed on state secrecy but only slightly. Some evidence was thrown out, a lesser Italian defendant or two was dismissed, but the case against the principals, including all of the Americans, was legitimated. Trial proceeded, after its fashion. It was like watching concrete cure.

Chapter 10

Martyrs

IF A PAIR of reporters from the *Chicago Tribune* can be believed, Abu
Omar worked for the CIA in Albania. The *Tribune* reporters, Tom
Hundley and John Crewdson, got the story from senior officers in
SHIK, the Albanian intelligence agency that arrested Abu Omar
in 1995 just before Egypt's foreign minister visited. In Abu Omar's
version of his arrest (told in Chapter 3), SHIK tried to make an
informer out of him but let him go when he refused. The officers'
story differed. They said the CIA asked them to detain a dozen or
so members of Gamaa and Islamic Jihad who might try to kill the
Egyptian minister, and they had done as asked. (At the time, three
years into Albania's first post-Communist government, the regime
was so pleased to have the United States for an ally that it let CIA
run SHIK practically as a subsidiary. "They worked in Albania,"
President Sali Barisha later said, "as if they were in New York or
Washington.") Abu Omar was not among the dozen men the CIA
wanted arrested, because neither the CIA nor SHIK suspected him
of terrorism. They may not even have known he existed. But the
CIA also asked SHIK to find four vehicles that seemed to be tied
to terrorists, and one of the vehicles was a Land Rover used by the
Human Relief and Construction Agency, the Islamic charity where
Abu Omar worked. The Land Rover, on investigation, turned out to
be registered to Abu Omar. Two CIA officers inspected it for traces

of explosives and found none, but they told SHIK to arrest Abu Omar anyway.

When he was brought in for interrogation, he at first refused to cooperate, but in the story told by the SHIK officers he soon changed his mind and talked—a lot. One of the officers described Abu Omar as "smooth and calm, probably because he wasn't under pressure from us. He was never aggressive with us. We didn't use a lot of physical pressure on him. He was well-behaved and gentle." What a SHIK officer might mean by "We didn't use a lot of physical pressure on him" is probably very different from what an FBI agent, or even a Chicago cop, might mean by the same phrase. Supposedly Abu Omar told the officers that he had been a member of Gamaa in Egypt and had come to Albania because it was a "safe hotel"—a place where exiled Islamists could stay a few years without fear of persecution. He said that Gamaa members in Albania would not attack the visiting minister because they did not want to invite reprisals that would shut down their hotel. He also identified the employees of Islamic charities in Tirana who belonged to Gamaa and told what he knew of their duties. Some of the charities, the CIA would eventually conclude, financed terrorism.

Abu Omar's chattiness surprised the SHIK officers. They had never had an Arab informer before. Now they had one who practically would not stop talking. "After a week," one interrogator said, "we had a full file." The CIA verified much of what was in the file and congratulated the SHIK men on their catch. The CIA's praise was greater still when SHIK asked Abu Omar to inform on his colleagues after his release and he said yes. Let go, he was true to his word. In return, SHIK helped him resolve a problem with his residency permit and may have helped settle a dispute with the landlord of the building where his bakery was to open. About three months into his career as an informer, however, he packed up his family and fled to Germany. The SHIK officers were surprised. They had thought him an essentially willing collaborator, but he had either fooled them to win his release or had a change of heart after he got out.

This history, if true, may explain why when the CIA rendered Abu Omar to Cairo in 2003 the Egyptian basha offered to return him to Italy if he would become an informer. Having once betrayed his friends, he might have been expected to recidivate. Certainly with the Iraq War about to start, the CIA would have appreciated an inside man who could say when and how Europe's Islamists were sending suicides to Iraq.

But the *Tribune's* story is not a sure thing. For one reason, the CIA seems not to have told DIGOS, the Carabinieri, or SISMI that Abu Omar had informed in Albania, which is odd because there was little reason to hide his collaboration. Odder still, if Bob Lady can be believed, even he did not know Abu Omar had been an informer. It is hard to imagine why the CIA would have kept the fact, if fact it was, from its own officer assigned to monitor the man. It is possible, then, that the CIA and SHIK concocted the informer story, although why they might have done so is not clear. One theory is that the CIA wanted to suggest that Abu Omar had not been kidnapped but had gone willingly to Cairo with the CIA, in which case Spataro's prosecution was moot. At the time the *Tribune* published the story, Spataro's first warrants had just been made public, and it was far from certain that his charges would advance to trial. Abu Omar, incommunicado in prison, could not offer his competing story of abduction and torture. It is a riddle that remains to be solved.

IN THE SPRING of 2007, a few weeks after Abu Omar was released from prison the second time, he began talking with reporters against the advice of the State Security Service. Clearly he was gambling that international celebrity would keep the government from re-arresting him, and in the first days at least, his gamble worked. I decided to go to Egypt to speak with him before his luck ran out. Before I left, I contacted his lawyer, Montasser El-Zayat. El-Zayat had once been Ayman al-Zawahiri's lawyer and had helped broker the nonviolence accords between Gamaa and the Egyptian government. Now he was brokering audiences with Abu Omar as tight-fistedly as a press agent for Angelina Jolie. He said through a translator that I could interview Abu Omar in Alexandria, but I must first visit him, El-Zayat, in Cairo, and I could not contact Abu Omar in the meantime. I arrived in Cairo and waited several days for him to honor our appointment. When finally he did, I beheld a mountain of a man in a finely tailored suit of light gray pin-stripe that had required the sacrifice of two or three bolts of tropic-weight wool. He loomed over a computer desk and answered my translated questions tersely while checking his e-mail. His manner implied a robust estimation of his own worth. At the end of the interview, he surrendered Abu Omar's mobile phone number.

Out on the street, my translator called Abu Omar in Alexandria and asked to set a date for the interview. Abu Omar replied, the translator told me, that he usually charged €4,000 for an interview but that since I was a freelancer he would talk to me for only €2,000.

I was not sure I had understood right.

"Did he say he's charging for the interview?"

"He did."

"Did he say two thousand *euros*?"

"He did."

The translator gave me a look that communicated both sympathy for me and a suspicion that he might have grossly undercharged for his services, which, however, had not been a bargain.

"Please tell him," I said, "that El-Zayat said nothing about paying for an interview, either just now or when I e-mailed him from home."

This was communicated, and a reply given.

"He says," my translator said, "that he doesn't know anything about the arrangements with El-Zayat. He says if you want to talk to him, you have to pay."

It was an excellent bait and switch. El-Zayat knew, as I later verified, that his client was selling his interviews, and Abu Omar knew that El-Zayat was letting him set the price.

I asked the translator to wait a moment while I debated whether to pay. The question was not whether to pay €2,000—that figure was obviously a starting point from which Abu Omar expected to be bargained down and which, in any event, I could not afford. The question was whether to pay something less. Over the years, I had always turned down such requests, mainly because paying can corrupt. Give a man $3,000 to tell you whether he was kidnapped by the CIA, and he may tell you he was kidnapped whether he was or not. Then, too, a reporter who pays $3,000 may be more inclined to hear what he hopes to hear. He wants his money's worth. In Abu Omar's case, however, there was already independent evidence attesting to his story, and I was not interested in breaking news that might be corrupted. I wanted chiefly to take the measure of the man and to get clarifying details about mostly undisputed events. Additionally, although most American publications refused to pay sources—partly to guard against corruption but also to guard their profits—some made exceptions. In 2001, for example, the *Wall Street Journal* paid $1,100 to the looter of a bombed al-Qaeda compound in Kabul who had retrieved a computer with important files that revealed how al-Qaeda worked. The *Journal* reported the contents of the files, acknowledged having paid $1,100 to get them, and let readers decide if it had done right. I thought the *Journal* had.

Reporters who interviewed Abu Omar before me had not. They had paid him, then neglected to report the fact. One international news network, I later learned off the record, paid €7,000 for an early interview. Other reporters paid from a few to several hundred euros. One reporter for a prominent European journal made a gift of some hundreds of euros to Abu Omar's wife to maintain the fiction that the interview had not been bought. My colleagues had betrayed their readers, to say nothing of setting me up.

It seemed to me, both in the seconds I thought this through and on later reflection, that Abu Omar was historically unique—in the class of the computer from Kabul. He was the only person in more than five years of the "War on Terror" to have been snatched by the CIA and to have emerged to tell the tale. (Two innocents, Khaled El-Masri and Maher Arar, had also survived rendition, but they had been arrested almost gently, not kidnapped, and could say nothing of the "black ops" aspect that seemed central to renditions. They also had not been taken to Egypt, America's leading offshore torture center.) If I could have been certain that Abu Omar would not have been arrested again soon, I would have waited a few months until his news value had cooled and he was willing to speak gratis to keep his story alive. But I could not be certain that Egypt would leave him be. My chief remaining concern was whether, if I paid him, he might convert his honorarium to terrorism. But I decided the possibility was an unlikely one. No doubt he was closely watched by the Egyptians, and in any case they would not have let him go if they suspected he was a serious threat.

"Tell him," I told my translator, "that I won't pay for just a single interview. Tell him I'm writing a book and need to hear his story in depth. I'll need many interviews—half a dozen or maybe even a dozen. If he'll agree to that, I'd give him a few hundred dollars."

This was relayed.

"He says a thousand dollars."

"Less."

"Seven hundred."

We settled on four hundred, the first interview to be the next evening, half the money to be paid at the outset. It added new meaning to "paying a visit."

I FOUND ALEXANDRIA bedraggled but not, despite the prevailing Islamism, disagreeable. There were a few inviting hookah bars, though their invitations were extended to men only, the street stalls bustled, and the breeze off the Corniche reached even the dismal, bug-ridden closet where I lodged to save money to pay Abu Omar's tithe. At the appointed hour, I walked with a new interpreter to Abu Omar's flat, which lay inland on a quiet side street. Chunks of plaster had fallen off nearby edifices, but the neighborhood was less shabby than most in town, and there were signs of a modest prosperity, like a tiny Internet café and pedestrians in clothes not long off the rack. The children who minded the small shop near Abu Omar's building had grown used to reporters standing puzzled in the street, trying to discern which building was his. "Abu Omar?" they said, and pointed to the right one. We rang him, and he said he would be down directly.

A minute later the great wooden door at the base of the building swung open, and in the doorway stood a tiny man in a gray galabia. He seemed a miniature copy of the Abu Omar I had seen in pictures, and I realized later that his reputation as a man of violence, combined with a fieriness of eye in the pictures, had enlarged him in my mind. (A woman who sat next to me on the flight to Egypt had caught a glimpse of one of those pictures and said, "Something is *not* right with that man.") There was no fire in Abu Omar's eyes today. His greeting was all smile.

Reporters who had interviewed him before me had described a near invalid who walked only with the greatest labor and was gasping before he reached the top of the four flights of stairs to his apartment. But the Abu Omar before us today practically leaped up the steps. Perhaps he had healed or, alternatively, had been lightened by the prospect of the two hundred American dollars that would greet him at the top. (Then, too, perhaps my colleagues had struck a better bargain than I.) If he had healed, he may subsequently have had a setback, whether to his health or to his fee, because reporters who came after me also saw more enfeeblement than I did. In general, few reports I read described his pain with nuance, I suppose because doing so might have made him seem less devastated by all he had endured. Reporters also tended to describe his apartment as cramped and its furnishings, save for two large, gold-colored chairs in the room where he held court, as spare. But the apartment I saw would have been considered normal in size in a comparable Western city, its crisply painted walls were probably adorned lightly because of Islamist views on art, not because of poverty, and among its fittings were a large, ornately carved dining room table and a desktop computer that was literally sparkling new: it had a transparent casing with innards that lit up when the machine whirred (the screen saver was a photo of Mecca). By the standards of Egypt, Abu Omar was making out, and even by the standards of the First World he was doing well.

We had not been seated a minute when he asked for the earnest money and reminded me he was doing me a favor by cutting his normal rate. I handed over two hundred and fifty dollars, the extra fifty a demonstration of good faith, unwarranted though it was. He counted the bills with the proficiency of a bank teller.

I asked how much English he spoke, and he said, "A lee-tul." I asked about Italian, and he said, "*Un po'.*" So we proceeded through my interpreter, a kindly medical student who was one of few Egyptians who did not try to extort the last dollar from my wallet.

Abu Omar spoke with his eyebrows, which had natural peaks, like *accents circonflexes*, that became exaggerated when he was impassioned. In extreme passion they crested to Matterhorns. He could also compress a lot of expression into the sweep of an arm or the stiffening of his spine. But although he told some parts of his story with animation, for long stretches of time he sank deep into his chair, flapped his legs idly together, and narrated without heat. If he had once been warmed by more of his tale, repetition had cooled him. He may also, like other survivors of trauma, have disassociated himself from the pain of the events. Perhaps because of this detachment and also because his voice had a thin, top-of-the-throat quality, I had a hard time imagining his captivating the Islamic flocks of Italy, no matter how much expression he packed

into his gestures. I wondered if something was being lost in translation, but my interpreter later said he did not find Abu Omar elo-
quent in Arabic or charismatic in general. He did, however, have a
clear, linear style of speech (*this* happened, then *that* happened, then
that) and a gallows humor, as when he said of the tendency of the
Egyptian police to beat first and ask questions later, "Violence is
the Egyptian way of showing love." Both traits must have served
him well in the pulpit.

Early in our interview, there came a gentle knock at the door
of our room, and Abu Omar went out and returned with tasty
yogurt-based drinks and cookies. His wife was our unseen hostess.
A couple of hours later, there was another soft knock, and he disappeared and came back with more drinks. The courses, if not quite a
bargain at $125 each, were still a nice touch.

Abu Omar's story was that which I have told in preceding chapters, fleshed out by and checked against other sources where possible. More than once he stressed that he had never been involved
with terrorists and had always loved Americans and other Westerners. Indeed, he still did, even after all he had been through, though
he thought less highly of their governments. Not long before my
arrival, he had called on terrorists in Iraq to release two German
hostages. "What are the German mother and the son guilty of?" he
had pled. "What have they got to do with the foreign policy of their
country?" (The mother was released.) He would later show a visitor
a bag of Christmas cards from well-wishers in Britain and said it
gave him strength to know such people existed.

He also emphasized that he had never informed for Albania's
SHIK or any other government, although during his torture in
Egypt he had blurted out all kinds of things, which he did not
now want to elaborate, that he thought his torturers might want
to hear. I asked him about a recent report in *GQ*, anonymously
sourced, that he had collaborated more willingly than that after
his rendition. The report said that CIA officers had watched the
first days of his interrogation in Cairo on a video feed outside the

interrogation room. He had not yet been tortured. From time to time his Egyptian interrogators emerged from the room and consulted with the CIA officers on how to get him to talk. During one of these consultations, the Americans said that before Abu Omar was kidnapped, his stepson, Nabila Ghali's son by prior marriage, had gotten into a fight with a friend and had asked Abu Omar what to do. Abu Omar told his stepson he must apologize. The CIA officers suggested that the interrogators tell Abu Omar they had a message from his stepson: he had heeded Abu Omar's advice and apologized. It might soften Abu Omar, somehow, to hear it. Sure enough, in the *GQ* story, when Abu Omar heard his son's "message," he wept and was moved to cooperate with his questioners. He talked for days. Torture had not been necessary. When he had talked himself out, the CIA officers left, and only then did the torture begin, apparently more for retribution than for information. To me, the *GQ* story sounded awfully convenient in exempting the CIA and more particularly Bob Lady—who had been in Cairo during this period and who was the source of other material in the article—from direct involvement in torture. In answer to my question, Abu Omar said his interrogators had indeed told him of his stepson's apology, but their disclosure had been preceded by torture and, rather than prompting him to talk, had caused him only to wonder why they had brought up this irrelevant vignette. It was bizarre. He assumed that since the information must have been obtained via a bug in Milan, a foreign intelligence agency must have been cooperating in his interrogation.

As for his current state, he said—and I believed—that he was depressed and had trouble concentrating, that he still awoke screaming at night and broke out trembling during the day, that the smallest irritant could send him into a rage, and that the tranquilizers he took afforded him only slight relief. He also took medicine for his heart, which apparently had been damaged by the electroshocks and other horrors of prison, and his bones and joints ached even at rest. If he was like other victims of torture, most of what ailed his body would heal, but his troubles of mind and spirit would persist. "Twenty-two years later," wrote Jean Améry, a Jew who was tortured by the Nazis in the Second World War, "I am still dangling over the ground by dislocated arms, panting and accusing myself." Améry eventually killed himself.

A couple of hours after we had begun, Abu Omar said he was fatigued and escorted us to the door. He had shown prior guests a small bag of clothes he kept in the foyer for when the police came to arrest him again. There was no bag now, from which I gathered he was gaining confidence in his emancipation.

WHEN WE CAME back the next night, I thought Abu Omar a little less buoyant climbing the stairs, and when we sat down with the yogurt drinks before us, he declared this was our last session. I was taken aback and reminded him we had agreed to several sessions and said I had many questions left to ask. (Indeed, I had hardly asked any: when an interviewee will talk on point unprompted, as Abu Omar had the previous night, a reporter learns more by letting him speak and asking follow-ups later.) Abu Omar was unmoved by my protest. He said I could have as many hours as I liked tonight, but none beyond. I protested some more, but he held defiant. As it is rude in Egypt to show a person the sole of your shoe, I tilted a foot up to him while we bickered, giving him a little more sole with each rebuff, but after I had given all the sole I had to give, he remained as immovable as the Temple of Ptah. I finally suggested, as a temporary fix, that we start the session and see how far we got, and he agreed.

He wanted to continue his narrative of the previous night, which had gotten as far as his first release from prison, but I preferred to ask about things he had glossed over. He tolerated my questions for a while, answering without much detail or interest, and when I pressed him about his probable terrorism (I had not yet read the transcripts of his conversations in Milan, so did not know just how likely a terrorist he was), he became still more clipped. Soon he announced he hadn't time for minutiae and said he would tell the rest of his narrative or nothing at all. We argued some more, and after getting no further than in our last tiff, I let him go ahead. An hour or so later, he was done and asked for the rest of the money.

Now it was my turn to refuse. I did. He insisted I pay, I refused again, and we went back and forth for some time. Eventually he turned from my interpreter, to whom he had been directing his conversation, and looked at me with the eyes of a seal pup in a Defenders of Wildlife ad.

"Steef," he said. "Pliz."

"No."

"Steef, pliz. I opened all. I tell you everything. Pliz, Steef. Pliz." Reverting to the interpreter, he said that he had no job and no prospect of one, that his medical bills were enormous, and that he was so very poor that, in effect, his whole family would starve if I did not honor my commitment. I brushed away a tear and said no. He stood up and paced a few moments, then removed a skeleton key from his pocket, stuck it in the door, and locked us inside the room.

This was a first. I had never before been locked in a room by or with a terrorist. Trying quickly to size up the situation, I decided he was unlikely to harm a reporter and an interpreter and earn himself a speedy return to prison. But this assumption was predicated on a rationality that neither I nor, by his own admission, he was certain he fully possessed. Also, I did not know what else was in his pocket, and I felt a keen obligation to my interpreter, who even before the appearance of the skeleton key had said, "This situation gives me a headache." In the end I told Abu Omar I would pay but added that since I had only fifty dollars in my wallet (the rest being in my sock), he would need to come with us to a cash machine. He demanded to see my wallet, which I produced. He inspected it, looked sad, and said that once we were outside we would run away or summon the police, which was true. He demanded I give him the fifty dollars, leave my passport as security, and go to the cash machine and return with the rest of the money. I countered with the fifty dollars and a credit card as security, which, after more haggling, he accepted as the best deal he could get. When he showed us to the door, there hung over our little group the feeling of paramours at the end of an unsatisfying fling, each party certain of never seeing the other again.

On the street, my translator, that honest soul, said, "There is an ATM down the block here."

When I said I was not going to honor my commitment, he seemed relieved. I asked him to wait a moment while I called my wife in Tennessee and told her a terrorist in Alexandria had just been enabled to buy crappy Kenmore appliances with our Sears card. She said she would cancel it. Then I took the money out of my sock, paid my interpreter the modest sum he had asked for, and offered him the hundred dollars I had not paid Abu Omar.

"No, no, keep it," he said. "You have been raped enough."

I have appreciated his hyperbole ever since. It reminds me there are people all over the world who are disturbed by even small injustices.

"MONICA COURTNEY ADLER" grew up in a large southern city and attended one of the paradoxical country day schools (paradoxical because they are never in the country) in which the region specializes. On being graduated from high school in the mid-1990s, she entered the flagship college of her home state, where she made the dean's list and Phi Beta Kappa and majored in international studies. Degree in hand, she moved to the Maryland suburbs of Washington, then moved across the Potomac to Arlington, much nearer CIA headquarters. When she left for Milan at the start of 2003, she was not more than twenty-five years old. She was probably a lookout on the day of the kidnapping. A year and a half after she returned, she married a young analyst who worked at a different government intelligence agency and who volunteered at a food bank (she volunteered for the Junior League) and served on the board of their neighborhood association. The neighborhood was a collection of mock townhouses marooned in a sea of parking, each home as anonymous as Monica had hoped, but failed, to be. A couple of years after the two were married, Monica's Facebook page showed a young mother, child in arms, smiling as radiantly as the Monica on her international driver's license in Milan. She had cut her hair since then. She seemed utterly ordinary.

Monica could be traced because in Italy she gave information about herself that was partly true. At one hotel, for example, she gave her address as an apartment building in Virginia that stood a block or so from a building in which she had once lived. By comparing information about past residents of buildings in the area with certain information from Monica's false identity, I found one real person who seemed to be the false Monica. In the winter of 2008 my assistant Jessica Easto called the probable Monica (whose real name was different) to ask if she was the Monica Courtney Adler of the kidnapping in Milan. The woman seemed to sputter a little, then said no.

"Do you work for the CIA?" Jessica said.

Monica declined to answer. "Um, you know," she said, "I just had a baby. I can't really talk about this right now."

"Do you know what an extraordinary rendition is?" Jessica said.

"Ummm—no."

Jessica gave her a brief tutorial, then asked about a close friend of Monica's who we had thought, early in our investigations, might have been Monica herself.

"I'd rather not have her involved in this," Monica said. "She's one of my best friends, and she has nothing to do with this." She suggested Jessica would do better to speak to the CIA's public relations department than to call individuals. Then she said goodbye and hung up.

I leave Monica her anonymity because of a law called the Intelligence Identities Protection Act, which was passed in response to the publication, in 1975, of a tell-all called *Inside the Company: CIA Diary*. Its author, Philip Agee, was a former CIA officer who was so disturbed by the CIA's violent subversions of Latin American democracies that he exposed dozens of the subversions and hundreds of the subverters, by name. The CIA and Ford White House wanted Agee's throat, but although they could prosecute him for breaking his contract with the CIA (which required employees and ex-employees to send their writings through a CIA censor), there was no law against revealing the names of a CIA officer per se. Someone outside the CIA, for example a reporter, could have published the entire personnel directory of the CIA without repercussion. At the time, the CIA was not in a position to correct this legal oversight, because Congress and reporters had just revealed that the agency had spied illegally on thousands of Americans, had abetted the Watergate burglars, had paid Mafia wiseguys to try to assassinate Fidel Castro, had helped overthrow the freely elected governments of Guatemala, Chile, and Brazil, and had done many other ugly things besides. But by 1982 the memory of these sins had faded, the American Right was again ascendant, and Congress and President Reagan enacted the Intelligence Identities Protection Act, which made it a crime to reveal the identity of an American spy. The act makes no exception for whistleblowing. A CIA officer can strangle infants in their cribs, rape whole convents of nuns, and assassinate the Queen of England, but to report the spy's name makes the reporter a felon. There is a strong First Amendment argument that the law is so indiscriminate as to be unconstitutional, but the current Supreme Court has subordinated the Constitution to an authoritarian idea of national security, and even were the court saner, to challenge the law would be the work of many years and thousands of dollars. I therefore leave Abu Omar's kidnappers their namelessness.

I DO NOT, however, leave their nature unknown. I wanted to find them, partly to know who America's warriors-on-terror were and partly to know whether they had hidden themselves at home with as little care as they had abroad. I was able to find the true identity of, I think, somewhat more than half of them. Some gave themselves away in the same way Monica had—that is, by giving out personal information in Italy that was true or nearly true. A few gave out so much true information that it took only a couple of hours to find them. One even gave an e-mail address that seemed to belong to his wife, who, consequently or not, left him after the kidnapping. Other spies betrayed themselves by calling family from Italy. Still others were undone, whether by themselves or by the CIA, by the way their fake identities were acquired. To get the components of those identities—driver's licenses, social security numbers, passports, credit cards—they had had to give addresses to government bureaus and credit card companies, some of which addresses became part of the public record and others of which could be had for a small fee. Often the addresses were unhelpful post office boxes, but sometimes they were street addresses. Even if the spies no longer lived there, there were usually forwarding addresses, deeds of sale, or other clues that eventually led to the spies. Almost always their traceability was a testimony less to my investigative powers than to the CIA's imprudence.

The spies were a varied lot—white, Latino, young, old, male, female—but were bound by the cord of suburbanity. Evidently the renderer, no less than the dentist or banker, believes he has given enough to his community in his working hours and wants isolation outside them. Some of the spies, like "Victor Castellano," who lived in a chipboard chateau on a newly divided tract of Texas scrubland near a military base, were described by their familiars in terms that suggested they were the "heavies"—the guys who, as a CIA chief of covert operations once said, would be out robbing banks if they weren't doing renditions. But the great majority of the spies I found could have been the bromidic guy or gal next door. It took far more planners, spotters, and drivers than brutes to kidnap a man steps from one of the busiest streets in one of Italy's biggest cities at high noon. One of the planners, who gave a name in Italy that was perhaps more true than false, inhabited an asbestos-sided Cape Cod in the Northeast, was a fan of the Beatles and old science-fiction TV serials, and seemed to have been in possession of a wife at the time he shared a room with a female colleague in Italy. Another planner, "Gregory Asherleigh," who was one of the two kidnappers who went to Norway to scout the abduction of Mullah Krekar, once listed his address as a mansion on the Atlantic that had a lion in bas relief that spouted water from his mouth. The mansion turned out to belong to his mother, who said, I think honestly, that she was not aware that her son worked for the CIA. Gregory proved to be tall, just a bit jowly, attractively silver-haired, and devoutly Christian. He gave money to the Republican Party and lived steps from a large military base and had a business that appeared in some measure real, although nobody ever answered the company phone when Jessica or I called. One of his children, coincidentally or not, worked for an FBI counterterror squad that had been dispatched to Iraq and other countries.

Few of the spies answered my call, e-mails, or letters. An exception was a youngish man who had perhaps been a planner in Milan and whose identity I had narrowed to one of two brothers. The brothers had grown up in a military family, enlisted in different branches, and thereafter left such a tangle of military addresses that it was hard to sort them out. One brother lived in Texas not far from "Victor Castellano," with whom the youngish planner had traveled closely in Italy. This brother called me in response to an e-mail I sent his wife. He seemed unsure what to say, so I said I was glad he had called.

"Well," he said, "I just didn't want you to waste any more time on me or my brother. You've got the wrong people."

"So you weren't involved in the rendition?"

"No."

"Do you know anything about the rendition?"

"No, nothing. Just that the action—you know, just from what you read on CNN or Fox or anything else on the Web—the action took place in 2005."

I told him that while the indictments had been issued in 2005, the "action" had taken place in 2003.

"In any case," I said, "how can you be sure that your brother wasn't involved and just didn't tell you about it?"

"No, not my brother, not my brother."

He reiterated that he had called only because he didn't want me to waste my time, but then he said, a bit contradictorily, "I was just saying to my wife, 'I'm really bored. I think I'll just call this guy up and see what he's got.'"

"You're interested in what I've got?"

"I'd be interested in seeing what documents you have, other than just word of mouth."

To my ears, he sounded a bit like a sixth-grader trying to wheedle the questions that would be on the exam out of the teacher. I told him where he could find the Italian court documents discussing what seemed to be his or his brother's involvement, and he sounded relieved that the evidence against him was merely Italian.

Toward the close of our short conversation, he said, "You can understand my being a little bit, uh, what's the word I should use? Cautious. It'd be like if you knocked on the door of an eighty-five-year-old man and said, 'The Italians say you took part in this thing.' It's just that strange."

IN ITALY some of the spies had given contact phone numbers or addresses that turned out to belong to front companies. "Eliana Isabella Castaldo" gave one such number in Norristown, Pennsylvania. When Jessica called it, a woman answered.

"Washburn and Company."

"May I speak with Eliana Castaldo?" Jessica said.

The woman hung up.

Jessica called back, and again a woman answered.

"Washburn and Company."

"May I speak with Eliana Castaldo?"

Click.

Other reporters who called "Washburn and Company" got different responses. Sometimes the woman who answered said the caller had reached an answering service. Other times she said that the number belonged to a business that she could not name. If the conversation got so far, she said no Eliana Castaldo worked or lived there.

The number turned out to belong to a youngish woman at a down-at-heel rowhouse who owned a "virtual assistant" business, a virtual assistant being someone who handles phones, faxes, and e-mail for other businesses without setting foot in their offices. She had been in business only six or seven months when Eliana Castaldo went to Italy and listed her phone number as her contact. A year or so after reporters started calling her, the woman's Web site said, "I am not working with clients at this time." Soon the site shut down entirely. The woman, however, remained active in the Virtual Assistance Chamber of Commerce, on whose Web site she described her clients as "nonprofits."

The CIA was better served by "Coachmen Enterprises," which other spies had listed as their contact. Calls to Coachmen went straight to an answering machine and were never returned.

I VISITED the family of another spy whom I will call Natalie because the name she used in Milan was so like her real one. She had a supporting role near Via Guerzoni on the day of the kidnapping, probably as a lookout. When not casing terrorists, Natalie lived in a Sun Belt subdivision of so sad a strain that I fancied I could smell the subprime mortgages in the cul-de-sacs. On the front door of her house were a Valentine's Day heart made out of polyester roses, a decal of a puppy dog with a butterfly on its nose (caption: "Forever Friends"), and a cutout of a family of holiday bears—mama bear in an apron, papa bear in pink bow tie, baby bear handing a valentine ("Love U") to mama. Natalie was not home, so I drove up the block and waited to see if she would arrive. Periodically an enormous man emerged from the house next to hers, smoked a cigarette, and glanced up the way at me. I left near midnight.

The next morning, Natalie still not having returned, I visited the house of her parents, who lived a mile or two away. I made the mistake of lingering outside to see if anyone might come out rather than going straight to the door, and a few minutes later a man who turned out to be Natalie's brother emerged. His musculature impressed me immediately, as did his stride, which indicated a state of upset. I got out of my car, and he demanded to know whether I was the same person who had staked out his sister's house last night. I felt as stupid as a CIA officer in Milan—the fat man had "made" me. I pled guilty and asked if he could help me find his sister. He said no, then told me to wait a minute and stepped off a few paces to call someone on his mobile phone. It seemed to be Natalie.

"Yeah, the guy's here. . . . Yeah, he's the same one."

He hung up without, as I had hoped, handing me the phone. We then had a rather tense discussion about why I was looking for his sister, and he expressed surprise, which I believed genuine, to hear she might be working for the CIA.

"Impossible," he said. "Just impossible."

But when I asked whether she worked for the military or for a company that contracted with the military, he did not answer. When I suggested such an employer might have sent her on a mission like the one in Milan, he said that was far-fetched, but he started to seem reflective. A little later he said he and his sister had been raised by hard-working parents with good American values, and I said I had no doubt their values were American. He took my card, and I left.

An hour later he called me from a blocked phone number. He said he had been researching the kidnapping on the Web, and he sounded a little troubled by what he had found. He said he was truly sorry that anyone might have gotten tortured out of this thing. That was bad. But he added with a sudden flash of anger that I had done bad too. My surveillance had violated his family. I had *terrorized* them, did I understand? *Terrorized.* And what did I think of that?

"JAMES ROBERT KIRKLAND" grew up in the Ohio Valley, took a bachelor's degree in a state adjoining his own, and dabbled in journalism and public relations before joining a police force. He served in many of the United States and rose through the ranks until, after twenty-five years, he was appointed the director of a force in a jurisdiction of a couple of million people. A few years later he left public service to become a consultant in private security and resettled in his homeland, where cottontails and Pentecostals were thick on the ground. (IF GOD IS YOUR CO-PILOT, a church marquee near his home proclaimed, CHANGE SEATS. THE TEN COMMANDMENTS AREN'T MULTIPLE CHOICE, a rival offered.) From a colonnaded ranch house he and his wife commanded a substantial acreage on which stood a great barn in fine trim and a taut wooden fence painted a crisp, happy color. The sum bespoke a well-ordered prosperity. After the kidnapping, the Kirklands bought a nearby colonial manor and turned it into a tastefully appointed country lodge, which seemed mainly the project of Mrs. Kirkland. Using the alias of one of her farm animals, she reviewed the lodge favorably on a travel Web site. (The hosts, she said, were superlatively nice.) Her day job, which I am reluctant to divulge specifically, involved evacuation flights not dissimilar to the ones on which Abu Omar was rendered.

One of the two SIMs that Mr. Kirkland had used in Italy had been activated at the start of December of 2002, which made him one of the earliest-arriving spies, which in turn suggested he was a senior planner. During his more than two months in Italy, he or someone using his SIM had been a prolific caller to the United States, calling numbers that belonged to his octogenarian mother, his then girlfriend (the present Mrs. Kirkland), the veterinarian who cared for their farm animals, an apparent stockbroker, an apparent accountant, and himself, which is to say the landline in his (and now Mrs. Kirkland's) home. He or someone using his SIM had also called an unregistered mobile phone in his home area code, which phone Jessica called five years later. A man answered, and Jessica told him about our search for a CIA officer or CIA hireling named James Robert Kirkland. The man replied that he didn't know anyone named James Robert Kirkland and that if he himself was a CIA agent, he didn't know that either.

"We think," Jessica said, "that this Kirkland might know someone who uses this cell phone. Have you had it since 2003?"

"Yes."

"Would you tell me your name?"

"I'd rather not."

"Do you know anyone named————?"—here mentioning Kirkland's real name.

There was a very long pause.

"Yes, I do," the man finally said. He sounded to Jessica, who has the exuberance of youth, "creeped the fuck out."

"Alright, well—" she began.

"Thank you," the man said, "goodbye."

We were pretty sure we had our Kirkland. I was further encouraged in this belief by a photo I had found of the real Kirkland that compared favorably with the very dark (and therefore indeterminate) copy of the photo on the passport he had used in Italy. The two men, or, rather more probably, one man, of the photos had the same shape of head, which was more long than round; the same ears, long also; the same hair, close-cropped or lacking; the same unobtrusively sized nose; the same distance between the eyes; the same crease running from a spot between the eyebrows down the bridge of the nose; and the same crooked smile, which tugged up at the left side. I traveled to the Kirklands' farm to see for myself.

When I arrived at the front door, Mrs. Kirkland, a slender woman of middle age, motioned through a window that I should walk around to the side of the house, where a large den had been added.

Her first words on opening the side door were "How did you find us?" It didn't seem like the greeting of an innocent.

I explained that I was interested in speaking with her husband about some of his law enforcement work, and she asked me to wait and left me in the den. It was homey—every surface draped in shawls, a watercolor in progress in one corner, a blaze in the hearth. Presently Mrs. Kirkland returned with her husband and a more composed countenance. The former was absurdly well pre-served. On an earlier attempt that day to find them at home, I had spied a bench press in one of the outbuildings, and it was not hard to imagine Mr. Kirkland using it to ward off his more than sixty years. He was more agile than brawny, however, and he spent half the interview with his legs draped over the side of an armchair.

The Kirklands encouraged me to sit, and while Mrs. Kirkland fetched me a Diet Coke, I told Mr. Kirkland about my search. He said he guessed he ought to ask if I had some identification to prove I was who I said I was, and I gave him my business card. He looked at it, then he guessed he ought to ask if I had other identification—a driver's license, say—and I gave him that too. He studied the watermark before transcribing my vitals, which I was sure were bound for the CIA. It was the only time in my career I have been carded.

Mrs. Kirkland returned, and both Kirklands professed great sur-prise that I had come to talk about a rendition. They knew almost nothing about renditions except that a movie called *Rendition* had been recently released. Was that the case I was looking into?

I said the movie seemed to be a composite of cases, but it had been poorly reviewed, so I hadn't seen it. I explained the essentials of Abu Omar's rendition and the phone calls that James Robert Kirkland had made from Italy to the family and associates of the real Kirkland in the Ohio Valley.

Mr. Kirkland said he had no idea why someone in Italy might have called his mother, his home, his wife, and other people he knew. For a few minutes he and Mrs. Kirkland hypothesized explanations. Finally he remembered that in or around 2003 his wallet had been stolen from a hotel room near Miami Beach. He had reported the robbery to the police, but nothing had come of it. Not long later, someone had tried to use his stolen credit cards, and he had had to change all of them and also several other accounts and his driver's license. I knew the passport of the Italian Kirkland had been issued in Miami, and I wondered if this story was meant to explain the new identity he had acquired there.

Mr. Kirkland also said that after his wallet was stolen, he and Mrs. Kirkland got a lot of strange phone calls. I asked what was strange about the calls, and he uhhhed and errred for a while, from which I surmised that he was unable to manufacture an answer. Eventually he said that, well, Mrs. Kirkland had said she received some strange calls. I turned to Mrs. Kirkland and asked what was strange about them, but she could offer nothing either—not that the callers hung up as soon as she answered, not that there was heavy breathing, not that someone asked her to describe her undergarments. The calls were just *strange*. Notwithstanding his decades in law enforcement, Mr. Kirkland never tried to find out whether the caller could be identified, let alone traced to the person who stole his wallet. As for how Kirkland's mother or his veterinarian or the others had come to be called, he now remembered that he kept in his wallet a list of numbers of people he often called. Evidently he had failed to memorize his mother's number, though it seems she had had it for many years.

I wasn't sure why the robber would want to call people close to Kirkland. "Wouldn't that just increase the chances the robber would be caught?" I said.

He explained that the robber was probably trying to establish himself in Kirkland's identity.

"From *Italy?*"

"It could happen."

A little later he said, "So tell me again what was the name of the man who was captured?"

"Abu Omar."

"Abu—Abu what?"

"Omar."

"Omar, Omar. You spell that "O-M?"—he searched his mind for what might come next—"A? R?"

"Yes."

"So where did all this take place, again?"

"Milan. Then they drove him to Aviano."

"What's Aviano?"

"An air force base."

"Oh, it's an air force base? Is it ours?"

He was trying too hard. But I was not actually embarrassed for him until he said, "And what will happen if the accused are tried in, in"—he paused and searched for the term. "In absentia? Is that what you call it?" There were not many senior law enforcers who, after a quarter century in the field, were unfamiliar with the term.

At another point he fretted that if I had been led to him in error, terrorists could be as well.

"It might sound paranoid," he said, "but we don't give them enough credit for how smart they are. No one thought 9/11 would happen, but it did."

I agreed.

"So what can we do about it?" he said. "How can we put this to bed?"

"I suppose you could contact the CIA."

"No, I don't want to get involved with the CIA. What else can we do?"

I suggested that a man with his years in law enforcement might know people better able than I to answer the question. He seemed to see reason in this, then said, "You seem responsible. You're not going to use our names, right?"

"How about I print your names and say you deny any involvement in the kidnapping?"

He did not think this sounded like a good idea. He said he and

Mrs. Kirkland would just be tarred by association, and he quoted a famous law enforcer he once worked with who said of such denials, "The truth never catches up to the lies." He did not seem to see the irony of deploying the aphorism in the present context.

Before I left, both Kirklands urged me to see *Vantage Point*, another recently released movie. In this one, swarthy terrorists killed Europeans by the hundred and nearly assassinated the visiting American president before being undone by a resourceful federal agent who, even before the movie began, had taken a bullet for the commander-in-chief. The Kirklands found it compelling in the utmost. I did not rush out to see it, as it had been even more poorly reviewed than *Rendition*, but on a plane home from Kirkland's trial in Milan, I saw it in all its dumbed-down glory and had no trouble seeing Kirkland picture himself as the heroic agent saving Western Civilization to presidential admiration.

I bade the Kirklands goodbye. To leave their property, I had to continue up the long driveway past the den to a turnaround loop, then drive back down past the den before heading out the front gate. On my first pass, the Kirklands stood by the fireplace and waved pleasantly, if restrainedly. On my second pass, Mrs. Kirkland had dropped to a chair and put a fist to her mouth, as though biting her knuckles. As I continued down the drive, I glanced over my shoulder and saw her head drop into her hands.

ON LEAVING her second-secretaryship at the U.S. embassy in Rome, Sabrina De Sousa bought a townhouse on a dead-end street off the Dulles Parkway, added a deck, and held her peace for several years. But in May of 2009, a year after her trial started in earnest, she brought suit against the State Department for neither defending her in court nor invoking diplomatic immunity on her behalf. She then gave unenlightening interviews to reporters in which she maintained she was not a spy. "You can keep hammering away at me," she told *Congressional Quarterly*'s espionage reporter, Jeff Stein, "but all I will say is I was a former federal employee. I worked for the State Department." She said her superiors at "State" had urged her not to travel abroad because she might be arrested, which, were that to happen, would put the United States in a difficult position. But she had family who lived overseas (she had been born in India), and she found it intolerable not to visit them, so she had resigned and brought suit. Three months after she did, Barack Obama's Justice Department said it would hire a lawyer of her choosing for the remainder of the trial, which, however, was by then only a few weeks from its end. But the administration would not invoke diplomatic immunity for her, no doubt because to have done so would have been construed a stronger endorsement of the kidnapping and would have provoked bigger headlines. She therefore continued her suit and denounced a government that let little people like her take the fall while the brass at Langley and the White House who had ordered the rendition got off. She had a point.

Lieutenant Colonel Joseph Romano, the security chief at Aviano, returned to the Pentagon after the kidnapping, was promoted to full colonel, then was posted to Lackland Air Force Base in San Antonio. Some months into his trial in Milan, while the other American defendants ignored the proceedings, he prevailed on the Air Force to give him a lawyer, who in turn argued that the NATO Status of Forces Agreement barred Italy from prosecuting him. SOFA, in the lawyer's opinion, gave the United States the primary responsibility for trying U.S. servicemen in Europe who were accused of crimes like those with which Romano was charged. Spataro rejoined that SOFA did not apply to the crimes in question and that in any case the United States, by ignoring the case for years, had abdicated its responsibility to try Romano. Judge Magi agreed, and the case against Romano continued.

Jeff Castelli, the CIA chief of station in Rome, also returned home to a promotion, in his case at headquarters in Langley. By some reports, he was being groomed to take over the CIA's important New York station. But after news of the sloppy rendition broke, he was admonished by a CIA review board and exiled to the

Air War College in Alabama. Off the record, some CIA officials said
that to win approval for the rendition, Castelli had misled headquarters into believing that DIGOS was keeping so poor a watch
on Abu Omar that he could have pulled off a terrorist attack before
anyone knew what was happening. The officials who said so, however, had an interest in throwing blame off headquarters and onto
Castelli. Eventually Castelli quit the CIA and joined a private firm
that, it seems, analyzed propaganda for the U.S. government.

IT IS BAD to lose your Italian estate but worse to lose it to the terrorist you kidnapped—a prospect that confronted Bob Lady because
of an Italian law that let victims of crimes recover damages from
their victimizers. If Lady were convicted at trial, and if the conviction withstood appeal, the Italian government would sell his villa
and send the net to Abu Omar. A man could live in Alexandria like
a pharaoh on the equity from a Piedmontese manse. The prospect
must have been all the more depressing to Lady because for some
time after he left Italy it was uncertain whether the trial would
occur and he continued to pay the estate's mortgage of $4,000 a
month.

After Lady was indicted, reporters from all over the world
wanted to talk to him, but initially he spoke to no one. In late 2006,
however, freelance reporter Matthew Cole achieved a fine *trionfo* by
chatting with him over coffee in a Florida strip mall. Cole's eventual portrait, published in sorrowful strokes in GQ, was of a martyred spy who had fought the good fight only to be abandoned by
his country. The govenment had not helped him with a lawyer, had
not contributed to his mortgage, and, so far as he could see, had not
pressed the Italians for a diplomatic solution. Sadder still, his wife
had abandoned him too, although Lady said he could not blame
her: he was powerless, frustrated, and had little to offer. He told
Cole he was speaking out at last because he had nothing left to lose
and hoped to shame the CIA into helping him. Also, he wanted it

known that the kidnapping was not his fault. He had warned Castelli of its foolishness, but Castelli had not listened.

After leaving Italy, Lady earned his living by consulting on security matters, mostly in Latin America. He was also spotted visiting the Libyan mission to the United Nations in Geneva. The Swiss government had known he was in the country and ordered the federal police to watch him, but since Switzerland was not a member of the European Union, it was not compelled by Spataro's warrants to arrest him.

For avocation, Lady essayfied. At least, it seemed to be he who published online, under the nom de plume of his dead father, a meditation on American leadership in time of war, with lessons culled from his upbringing in Honduras. Although the author of the tract did not mention the CIA, he seemed to have in mind a certain botched mission when he wrote, "At this time, we can't help but vote for a party that knows how to deal with the uncertainties, the mistakes, and the sacrifices of real warfare." That party, he clarified, was not the Democratic, which had become "flimsy, senseless, and prone to the vapors . . . in the perfumed salons of Manhattan and academia" and "whose notion of warfare is to wallop Christmas trees and boy scouts with stacks of legal papers." He allowed, however, that in a time of peace one might consider whether the Republicans had screwed the working class, for example by repealing the estate tax.

Lady disappeared again from public view, but toward the end of 2007 his name appeared as the co-purchaser on a deed of sale of a house in Abita Springs, a mossy suburb of New Orleans where the driveways tended to dirt and a double-wide would not have insulted the prevailing architecture. Some people might have thought it a comedown from the estate in Penango. No one was home when I visited, nor did anyone answer queries I sent.

Two years later, as his trial drew to a close, Lady emerged once more and spoke via Skype to Luca Fazzo of *Il Giornale*, a rightist newspaper owned by the brother of Silvio Berlusconi. Lady said he assumed he would be convicted, but he wanted to underscore that his role in the rendition had been exceedingly small. CIA chiefs like him, he explained, were too well known by local law enforcers to be used in renditions. If things went awry, it would be bad for both the chiefs and the CIA. So the CIA imported out-of-towners to do all the real work, and it was they who were responsible for the mistakes in Abu Omar's rendition. His account, while not entirely devoid of truth, was rather at odds with his recruitment of Ludwig, his flight to Cairo, and his possession of surveillance photos of Abu Omar.

He had a fallback argument, though. Whatever his role in the kidnapping, he said, "I am responsible only for carrying out an order I received from my superiors"—a defense whose pedigree was succinctly summarized by one commentator as "I vas only following ze orders."

"I worked in intelligence for twenty-five years," Lady continued, "and almost none of my activities in these twenty-five years were legal in the country where I was carrying them out. . . . It's a life of illegality, if you want to look at it that way. But governments all over the world have professionals in my field, and it falls to us to do our duty. When Achilles attacked Troy, it was an illegal operation, but it was what he and the others thought they had to do."

I thought he had his analogy wrong. Lady in Milan had played the role of Paris, with Abu Omar his abducted Helen. Spataro was Achilles, or better still Agamemnon, out to punish Paris and the other Trojans for their crime.

"Humanly," Fazzo said, "what effect has all of this had on you?"

"I can't say I'm angry," Lady replied. "But I'm tired, very tired. . . . I console myself by remembering that I was a soldier. I was in a war against terrorism. I could not debate orders that were given to me. They tell me to do this, and what can I do? But there is one thing I can't swallow."

"And that is?"

"I love Italy. I decided to live my life in Italy. My whole family loves Italy. I thought that I could serve there professionally, and then at sixty-five I'd be making my own Barbera in my grand house near Asti—ten acres of vineyards, a stupendous place. Instead, I had to flee."

ON THE NIGHT in 2008 that Barack Obama was elected president, Spataro watched the returns at a party held by the U.S. consulate in a Milan disco. He had been delighted to accept the consul's personal invitation.

"Good Morning America!" he e-mailed friends a few hours after the party wound down. "I'd like to express my happiness for a dream which comes true. . . . Nearly all attendees, Italians and Americans, supported Obama and all good news on him were greeted with cheers. Today the world is living a bright and unforgettable morning."

A year later Spataro made his closing argument at trial and asked Judge Magi to sentence Jeff Castelli and SISMI director Nicolò Pollari to thirteen years apiece, Bob Lady and Sabrina De Sousa to twelve years apiece, and the other Americans and Italians to ten or so years apiece depending on their degree of involvement. A few weeks later Magi returned convictions for twenty-three of the twenty-six Americans: Lady got eight years, De Sousa and the other Americans five. Castelli, First Secretary Ralph Russomando, and Second Secretary Betnie Medero-Navedo were acquitted because, Magi said, their jobs at the U.S. embassy in Rome bestowed a wide immunity on them. Lady and De Sousa, working from the consulate in Milan, were less immune. Magi also acquitted SISMI's Pollari and his senior aide Marco Mancini because the Constitutional Court's rulings on state secrecy kept him from considering important evidence against them. Pio Pompa and another SISMI official got three years each. (Maresciallo Luciano Pironi, pseudonymously

Ludwig, had earlier received a suspended sentence. He finished his tour at the Italian embassy in Belgrade, then was assigned to a military academy in Turin, where he trained recruits how to be Carabinieri.) Judge Magi ordered the convicts to collectively repair Abu Omar and his wife with €1.5 million, but the reparations would have to withstand appeal, and most of the repairers were beyond the grasp of Italian courts. Lady's estate remained in escrow.

De Sousa responded to her conviction by suing Lady and Castelli for getting her into the mess, and Colonel Romano opined through his lawyer that the verdict "should be an embarrassment to Italy." The *Wall Street Journal,* speaking for rightists the world over, declared the ruling "one more dubious milestone in the legal war against the war on terror" and warned that "innocent people may eventually pay for Mr. Spataro's 'victory.' " Spokesmen for the State and Defense departments said Magi's decision "disappointed" the Obama administration.

THE NUMBER of men rendered to torture by the United States under George W. Bush is still not known. Reporters on the beat have guessed from one hundred to several hundred; a few outliers think more than a thousand. Many decent Americans believed that when Bush left office their long national nightmare would be over. They were apparently under the impression that Democrats had not connived in the outsourcing of torture. Two days after Obama became president, he issued an executive order banning the United States from torturing people directly but not—contrary to many confused reports—from sending captives elsewhere to be tortured. What created the confusion (intentionally, I suspect) was that Obama ordered a task force to study extraordinary rendition with the *goal* of ensuring that the United States did not send people to torture. The task force, of course, had no power to ensure the goal was met, but hopeful reporters read what they wanted into the order. Later Obama's CIA director, Leon Panetta, explained that the CIA would still extraordinarily render people. He added, as a kind of balm, "If we render someone, we are obviously going to seek assurances from that country that their human rights are protected and they are not mistreated." It was precisely what the Bush administration had said.

Toward the end of 2009 the president's task force recommended that the United States protect the victims of its renditions by visiting them in the dungeons it had rendered them to.

Simultaneously Obama's Justice Department was arguing in federal court, again exactly as Bush's had, that lawsuits against the government by victims of rendition must be dismissed because they would reveal secrets vital to the nation's security. The lead plaintiff in the most important suit, Binyam Mohamed, had been rendered by the CIA to Morocco, where his genitals had been sliced open dozens of times and caustic liquid poured in the wounds.

As for Abu Omar's kidnappers, Obama's people said off the record that should Italy request their extradition, the president would not comply. Bush's people had at least had the courage to say so on the record.

EGYPT DID NOT re-arrest Abu Omar, perhaps because his torment had already been made public and jailing him again would only draw more attention to it. Unable to work or preach, he was at a loss to fill his time. He said he might run for elected office, but then did not. He started a blog to tell his life story, but what he told was unilluminating and he soon quit the chore. Five years to the day after he was kidnapped, one month after "Monica Courtney Adler" gave birth to a daughter, his wife gave birth to a son.

Significant Characters

Islamic Radicals and Acquaintances

Abu Imad (Arman Ahmed El Hissini Helmy). Imam of the mosque on Viale Jenner.

Abu Omar (Osama Mustafa Hassan Nasr). Victim of the kidnapping in Milan.

Abu Saleh (Mahmoud Abdelkader Es Sayed). Leader of Milan's al-Qaeda cell before Abu Omar's arrival.

Abu Talal (Talaat Fuad Qassim). Leader of Gamaa and the Islamic Brigade in Bosnia; first victim of a U.S. extraordinary rendition.

Ali Sharif (Ali Abdel Al Ali). Administrator of the mosque on Via Quaranta.

Blind Sheikh (Omar Abdel-Rahman). Leader of Gamaa in prison in the United States.

Mohammed Reda Elbadry. Teacher at the mosque on Via Quaranta.

Karim Said Atmani. Associate in terrorism with Anwar Shaaban and Fateh Kamel.

Nabila Ghali. Second wife of Abu Omar.

Marsela Glina. First wife of Abu Omar.

Hayam Abdelmoneim Mohamed Hassanein. Friend of Merfat Rezk.

Fateh Kamel. Associate in terrorism with Anwar Shaaban and Karim Atmani.

Merfat Rezk. Witness to the kidnapping.

Shawki Bakry Salem. Husband of Merfat Rezk.

Sayed Shaban. Man who told Abu Imad that he knew someone who had seen the kidnapping.

Anwar Shaaban. Early leader of the mosque on Viale Jenner and the Islamic Brigade in Bosnia.

Italian Officials

Stefano D'Ambrosio. SISMI's chief in Milan.
Stefano Dambruoso. First magistrate to investigate the kidnapping.
Renato Farina. Journalist paid by SISMI.
Marco Mancini. SISMI's chief of northern Italy.
"Massimo." Police official and CIA mole.
Bruno Megale. DIGOS's chief of counterterrorism in Milan.
Gustavo Pignero. SISMI's chief of counterterrorism.
Luciano Pironi, aka Ludwig. Marshal of the Carabinieri.
Nicolò Pollari. SISMI's director.
Pio Pompa. SISMI agent who ran an off-the-books spy shop.
Armando Spataro. Second magistrate to investigate the kidnapping.

American Officials and Officers

Embassy and consular officials:
    Jeff Castelli. CIA chief in Italy.
    Sabrina De Sousa. Second secretary at the U.S. embassy in Rome.
    Betnie Medero-Navedo. Second secretary at the U.S. embassy in Rome.
    Bob Lady. CIA chief in Milan.
    Joseph Romano III. Air Force lieutenant colonel at Aviano Air Base.
    Ralph Russomando. First secretary at the U.S. embassy in Rome.

Agents who were in Dergano, Abu Omar's neighborhood, during the time of the kidnapping:
    Monica Courtney Adler.
    Gregory Asherleigh.
    Raymond Harbaugh. Apparent co-leader of the kidnappers.
    James Thomas Harbison.
    Ben Amar Harty.
    George Purvis. Apparent co-leader of the kidnappers.
    Pilar Maria Rueda.
    Joseph Sofin.

Agents who were in the caravan that took Abu Omar to Aviano Air Base:
    Lorenzo Gabriel Carrera.
    Drew Carlyle Channing.
    Vincent Faldo.
    Cynthia Dame Logan.
    Michalis Vasiliou.

Agents who helped scout the kidnapping:

Eliana Isabella Castaldo.
Victor Castellano.
John Kevin Duffin.
John Thomas Gurley.
Brenda Liliana Ibanez.
James Robert Kirkland.
Anne Linda Jenkins.

Acknowledgments

I WAS FORTUNATE to have the help of two able research assistants, Jessica Easto of Knoxville and Alice Annicchiarico of Milan, and of a skilled translator of Arabic, Andrea Okorley of Philadelphia, whom I found through the excellent Translations for Progress. I also had adept interpreters in Egypt, whom I do not wish to jeopardize with individual thanks. Aida Seif El Dawla, the vocal director of Cairo's El Nadim Center for the Rehabilitation of Victims of Violence, gave me important help in understanding torture in Egypt. The staff of Human Rights Watch, particularly Elijah Zarwan, helped me make connections in Cairo and Alexandria without which I would have been lost. Reporter Caryle Murphy and researchers Lorenzo Vidino and Daniele Ganser read parts of the manuscript and made valuable editorial suggestions. Reporter Guido Olimpio generously shared with me the fruits of his investigations into the spies of Milan. My editor at W. W. Norton, Alane Salierno Mason, gave wise counsel and has my gratitude for enduring my many delays. Her assistant, Denise Scarfi, steered the book's production with superlative competence, and copy editor Fred Wiemer expertly cleaned up many of my blunders of style. My agent Andrew Wylie advocated for this book with an enthusiasm as contagious as it was influential; I landed fortunately when he decided to take me under his wing. Jofie Ferrari-Adler of Grove/

Atlantic still has my thanks for introducing me to Andrew. Stefania Zamagni, Daniel Stephens, and the staff of Madrelingua Language School in Bologna are responsible for great improvements in my poor Italian. Diana Zimmerman of Lewis and Clark Library in Helena, Montana, gave me her usual cheerful, efficient aid with interlibrary loans, and the staff of the Knox County Public Library in Knoxville, Tennessee, helped as well. Judy Bovington, Tim Davis, Doug Andreasen, Melissa Cohen, Emma Takvoryan, the teachers of Garden Montessori, Stefania Ragusa, and Lorenza Moscarella gave me miscellaneous irreplaceable support in holding family and self together. So did my wife Jennifer and son Elliott, who saw me through the usual writerly melodramas and a rather disagreeable depression. My debt to them is tremendous but a pleasurable one to repay.

Notes

On Sources and Language

My book would have been much the poorer without the works
I cite below, and I am grateful to their authors. For brevity's sake
and because I have aimed the book at the general reader, I have not
cited sources for many well-established facts. For the same reasons,
I have preferred to cite books that synthesize articles and other
sources instead of citing those articles and sources individually. I
have made exceptions for original sources critical to the book.

Many quotations that appear in English in the book originally
appeared in Italian. If a quotation is cited below to a work with a
title in Italian, I translated the quotation. If the quotation is cited
below to a work with a title in English, the author of that work
made the translation—although where I thought the translation of
certain words or phrases could be improved, I have amended them.
Italian police translated almost all of the conversations in the book
that originally took place in Arabic. Throughout the book, when
transliterating Arabic names into English, I have preferred commonly known spellings even when they were not the most translit-
eratively correct. Thus, for example, I have used "Osama bin Laden"
instead of "Usama bin Ladin."

This book tells many stories whose participants would not talk
to me or other investigators, who lied when they did talk, or who
through honest confusion told different stories at different times.

I have noted instances in which I was unsure whether I had teased out the truth. Most of the people I interviewed would not speak on the record and so have not been cited below. I almost never reproduced what I was told off the record unless I could verify it with another source on the record. I have noted the few exceptions. Where I have made errors of fact, I welcome corrections and will ask my publisher to make them in future editions of this book.

Sources

In General

For an overview of aspects of the CIA relevant to my book: Tim Weiner, *Legacy of Ashes: The History of the CIA*, Doubleday, 2007 (the Bible of the field); Jane Mayer, *The Dark Side: The Inside Story of How the War on Terror Turned into a War on American Ideals*, Doubleday, 2008; Robert Baer, *See No Evil: The True Story of a Ground Soldier in the CIA's War on Terrorism*, Three Rivers, 2003; Ronald Kessler, *Inside the CIA: Revealing the Secrets of the World's Most Powerful Spy Agency*, Pocket Books, 1992, and *The CIA at War: Inside the Secret Campaign Against Terror*, St. Martin's, 2003 (Kessler is more infatuated with the CIA and the "War on Terror" than I); Tyler Drumheller, *On the Brink: An Insider's Account of How the White House Compromised American Intelligence*, Carroll & Graf, 2006; Lindsay Moran, *Blowing My Cover: My Life as a CIA Spy*, Berkley Trade, 2005.

For an overview of Islamic terrorism: Lawrence Wright, *The Looming Tower: Al-Qaeda and the Road to 9/11*, Vintage, 2007; Jason Burke, *Al-Qaeda: The True Story of Radical Islam*, I. B. Tauris, 2004.

For an overview of Italian politics and society: Tobias Jones, *The Dark Heart of Italy*, North Point Press, 2004; Paul Hoffman, *That Fine Italian Hand*, Henry Holt, 1990; Paul Ginsborg, *Italy and its Discontents: Family, Civil Society, State: 1980-2001*, Palgrave Macmillan, 2003, and *A History of Contemporary Italy: Society and Politics 1943-1988*, Palgrave Macmillan, 2003; Luigi Barzini, *The Italians*, Touchstone, 1964.

Chapter 1: A Kidnapping

For Luciano Peroni, alias Ludwig: PIRONI Luciano, Verbale di interrogatorio di persona sottoposta ad indagini, N. 10838/05 R.G.N.R. mod. 21, Procura della Repubblica presso il Tribunale Ordinario di Milano, Apr. 14, 2006; Untitled deposition of Luciano Pironi, Proc. Pen. N. 1966/05 R.G.G.I.P., Sept. 30, 2006.

For "Massimo": Guido Olimpio, *Operazione Hotel California*, Feltrinelli, 2005. I interviewed a man who claimed to be Massimo, but as he told me no more than what was in Olimpio's report, I am inclined to believe he was a pretender.

Chapter 2: A Sirocco

For Flaubert's statement "We have had bands of ten or twelve Arabs . . .": Gustave Flaubert, *Flaubert in Egypt*, ed. Francis Steegmuller, Penguin, 1979.

For the rise of Islamism and Islamic terrorism in Egypt and beyond (including Pakistan and Afghanistan): Lawrence Wright, *The Looming Tower: Al-Qaeda and the Road to 9/11*, Vintage, 2007; Jason Burke, *Al-Qaeda: The True Story of Radical Islam*, I. B. Tauris, 2004; Caryle Murphy, *Passion for Islam: Shaping the Modern Middle East: The Egyptian Experience*, Scribner, 2002; Geneive Abdo, *No God but God: Egypt and the Triumph of Islam*, Oxford University Press, 2000; Gilles Kepel, *Muslim Extremism in Egypt: The Prophet and the Pharaoh*, University of California Press, 1985; Richard P. Mitchell, *The Society of the Muslim Brothers*, Oxford University Press, 1969.

For Abu Omar's youth and travels before coming to Italy: Author interviews of Abu Omar, Alexandria, Egypt, Apr. 2007; Abu Omar, "Abu Omar Al-Masri" (blog), http://abuomarelmasri.blogspot.com.

For the history of postwar Milan: John Foot, *Milan since the Miracle: City, Culture and Identity*, Berg, 2001.

Chapter 3: The Enemy Within

For Omar Abdel-Rahman's statement "We must be terrorists . . .": Andrew C. McCarthy, "Prosecuting the New York Sheikh," *Middle East Quarterly*, vol. 4, no. 1, Mar. 1997.

For the growth of Islamic terrorism in Milan: Lorenzo Vidino, *Al Qaeda in Europe: The New Battleground of Jihad*, Prometheus, 2006, and, "Islam, Islamism, and Jihadism in Italy," *Current Trends in Islamist Ideology*, vol. 7, Aug. 4, 2008; Alison Pargeter, *The New Frontiers of Jihad: Radical Islam in*

Europe, University of Pennsylvania Press, 2008; Stefano Dambruoso with Guido Olimpio, *Milano-Bagdad: Diario di un magistrato in prima linea nella lotta al terrorismo islamico in Italia*, Mondadori, 2004; Guido Olimpio, *La rete del terrore*, Sperling & Kupfer Editori, 2002; and many reports by Paolo Biondani of *Corriere della Sera*.

The U.S. Treasury Department declared Idris Ahmed Nasreddin, the Eritrean businessman who staked the mosque on Viale Jenner, a financier of terrorists in 2002. In 2007, after Nasreddin changed some of his business practices, the Treasury Department said he was no longer financing terrorists.

For links between Islamists in Milan (particularly Anwar Shaaban) and the Islamic Brigade of the Bosnian War: the several works, *supra*, on the growth of Islamic terrorism in Milan; Evan F. Kohlmann, *Al Qaeda's Jihad in Europe: The Afghan-Bosnian Network*, Berg, 2004; John R. Schindler, *Unholy Terror: Bosnia, al-Qa'ida, and the Rise of the Global Jihad*, Zenith, 2007.

The terrorist who described the elaborate arms purchases for the Islamic Brigade was Sekseka Habib Waddani. See Lucy Komisar, "Police spoke to U.S. terror suspect," Sept. 16, 2002, http://thekomisarscoop.com/2002/09/police-spoke-to-us-terror-suspect/. Waddani said he was being blackmailed. He wanted the Italian police to protect him, but they seem to have turned him away. He later (see Chapter 4, "Beloved by God") became a martyr in Iraq.

For the butchery of the Islamic Brigade in the Bosnian War: John-Thor Dahlburg, " 'Holy Warriors' Brought Bosnians Ferocity and Zeal," *Los Angeles Times*, Aug. 6, 1996; and Kohlmann, *supra*, citing, among others, Suzana Andjelic, " 'Uragan 95' and Mujahedeen," *Slobodna Bosna*, Sept. 13, 2001.

For the number of phones tapped in Italy and elsewhere: Arik Hesseldahl, "Big Brother Isn't Here Yet," Forbes.com, Digital Life section, May 6, 2005.

For the traffic in stolen passports by Serbian gangs: Craig Pyes, Sebastian Rotella, and David Zucchino, "Fraudulent Passports Key Weapon for Terrorists," *Los Angeles Times*, Dec. 16, 2001.

For L'Houssaine Kherchtou: Sean O'Neill, "The terrorist trained to fly bin Laden's plane," *Daily Telegraph*, Sept. 21, 2001.

For Operation Sphinx: Vidino (both), *supra*; Kohlmann, *supra*.

For Fateh Kamel and Karim Said Atmani: Kohlmann, *supra*; Schindler, *supra*; Marc Sageman, *Understanding Terror Networks*, University of Pennsylvania Press, 2004; "Mustapha the terrorist," *National Post* (Toronto), Feb. 24, 2001; Stewart Bell, "Terrorist Returns: Tory urges Ottawa to consider revoking citizenship," *National Post* (Toronto), Feb. 26, 2005.

For Abu Talal (Talaat Fuad Qassim): Michael Taarnby Jensen, "Jihad in Denmark: An Overview and Analysis of Jihadi Activity in Denmark, 1990–2006," DIIS Working Paper 2006/35, Danish Institute for International Studies, 2006, http://www.diis.dk/sw30537.asp; untitled, undated articles from the Danish newspaper Politiken, translated by Center for Human Rights and Global Justice of New York University School of Law, http://www.chrgj.org/press/docs/Politiken.pdf; Youssef M. Ibrahim, "Egypt Says Militant Muslim Is Seized in Croatia," *New York Times*, Sept. 25, 1995; "Islamists Hit Back," *Intelligence Newsletter*, no. 276, Indigo Publications, Nov. 23, 1995.

For Abu Talal's statement "The Muslim has a duty to be a terrorist...": Vidino, *Al Qaeda in Europe.*

For Denmark's grant of asylum to Abu Talal's colleagues: "NYC bomb suspects get asylum in Denmark," *Cleveland Plain Dealer*, June 29, 1995.

For the history of U.S. renditions, ordinary and extraordinary: Margaret L. Satterthwaite and Angelina Fisher, "Tortured Logic: Renditions to Justice, Extraordinary Rendition, and Human Rights Law," *The Long Term View* (Massachusetts School of Law), vol. 6, no. 4, 2006, http://www.mslaw.edu/MSLMedia/LTV/6.4.pdf; D. Cameron Findlay, "Abducting Terrorists Overseas for Trial in the United States: Issues of International and Domestic Law," *Texas International Law Journal*, vol. 23, no. 1, 1988; Joseph F. C. DiMento and Gilbert Geis, "The Extraordinary Condition of Extraordinary Rendition: The C.I.A., the D.E.A., Kidnaping, Torture, and the Law," *War Crimes, Genocide & Crimes against Humanity*, vol. 2, 2006; "Torture by Proxy: International and Domestic Law Applicable to 'Extraordinary Renditions,' " Committee on International and Human Rights of the Association of the Bar of the City of New York and Center for Human Rights and Global Justice of New York University School of Law, June 2006.

For the U.S. Supreme Court cases on renditions: *Ker v. Illinois*, 119 U.S. 436 (1836); *Frisbie v. Collins*, 342 U.S. 519 (1952); *United States v. Alvarez-Machain*, 504 U.S. 655 (1992).

For the appellate court's statement "conduct of a most shocking...": *United States ex rel. Lujan v. Gengler*, 510 F.2d 62 (2d Cir. 1975), *cert. denied*, 421 U.S. 1001 (1975); the court was clarifying its earlier decision in *United States v. Toscanino*, 500 F.2d 267 (2d Cir. 1974), petition for rehearing en banc denied, 504 F.2d 1380 (1974).

For the *Achille Lauro* and TWA hijackings: Philip B. Heymann, *Terrorism and America: A Commonsense Strategy for a Democratic Society*, MIT Press, 1998.

For Reagan's National Security Decision Directive 207: John Walcott and

Andy Pasztor, "Reagan Ruling to Let CIA Kidnap Terrorists Overseas Is Disclosed," *Wall Street Journal*, Feb. 20, 1987 (the number of the directive was not known at the time of the *Journal's* article).

For the rendition of Fawaz Yunis: Findlay, *supra*; Duane Clarridge with Digby Diehl, *A Spy for All Seasons: My Life in the CIA*, Scribner, 1997 (Clarridge says the female FBI agents on the yacht were wearing bikinis, not halter tops); "A Byte Out of History: The Case of the Yachted Terrorist," Headline Archives, FBI, Sept. 15, 2004, http://www.fbi.gov/page2/sept04/yachted091504.htm.

For William Webster's views on renditions: Walcott and Pasztor, *supra*; David B. Ottaway and Don Oberdorfer, "Administration Alters Assassination Ban: In Interview, Webster Reveals Interpretation," *Washington Post*, Nov. 4, 1989.

For the opinion of the first President Bush's Justice Department on FBI renditions: "Authority of the Federal Bureau of Investigation to Override International Law in Extraterritorial Law Enforcement Activities," 13 Op. Off. Legal Counsel 163 (1989).

For Richard Clarke's statement "The first time I proposed a snatch . . .": Richard A. Clarke, *Against All Enemies: Inside America's War on Terror*, Free Press, 2004. It seems that in this case Clarke was proposing an ordinary, rather than an extraordinary, rendition, but it is not clear because he uses the imprecise term "snatch" and because he himself is confused about (or unaware of) the difference between ordinary and extraordinary renditions—he calls them all "extraordinary renditions," erroneously citing for example the capture of Ramzi Yousef.

For the Rijeka car-bombing: Fabrizio Gatti, "1995: da Milano parte un' autobomba per Fiume," *Corriere della Sera*, Nov. 11, 2001; Kohlmann, *supra*. Sometimes the bomber's name is listed as Jon (rather than John) Fawzan.

For the statement of Abu Saleh (Mahmoud Abdelkader Es Sayed) "I told them . . . that my three brothers were in prison . . . ": "Egiziano sfuggito alla cattura: 'L'Italia è un paese terrorista,' " *La Repubblica*, Nov. 29, 2001. The Syrian minister of defense who supposedly helped Abu Saleh was Mustafa Tlass.

For the statement of the instructor from Munich "Do you see this?": Vidino, *Al Qaeda in Europe, supra*.

The young Tunisian who scouted potential terrorist targets in Italy was a thirty-four-year-old whom Magistrate Stefano Dambruoso refers to as Yasir: Dambruoso, *supra*.

When Abu Imad asked, "Is it alright to kill a person . . . ," he was repeating a question from a member of an audience at a conference. It was an accurate reflection of his own views, which, presumably, is why he repeated rather than repudiated the noxious question. The speaker who said "Between us and the unbelievers there is hatred" was Mohammed al-Fizazi, who had preached, among other places, in Hamburg's Al-Quds Mosque, which later became notorious as the radicalizing sanctum of Mohamed Atta and other hijackers. See Fausto Biloslavo, "Così gli imam predicano l'odio in Italia," *Il Giornale*, Feb. 12, 2006, http://www.ilgiornale.it/esteri/cosi_imam_predicano_odio_italia/12-02-2006/articolo-id=64426-page=0-comments=1.

For Abu Saleh's statement "If the brothers want to hide . . ." and his subsequent statements: Sandro Contenta, "Catching terror on tape: Milan wiretaps offer sensational glimpse into alleged terrorists' life," *Toronto Star*, Dec. 1, 2002; Sebastian Rotella, "Chilling 'Chatter' of Jihad," *Los Angeles Times*, Sept. 23, 2002.

For Abdulsalam Ali Abdulrahman al-Hilal (sometimes Abd al-Salam Ali al-Hila): Human Rights Watch, "Black Hole: The Fate of Islamists Rendered to Egypt," May 9, 2005, http://www.hrw.org/en/reports/2005/05/09/black-hole.

For Abdulrahman and Abu Saleh's betrayal of the al-Qaeda turncoat: Andrew Higgins and Alan Cullison, "Friend or Foe: The Story of a Traitor to al Qaeda: Murky Loyalties in Yemen Undo the Betrayer, Who Finds Himself Betrayed: Ominous Words Before 9/11," *Wall Street Journal*, Dec. 20, 2002.

For Abu Saleh's conversation with Abdulrahman after the latter's arrival in Bologna: Vidino, *Al Qaeda in Europe*. Because of the noise of Abu Saleh's car, DIGOS needed some months to transcribe the conversation, but the FBI apparently received it months before the Sept. 11 attacks.

For Egypt's warning that al-Qaeda intended to attack the G8 summit in Genoa: Daniel McGrory and Dominic Kennedy, "Raids Crush Terrorist Cells and Foil Plot to Kill Bush," *Times* (London), Sept. 27, 2001.

For the steganographic images on the computers of the Via Quaranta mosque: Alexandra Salomon, "Coded Porn Found in Terror Cell: Coded Pornography, WTC Pictures Found on Terror Cell Computers," ABC News, May 8, 2003; Stefano Dambruoso with Guido Olimpio, *Milano-Bagdad: Diario di un magistrato in prima linea nella lotta al terrorismo islamico in Italia*, Mondadori, 2004; Vidino, *Al Qaeda in Europe*.

For Father Jean-Marie Benjamin's advance warning of the attacks of September 11: "Days Before, Priest Predicted Plane Attacks on U.S.: Says

Organization of Terrorist Groups Has Changed," *Zenit*, Sept. 16, 2001, http://www.zenit.org/article-2377?l=english.

Chapter 4: Beloved by God

For Abu Omar's life in Milan, including the many tapped conversations of and about him: Guido Salvini, "Ordinanza di applicazione della misura dell custodia cautelare in carcere," N.5236/02 R.G.N.R., N.1511/02 R.G.GIP (NASR Osama Mostafa Hassan), Tribunale Ordinario di Milano, Ufficio del Giudice per le indagini preliminari, June 24, 2005 (this document is derived largely from Armando Spataro, "Richiesta per l'applicazione di misure cautelari," N. 5236/02.21 (NASR Osama Mostafa Hassan), Procura della Repubblica presso il Tribunale Ordinario di Milano, Apr. 4, 2005); author interviews of Abu Omar, Alexandria, Egypt, Apr. 2007. The terrorist who told police, "I and all the other people in the group . . ." was Riadh Jelassi. Abu Omar's interlocutor Hammadi was Bouyahia Hammadi Ben Abdelaziz.

For Kamal Morchidi and the Tunisian suicide whose family was to be rewarded with €8,000: Salvini, *supra*; Paolo Biondani, " 'Festeggio il martirio di mio figlio,' " *Corriere della Sera*, Dec. 2, 2003; Magdi Allam, *Kamikaze Made in Europe: Riuscirá l'Occidente a sconfiggere i terroristi islamici?*, Mondadori, 2004. There are competing claims about whether Morchidi died as a suicide or was killed by American troops. The Tunisian was Sekseka Habib Waddani, the same who told police about the elaborate arms shipments from Russia to Italy to Bosnia in the early 1990s.

For the jailhouse conversation of Ciise and Merai: Gianni Cipriani, " 'Sarò un martire,' così parlano gli islamici in manette," *Il Nuovo*, Dec. 5, 2003; Lorenzo Vidino, *Al Qaeda in Europe: The New Battleground of Jihad*, Prometheus, 2006.

For the initial investigation, in 2003, into the disappearance of Abu Omar: Chiara Nobili, "Ordinanza di applicazione della misura dell custodia cautelare in carcere," N. 10838/05 R.G.N.R., N. 1966/05 R.G.GIP (ADLER Monica Courtney et al.), Tribunale di Milano, Sezione Giudice per le indagini preliminari, June 22, 2005 (English translation, Nov. 5, 2005); author interviews of Armando Spataro, Milan, Italy, 2007 to 2009; author interview of Stefano Dambruoso, Milan, Italy, Nov. 2007.

For Merfat Rezk's story: REZK Merfat, Verbale di sommarie informazioni testimoniali rese, Questura di Milano, Divisione Investigazioni Generali Operazioni Speciali (DIGOS), Feb. 26, 2003; REZK Merfat, Verbale di assunzione informazioni, Nr. 20287/03 R.G.N.R. Mod. 44, Nr. 12 Reg. int.

P.M., Procura della Repubblica presso il Tribunale Ordinario di Milano, Mar. 4, 2003.

For Hayam Hassanein's story: HASSANEIN Hayam Abdelmoneim Mohamed, Verbale di sommarie informazioni testimoniali rese, Questura di Milano, Divisione Investigazioni Generali Operazioni Speciali (DIGOS), Feb. 15, 2005.

For Shawki Salem's story: SALEM Shawki Bakry, Verbale di assunzione informazioni, N. 20287/03 Mod. 44, Procura della Repubblica presso il Tribunale Ordinario di Milano, Mar. 15, 2005; SALEM Shawki Bakry, Verbale di assunzione informazioni, N. 20287/03 R.G.N.R. Mod. 44, Procura della Repubblica presso il Tribunale Ordinario di Milano, Mar. 18, 2005.

For Stefano Dambruoso: Author interview of Dambruoso, *supra*; Jeff Israeli, "Cracking Down on al-Qaeda: Stefano Dambruoso, Italy," *Time Europe*, Apr. 20, 2003.

The administrator at Via Quaranta who said that Abu Omar's wife had said he was being followed was Sherif Hafez El Ashmawi. See Nobili, *supra*.

Chapter 5: Torment

For the transport of Abu Omar from Milan to Cairo: Chiara Nobili, "Ordinanza di applicazione della misura dell custodia cautelare in carcere," N. 10838/05 R.G.N.R., N. 1966/05 R.G.GIP (ADLER Monica Courtney et al.), Tribunale di Milano, Sezione Giudice per le indagini preliminari, June 22, 2005 (an English translation of this order was made Nov. 5, 2005); author interviews of Abu Omar, Alexandria, Egypt, Apr. 2007; Abu Omar, "The Account of an Islamist Kidnapped from the Streets of Milan," undated, reproduced (in a rough English translation) as "My CIA rendition," Stephen Grey's *Ghost Plane* (Web site), http://www.ghostplane.net/abuomar, and excerpted in Paolo Biondani and Gianni Santucci, "Il memoriale di Abu Omar: 'Rapito e picchiato da italiani,'" *Corriere della Sera*, Nov. 9, 2006. There are several accounts by reporters who interviewed Abu Omar about his ordeal. One of the better is a series by Matthias Gebauer: "Rendition Victim Speaks Out," "Abu Omar's Abduction in Milan," "Abu Omar's Arrival in Cairo," "Before the Trial," "CIA Activities in Italy," *Der Spiegel*, Mar. 19, 2007, http://www.spiegel.de/international/europe/0,1518,657431,00.html.

My description of certain tortures generally and of Abu Omar's tortures particularly was enlightened by the accounts of survivors, including several in Egypt, who prefer to remain anonymous. Cairo's El Nadim Center for the Rehabilitation of Victims of Violence has documented and made public the stories of other survivors. Other helpful accounts were Munú Actis et al., *That Inferno: Conversations of Five Women Survivors of an Argentine Torture Camp*, Vanderbilt University Press, 2006; Henri Alleg, *The Question*, George Braziller, 1958; Jean Améry, *At the Mind's Limits: Contemplations by a Survivor of Auschwitz and its Realities*, Indiana University Press, 1998; William F. Schulz, ed., *The Phenomenon of Torture: Readings and Commentary*, University of Pennsylvania Press, 2007; Eric Lomax, *The Railway Man*, W. W. Norton, 1980; John Conroy, *Unspeakable Acts, Ordinary People: The Dynamics of Torture*, Knopf, 2000; Edward Peters, *Torture*, University of Pennsylvania Press, 1996; Kate Millett, *The Politics of Cruelty: An Essay on the Literature of Political Imprisonment*, W. W. Norton, 1994; Lawrence Weschler, *A Miracle, a Universe: Settling Accounts with Torturers*, Pantheon, 1990; Elaine Scarry, *The Body in Pain: The Making and Unmaking of the World*, Oxford University Press, 1985; and others cited below.

For the history of torture: John H. Langbein, *Torture and the Law of Proof: Europe and England in the Ancien Régime*, University of Chicago Press, 1977; Peters, *supra*; Conroy, *supra*; Millett, *supra*; Weschler, *supra*; Schulz, *supra*.

For the possibly fatal experiments on captured spies in Germany, Japan, and the Panama Canal Zone: Tim Weiner, *Legacy of Ashes: The History of the CIA*, Doubleday, 2007.

For the study and practice of torture by the CIA and Department of Defense throughout this chapter, including the experiments at McGill and the Phoenix program: Alfred W. McCoy, *A Question of Torture: CIA Interrogation, from the Cold War to the War on Terror*, Metropolitan Books, 2006; Conroy, *supra*; Schulz, *supra*. See also John Marks, *The Search for the "Manchurian Candidate": The CIA and Mind Control*, Times Books, 1978.

For the statement of the Defense researchers "Any fixed position which is maintained . . .": Lawrence Hinkle and Harold Wolff, "Communist Interrogation and Indoctrination of 'Enemies of the State,'" *Archives of Neurology and Psychiatry*, vol. 76, no. 2, Aug. 1956.

For Menachem Begin's statement "to sleep, to sleep just a little . . .": Menachem Begin, *White Nights*, Harper & Row, 1979. On sleep deprivation, see also Artur London, *The Confession*, William Morrow, 1970.

For Frank Olson's death: The Frank Olson Legacy Project, "Family Statement on the Murder of Frank Olson," Frederick, Maryland, Aug. 8, 2002, http://www.frankolsonproject.org/Statements/FamilyStatement2002.html.

For the CIA's statement "when his mental and physical resistance is at its lowest": CIA, *Kubark Counterintelligence Interrogation*, July 1963, subsequently amended as CIA, *Human Resource Exploitation Training Manual*, 1983.

The Army's statement "Use of torture is not only illegal . . ." is stated in slightly varying forms in different field manuals, beginning (at least) with: Army Intelligence Center's FM 34-52: *Intelligence Interrogation*, Sept. 1992. A more recent version is FM2-22.3 (FM 34-52): *Human Intelligence Collector Operations*, 2006.

For Major Sherwood Moran's manual: Stephen Budiansky, "Truth Extraction," *The Atlantic*, June 2005.

The CIA commander who told McCoy, "The truth is that never in the history of our work in Vietnam . . ." was Ralph W. McGehee.

The purported witness in Uruguay who said, "The special horror of the course . . ." was Manuel Hevia Cosculluela. See McCoy, *supra*. Hevia, a CIA agent, defected to Cuba, where he told his story. His claims were earlier corroborated by a high official in the Uruguayan police who said that the CIA's trainer, who died in 1980, had taught "violent techniques of torture and repression."

The Honduran sergeant trained in Texas who said, "They taught us psychological methods . . ." was Florencio Caballero. See James LeMoyne, "Testifying to Torture," *New York Times Magazine*, June 5, 1988.

For the CIA's hiring of Nazis to train security services in the Middle East: Christopher Simpson, *Blowback: America's Recruitment of Nazis and Its Effects on the Cold War*, Weidenfeld & Nicholson, 1988; Peter Grose, "Uncle Sam's Nazis," *Washington Post Book World*, Apr. 24, 1988; Miles Copeland (who was the officer on loan from the CIA to Nasser), *The Game of Nations*, Simon & Schuster, 1974. For a mildly dissenting view (arguing that the CIA recruited the Nazis but had little role in sending them to Egypt): Richard Breitman et al., *US Intelligence and the Nazis*, Cambridge University Press, 2005.

For the complicated relationship between the CIA and Nasser: Weiner, *supra*; Miles Copeland, *Without Cloak or Dagger: The Truth About the New Espionage*, Simon & Schuster, 1974; and Copeland, *The Game of Nations*.

For Ambassador Edward Walker's statement "Too many people . . . died while fleeing": Stephen Grey, *Ghost Plane: The True Story of the CIA Torture Program*, Henry Holt, 2006.

For Robert Baer's statement "If you want a serious interrogation . . .": Stephen Grey, "America's Gulag," *New Statesman*, May 17, 2004.

For the Convention Against Torture, as adopted by the United States: Foreign Affairs Reform and Restructuring Act of 1998, § 2242(a), in Omnibus Consolidated and Emergency Supplemental Appropriations Act of 1999, Pub. L. No. 105-277 (1998). For commentary on U.S. obligations: David Weissbrodt and Amy Bergquist, "Extraordinary Rendition and the Torture Convention," *Virginia Journal of International Law*, Summer 2006; "Torture by Proxy: International and Domestic Law Applicable to 'Extraordinary Renditions,'" Committee on International and Human Rights of the Association of the Bar of the City of New York and Center for Human Rights and Global Justice of New York University School of Law, June 2006.

For a partial account of conditions in Egyptian prisons: Human Rights Watch, "Prison Conditions in Egypt: A Filthy System," Feb. 1993, http://www.hrw.org/reports/pdfs/e/egypt/egypt.932/egypt932full.pdf.

For Abu Omar's torture: Author interviews of Abu Omar, *supra*; Abu Omar, *supra*; Gebauer, *supra*. There is some doubt over the order and duration of Abu Omar's torments after he reached Cairo, probably because he has told them in different order to different reporters. He did not grant me (or, to my knowledge, any other reporter) a long enough interview to sort them out. No credible American or Egyptian official, however, has disputed his claims to torture, and his claims are similar to those of other victims of torture in Egypt. Abu Omar believes his first seven months of imprisonment and torture took place at the headquarters compound of the Mukhabarat, but he is not sure.

Chapter 6: Inquest

For the investigation of the movements and identities of Abu Omar's kidnappers and of Abu Omar's emergence from prison in 2004: Chiara Nobili, "Ordinanza di applicazione della misura dell custodia cautelare in carcere," N. 10838/05 R.G.N.R., N. 1966/05 R.G.GIP (ADLER Monica Courtney et al.), Tribunale di Milano, Sezione Giudice per le indagini preliminari, June 22, 2005 (English translation, Nov. 5, 2005); Enrico Tranfa et al., untitled order appealing Chiari's order of June 22, 2005, No. 1413/2005 RG TRD, N. 10838/2005 R.G.N.R., 1966/2005 R.G. A.G. (CASTALDO Eliana et al.), Tribunale di Milano, Section XI criminal court, July 20, 2005 (English translation, Nov. 5, 2005); Chiara Nobili, "Ordinanza di applicazione della misura dell custodia cautelare in carcere," N. 10838/05 R.G.N.R., N. 1966/05 R.G.GIP (MEDERO Betnie et al.), Tribunale di Milano, Sezione Giudice per le indagini preliminari, Sept. 27, 2005 (English translation, untitled, Nov. 5, 2005); Enrico Manzi, "Decree for the Application of Coercive Measures," N. 10838/05 R.G.N.R., N. 1966/05 R.G.GIP (CASTELLI Jeffrey et al.), Tribunale di Milano, Sezione Giudice per le indagini preliminari, Jul. 7, 2006; author interviews of Armando Spataro, Milan, Italy, 2007 to 2009; off-the-record author interviews of police officials, Milan, Italy. See also Guido Salvini, "Ordinanza di applicazione della misura dell custodia cautelare in carcere," N.5236/02 R.G.N.R., N.1511/02 R.G.GIP (NASR Osama

Mostafa Hassan), Tribunale Ordinario di Milano, Ufficio del Giudice per le indagini preliminari, June 24, 2005, which document is derived largely from Armando Spataro, "Richiesta per l'applicazione di misure cautelari," N. 5236/02.21 (NASR Osama Mostafa Hassan), Procura della Repubblica presso il Tribunale Ordinario di Milano, Apr. 4, 2005.

For Abu Omar's last months in prison in 2004: Author interviews of Abu Omar, Alexandria, Egypt, Apr. 2007; author interview of Montasser El-Zayat, Cairo, Egypt, Apr. 2007; Abu Omar, "The Account of an Islamist Kidnapped from the Streets of Milan," undated, reproduced (in a rough English translation) as "My CIA rendition," Stephen Grey's *Ghost Plane* (Web site), http://www.ghostplane.net/abuomar. I have been unable to verify a few small details about Abu Omar's various releases from prison (discussed in this and a later chapter), for example whether it was his brother Hitham or, instead, Hitham's wife who received the call from the police on April 19, 2004.

For Emilio Alessandrini: Author interviews of Spataro, *supra*; Armando Spataro, "In ricordo di Emilio Alessandrini," Giustizia e Carità, Dec. 6, 2000, http://www.giustiziacarita.it/professioni/aless2.htm; "Schede/1979/ Alessandrini," Associazione Italiana Vittime del Terrorismo, http://www .vittimeterrorismo.it/memorie/schede/alessandrini.htm.

For Guido Galli: Author interviews of Spataro, *supra*; Armando Spataro, "In ricordo di Guido Galli," Giustizia e Carità, undated, http://www .giustiziacarita.it/professioni/gallis.htm; "Schede/1980/Galli," Associazi-one Italiana Vittime del Terrorismo, http://www.vittimeterrorismo.it/ memorie/schede/galli.htm.

The fifty-four SIMs (and several landlines) of the alleged conspirators that DIGOS discovered may not have represented all of the conspirators. A conspirator who did not use a SIM or who used one very discreetly would not have been recorded.

For Gregory Asherleigh and Cynthia Dame Logan's travels to Norway: John Crewdson, "Frequent-flier miles expose CIA operation," *Chicago Tribune,* July 23, 2006; Jonathan Tisdall, "Suspect CIA agents were in Norway," *Aftenposten,* July 24, 2006, http://www.aftenposten.no/english/local/ article1397884.ece?service=print; Kristjan Molstad, "Bonuspoeng avs-lørte CIA-agenter," *Aftenposten,* July 24, 2006, http://www.aftenposten .no/nyheter/uriks/article1397211.ece; "Norsk etterretning kjente til CIA-agenter," *Aftenposten,* Aug. 1, 2006, http://www.aftenposten.no/nyheter/ iriks/article1406229.ece.

For Brynjar Meling's statement "A lot of people with integrity in the govern-ment . . .": Crewdson, *supra*.

Chapter 7: Flight

For the investigation of the flights on which Abu Omar was transported: Chiara Nobili, "Ordinanza di applicazione della misura dell custodia cautelare in carcere," N. 10838/05 R.G.N.R., N. 1966/05 R.G.GIP (ADLER Monica Courtney et al.), Tribunale di Milano, Sezione Giudice per le indagini preliminari, June 22, 2005 (English translation, Nov. 5, 2005); Chiara Nobili, "Ordinanza di applicazione della misura dell custodia cautelare in carcere," N. 10838/05 R.G.N.R., N. 1966/05 R.G.GIP (MEDERO Betnie et al.), Tribunale di Milano, Sezione Giudice per le indagini preliminari, Sept. 27, 2005 (English translation, untitled, Nov. 5, 2005); Enrico Manzi, "Decree for the Application of Coercive Measures," N. 10838/05 R.G.N.R., N. 1966/05 R.G.GIP (CASTELLI Jeffrey et al.), Tribunale di Milano, Sezione Giudice per le indagini preliminari, Jul. 7, 2006; author interviews of Armando Spataro, Milan, Italy, 2007 to 2009.

There is confusion about the precise times that Spar 92 landed at Ramstein and N85VM took off from there. I use the times Italian investigators settled on. Other sources put the landing time of Spar 92 as early as 7:30 P.M. and the departure time of N85VM as early as 7:52 P.M. See Stephen Grey, *Ghost Plane: The True Story of the CIA Torture Program*, Henry Holt, 2006; Edward Horgan, "Irish Complicity in CIA Rendition: CIA Plane Movements Through Irish Airports," version 1.3, ShannonWatch, Feb. 9, 2008, http://www.shannonwatch.org/docs/CIA_Shannon_Report_9_2_09.pdf.

For the Red Sox plane (N85VM, later changed to N227SV), including Mahlon Richards's statement "I don't ask my customers why . . ." and Philip Morse's statement "It just so happens one of our customers . . .": John Crewdson and Tom Hundley, "Jet's Travels Cloaked in Mystery," *Chicago Tribune*, Mar. 20, 2005; Gordon Edes, "CIA uses jet, Red Sox partner confirms," *Boston Globe*, Mar. 21, 2005; Horgan, *supra*.

For Lady's background: William Lady (all but certainly the nom de plume of Bob Lady), "Coyotes From the Same Hill," *Dead Mule* (online), Oct. 1, 2005, http://www.deadmule.com/content/2005/10/01/coyotes-from-the-same-hill/; off-the-record author interviews of police officials, Milan, Italy; Guido Olimpio, "Chi ha coperto Bob, 007 senza limiti?" *Corriere della Sera*, June 24, 2005; Matthew Cole, "Blowback," *GQ*, Mar. 7, 2009; Nobili (both), *supra*.

La Repubblica's reporters who broke the story of Spataro's inquiry in early 2005 are the excellent Carlo Bonini and Giuseppe D'Avanzo.

For the conversation between Martha and Bob Lady after their house in Penango was raided: John Crewdson and Alessandra Maggiorani, "CIA chiefs reportedly split over cleric plot: Agency schisms come to light in Italy probe," *Chicago Tribune*, Jan. 8, 2007.

For the CIA's past betrayal of its agents in Iran, its botched smear of the ambassador to Guatemala (Marilyn McAfee), and its see-no-evil view of Aldrich Ames: Tim Weiner, *Legacy of Ashes: The History of the CIA*, Doubleday, 2007.

Chapter 8: Gladiators

For the Peteano bombing and cover-up: Franco Ferraresi (the nonpareil on violent Italian rightists), *Threats to Democracy: The Radical Right in Italy after the War*, Princeton University Press, 1996; Franco Ferraresi, "A secret structure codenamed Gladio," in Stephen Hellman and Gianfranco Pasquino, eds., *Italian Politics: A Review*, Pinter Pub., vol. 7, 1992; Daniele Ganser, *NATO's Secret Armies: Operation Gladio and Terrorism in Western Europe*, Frank Cass, 2006; Marcella Andreoli, "Che bomba di esparto!" *Panorama*, Nov. 18, 1990. The arms cache near Peteano was found in Aurisina.

For the CIA's efforts to influence Italian elections: Tim Weiner, *Legacy of Ashes: The History of the CIA*, Doubleday, 2007; Ganser, *supra*; Ray S. Cline, *Secrets, Spies and Scholars: Blueprint of the Essential CIA*, Acropolis, 1976; "The CIA in Italy: An Interview with Victor Marchetti," Philip Agee and Louis Wolf, eds., *Dirty Work: The CIA in Western Europe*, Lyle Stuart, 1978; *CIA: The Pike Report*, Spokesman Books, 1977 (containing selections from a report by the U.S. House Committee on Intelligence that has never been released to the public but was leaked to reporter Daniel Schorr and subsequently published in the *Village Voice*); Paul Ginsborg, *A History of Contemporary Italy: Society and Politics 1943-1988*, Penguin, 1990; William R. Corson, *The Armies of Ignorance: The Rise of the American Intelligence Empire*, The Dial Press/James Wade, 1977; William Colby and Peter Forbath, *Honorable Men: My Life in the CIA*, Simon & Schuster, 1978; John Prados, *Lost Crusader: The Secret Wars of William Colby*, Oxford University Press, 2003; Richard N. Gardner, *Mission Italy: On the Front Lines of the Cold War*, Rowman & Littlefield, 2005.

F. Mark Wyatt, who became the head of the CIA's Italian desk, is quoted in Weiner, *supra*.

For Marchetti's estimate that the CIA gave Italian politicians $20 million to $30 million a year in the 1950s: "The CIA in Italy: an Interview with Victor Marchetti," *supra*. The U.S. government also gave Italy $176 million in well-publicized aid in the months before the 1948 elections and announced that such aid would end if Italians empowered Communists. See Ginsborg, *supra*.

For Gladio generally: Allan Francovich, director, *Gladio*, three-part documentary, Timewatch program, British Broadcasting Corp., BBC2, June 10, 1992 (date of first episode); Ganser, *supra*; Ferraresi, both works *supra*; Jan Willems, ed., Gladio, EPO Dossier (publisher), Brussels, 1991; Philip Willan: *Puppetmasters: The Political Use of Terrorism in Italy*, iUniverse, 2002; Arthur E. Rowse, "Gladio: The Secret U.S. War to Subvert Italian Democracy," *CovertAction*, no. 49, summer 1994. The foregoing sources vary greatly in their reliability. Readers should tread carefully in the literature of Gladio, as it is rife with inaccuracies and bald untruths.

For a couple of the many estimates of the number of Gladiators, regular and irregular: Ferraresi, "A secret structure codenamed Gladio," *supra*; William Scobie, "Gladio: The War That Never Was," *World Press Review*, Feb. 1991.

For the discussion in the U.S. embassy about the possibility of armed intervention should Socialists come to power in 1963: Ferraresi, *Threats to Democracy, supra*; Yves Cartuyvels, "L'intervention américaine en Italie et les interêts supérieurs du Pacte atlantique (1942-1962)," in Willems, *supra*. A supposed participant in the discussions, Colonel Vernon Walters (then military attaché, later deputy director of the CIA), denied that armed intervention was considered.

For the threatened coup of 1964 (called Plan Solo) by Giovanni De Lorenzo: Ferraresi, both works *supra*; Richard Collin, *The De Lorenzo Gambit: The Italian Coup Manqué of 1964* (monograph), Sage Research Papers in the Social Sciences No. 90-034, Sage Pubs., 1976; Paul Ginsborg, *supra*; Ganser, *supra*. De Lorenzo's statement that the United States and NATO suggested he collect the illegal dossiers is in Ganser.

For Junio Borghese's "Tora, Tora" coup: Jack Greene and Alessandro Massignani, *The Black Prince and the Sea Devils: The Story of Valerio Borghese and the Elite Units of the Decima MAS*, Da Capo, 2004; "Zio Sam sapeva del golpe di Borghese," *La Repubblica*, Dec. 6, 2000; Giovanni Maria Bellu et al., "Golpe Borghese, gli Usa sapevano," *La Repubblica*, Dec. 19, 2004; Giovanni Maria Bellu, "E la Cia disse: sì al golpe Borghese ma soltanto con Andreotti premier," *La Repubblica*, Dec. 5, 2005.

For the statement that Vito Miceli was "linked to antidemocratic elements of the Right": *CIA: The Pike Report, supra*.

For Vito Miceli's statement "A Super SID on my orders?": Ganser, *supra*.

For Edgardo Sogno's planned coup: Ferraresi, *Threats to Democracy, supra*; Jeffrey McKenzie Bale, *The "Black" International—Neo-Fascist Paramilitary Networks and the "Strategy of Tension"* (doctoral dissertation), University of California at Berkeley, UMI Dissertation Service, 1994.

For Sogno's statement "When FIAT stopped financing us . . .": Ferraresi, *Threats to Democracy, supra* (the quotation, however, is my translation from the original Italian version of the book).

For Sogno's statement "I told him that I was informing him . . .": Philip Willan, "Terrorists 'helped by CIA' to stop rise of left in Italy," *The Guardian*, Mar. 26, 2001, http://www.guardian.co.uk/world/2001/mar/26/terrorism.

For the bombing of Piazza Fontana: Ferraresi, *Threats to Democracy, supra*; Carlo Lucarelli, *Piazza Fontana* (transcript of RAI [Radiotelevisione Italiana] TV program of the same name), Giulio Einaudi, 2007.

For the count of 491 dead and 1,181 wounded in the Years of Lead: Ganser, *supra*. The numbers vary, depending on one's definition of a political attack, and assigning blame for some attacks to leftists or rightists is still more complicated.

For Vincenzo Vinciguerra's statement "There exists in Italy a secret parallel . . . ": Ferraresi, *Threats to Democracy, supra*.

For Vinciguerra's statement " . . .in the absence of a Soviet military invasion . . . ": Ed Vulliamy, "Secret agents, freemasons, fascists . . . and a top-level campaign of political 'destabilisation' " (ellipsis in original), *The Guardian*, Dec. 5, 1990.

For Gerardo Serravalle's statement " . . . the subject of internal control . . .": Francovich, *supra*. This claim corresponds to that of General Antonio Podda, vice-director of SIFAR from 1966 to 1970, and of a Gladio document from 1958. See Ferraresi, "A secret structure codenamed Gladio," *supra*. Another Gladio document, on a 1972 meeting between Gladio chiefs and the CIA's Stone, reported that Stone warned of a possible insurrection in southern Italy. Were it to occur, he said, Gladio would have to operate in "exactly the same way" that the CIA had in Vietnam. See Paul Ginsborg, *Italy and Its Discontents: Family, Civil Society, State: 1980-2001*, Palgrave Macmillan, 2003.

For Paolo Taviani's statement "It seems to me certain . . .": Philip Willan, "Paolo Emilio Taviani" (obituary), *The Guardian*, June 21, 2001, http://www.guardian.co.uk/news/2001/jun/21/guardianobituaries.philipwillan.

For Giandelio Maletti, including his statement " . . . the CIA, following the directives . . .": Philip Willan, "Terrorists 'helped by CIA' to stop rise of left in Italy," *The Guardian*, Mar. 26, 2001, http://www.guardian.co.uk/world/2001/mar/26/terrorism; Daniele Mastrogiacomo, "Maletti, la spia latitante La Cia dietro quelle bombe," *La Repubblica*, Aug. 4, 2000.

For other claims implicating the United States and/or NATO in foreknowledge of or participation in the bombings of Piazza Fontana, Brescia, and

Bologna: Philip Willan, "US 'supported anti-left terror in Italy,'" *The Guardian*, June 24, 2000; Ed Vulliamy, title of article unknown, *The Guardian*, Jan. 16, 1991, cited in Statewatch, "Operation Gladio," Statewatch Archive, http://database.statewatch.org/searchdisplay.asp?grpid=39.

Chapter 9: In Absentia

For Armando Spataro: Author interviews of Armando Spataro, Milan, Italy, 2007 to 2009; personal papers of Armando Spataro provided to author.

For the *Wall Street Journal*'s statement "a rogue": "The Italian Job," *Wall Street Journal*, Feb. 26, 2007, http://online.wsj.com/article/SB117245796674319001.html?mod=opinion_main_review_and_outlooks.

For Luciano Peroni, alias Ludwig: PIRONI Luciano, Verbale di interrogatorio di persona sottoposta ad indagini, N. 10838/05 R.G.N.R. mod. 21, Procura della Repubblica presso il Tribunale Ordinario di Milano, Apr. 14, 2006; Untitled deposition of Luciano Pironi, Proc. Pen. N. 1966/05 R.G.G.I.P., Sept. 30, 2006.

For Stefano D'Ambrosio: D'AMBROSIO Stefano, Verbale di assunzione informazioni, N. 10838/05 R.G.N.R. mod. 21, Procura della Repubblica presso il Tribunale Ordinario di Milano, Apr. 20, 2006; D'AMBROSIO Stefano, Verbale di assunzione informazioni, N. 10838/05 R.G.N.R. mod. 21, Procura della Repubblica presso il Tribunale Ordinario di Milano, Jul. 12, 2006.

For Bob Lady's denial of D'Ambrosio's claims about their conversation: Luca Fazzo, "L'ex capo Cia: 'Così rapimmo Abu Omar,'" *Il Giornale*, June 30, 2009.

For the bugged conversations of Gustavo Pignero and Marco Mancini: Enrico Manzi, "Decree for the Application of Coercive Measures," N. 10838/05 R.G.N.R., N. 1966/05 R.G.GIP (CASTELLI Jeffrey et al.), Tribunale di Milano, Sezione Giudice per le indagini preliminari, Jul. 7, 2006; "Secret Agents Spilling Secrets," *Washington Post*, Dec. 8, 2006.

For SISMI's offer to help the CIA with the kidnapping of Abu Omar: Manzi, *supra*; PIGNERO Gustavo, Interrogatorio Indagato, Proc. Pen. N. 10838/05 Mod. 21 R.G.N.R., Procura della Repubblica presso il Tribunale Ordinario di Milano (but the statement was taken in Rome), July 13, 2006.

For Renato Farina and Pio Pompa: Author interviews of Spataro, *supra*; Manzi, *supra*; FARINA Renato, Interrogatorio Indagato, Proc. Pen. N. 10838/05, Procura della Repubblica presso il Tribunale Ordinario di Milano, July 7, 2006; John Foot, "The Rendition of Abu Omar," *London Review of Books*,

Aug. 2, 2007; John Hooper, "The editor who spooked Italy," *The Guardian*, Jan. 29, 2007, http://www.guardian.co.uk/media/2007/jan/29/mondayme diasection.italy; Statewatch, "Italy: Renditions: Judge notifies defendants of the state of play in investigations into Abu Omar rendition: High-level SISMI and CIA officials involved," Statewatch News, http://www.state watch.org/news/2006/oct/10italy-omar-case.htm.

For Farina's article trying to blame the Yellowcake Affair on France: Renato Farina, "A caccia dell'italiano d'America regista del trappolone anti-Bush," *Libero*, Aug. 10, 2004.

For Farina's confession: FARINA Renato, *supra.*

For Pignero's confession: PIGNERO Gustavo, *supra.*

For Farina's statement "fighting the fourth world war . . ." and Silvio Berlusconi's statement that Farina was "a guerrilla fighter for liberty": Foot, *supra.*

For Pompa's minimal response to Spataro's inquiry: Pio Pompa, letter to Armando Spataro and Ferdinando Pomarici, Procura della Repubblica presso il Tribunale Ordinario di Milano, July 7, 2006.

For the Telecom shop allegedly run by Mancini and others: Elizabeth Filippouli, "Italy Gate," *People & Power* program, Al Jazeera TV network, Aug. 1, 2007.

For the statement of Pollari's lawyer (Titto Maddia) "Evidently. It wasn't the doorman": Ian Fisher and Elisabetta Povoledo, "Italy Braces for Legal Fight Over Secret C.I.A. Program," *New York Times*, June 8, 2007.

For Gianfranco Battelli's statement that he would have told the prime minister: Ammiraglio Gianfranco BATTELLI, Verbale di assunzione informazioni, N. 10838/05 R.G.N.R. mod. 21, Procura della Repubblica presso il Tribunale Ordinario di Milano, July 18, 2006.

For Silvio Berlusconi's statement "There has not been, I repeat . . .": "Berlusconi: 'Smentisco per l'ennesima volta.' " *Corriere della Sera*, Dec. 7, 2005, http://www.corriere.it/Primo_Piano/Politica/2005/12_Dicembre/07/berlu_smentita.html.

For Vincent Cannistraro's statement "Are you kidding?": Claudio Fava, *Quelli Bravi Ragazzi*, Sperling & Kupfer, 2007.

For Spataro's charges against Castelli, De Sousa, and Romano: Manzi, *supra.*

For Abu Omar's statement "My name is Osama Mustafa Hassan Nasr . . .": Abu Omar, "The Account of an Islamist Kidnapped from the Streets of Milan," undated, reproduced (in a rough English translation) as "My CIA rendition," Stephen Grey's *Ghost Plane* (Web site), http://www.ghostplane.

net/abuomar, and excerpted in Paolo Biondani and Gianni Santucci, "Il memoriale di Abu Omar: 'Rapito e picchiato da italiani,' " *Corriere della Sera*, Nov. 9, 2006.

For the account of Abu Omar's journey from prison to prison between 2004 and 2007 and of Nabila Ghali's visits with him: Manzi, *supra*; author interviews of Abu Omar, Alexandria, Egypt, Apr. 2007

For the CIA's near offer of hush money to Khaled El-Masri: Jane Mayer, *The Dark Side: The Inside Story of How the War on Terror Turned into a War on American Ideals*, Doubleday, 2008.

For the length of Italian trials: Alexander Stille, "Italy Against Itself," *New York Review of Books*, Dec. 4, 2008. Furthermore: "Claims for damage done by Garibaldi and his Redshirts to property in Sicily in 1860 . . . were still being paid in 1954, ninety-six years later, in lire which had lost all value and meaning, to heirs who barely remembered the reason why they were entitled to receive such pitifully small sums of money" (Luigi Barzini, *The Italians*, Touchstone, 1964).

For the chronology of the kidnappers' trial and for the appeals: Armando Spataro, "Abu Omar trial: Updating" nos. 1 through 30, e-mails to reporters, Mar. 2008 to Nov. 2009.

Chapter 10: Martyrs

For the report that Abu Omar informed for Albania's SHIK: John Crewdson and Tom Hundley, "Abducted imam aided CIA ally," *Chicago Tribune*, July 3, 2005; Tom Hundley and John Crewdson, "Wife was left behind with Children," *Chicago Tribune*, July 3, 2005.

For Sali Barisha's statement "They worked in Albania . . ." and for CIA operations in post–Cold War Albania generally: Andrew Higgins and Christopher Cooper, "Cloak and Dagger: A CIA-Backed Team Used Brutal Means to Crack Terror Cell," *Wall Street Journal*, Nov. 20, 2001. See also "How 'Albanian' Egyptians Operate," *Intelligence Newsletter*, Indigo Publications, no. 347, Nov. 26, 1998.

For Bob Lady's claim that he did not know Abu Omar had informed in Albania: Luca Fazzo, "L'ex capo Cia: 'Così rapimmo Abu Omar,' " *Il Giornale*, June 30, 2009.

For Montasser El-Zayat: Author interview of Montasser El-Zayat, Cairo, Egypt, Apr. 2007.

One of the fruits of the $1,100 paid by the *Wall Street Journal* to a Kabul looter was the story of how Abdulrahman and Abu Saleh betrayed an al-Qaeda turncoat in Yemen (see Chapter 3, "The Enemy Within"). See Andrew Higgins and Alan Cullison, "Friend or Foe: The Story of a Traitor to al Qaeda: Murky Loyalties in Yemen Undo the Betrayer, Who Finds Himself Betrayed: Ominous Words Before 9/11," *Wall Street Journal*, Dec. 20, 2002. See also Andrew Higgins and Alan Cullison, "Computer in Kabul Holds Chilling Memos," *Wall Street Journal*, Dec. 31, 2001.

For Abu Omar's statement "What are the German mother and son . . .": Deutsche Presse-Agentur, "Egyptian Islamist Urges Militants to Free German Hostages in Iraq," *EarthTimes*, Mar. 11, 2007, http://www.earthtimes .org/articles/show/38956.html.

For Abu Omar in Alexandria: Author interviews of Abu Omar, Alexandria, Egypt, Apr. 2007. For the report in *GQ* that CIA officers watched part of Abu Omar's interrogation on a video feed: Matthew Cole, "Blowback," *GQ*, Mar. 2007.

For Jean Améry's statement "Twenty-two years later . . .": Jean Améry, *At Mind's Limits: Contemplations by a Survivor of Auschwitz and its Realities*, Indiana University Press, 1998.

Jessica Easto and I interviewed the U.S. spies in 2007 and 2008.

For the cause and consequence of the flap over exposure of CIA officers in the 1970s: Philip Agee, *Inside the Company: CIA Diary*, Bantam, 1984; Intelligence Identities Protection Act of 1982, 50 U.S.C. § 421-26 (2006).

The CIA chief who said the snatch teams would be out robbing banks if they weren't doing renditions was Tyler Drumheller. See Tyler Drumheller with Elaine Monaghan, *On the Brink: An Insider's Account of How the White House Compromised American Intelligence*, Carroll & Graf, 2006.

For an account of another reporter who phoned "Washburn and Company": Greg Miller, "Shades of Cover," *Los Angeles Times*, July 16, 2005.

For Sabrina De Sousa's statement "You can keep hammering . . .": Jeff Stein, "CIA Woman Outraged by Belated U.S. Legal Help," CQ Politics: SpyTalk (blog), Aug. 28, 2009, http://blogs.cqpolitics.com/spytalk/2009/08/cia-woman-outraged-by-belated.html.

For Jeff Castelli's life after the rendition of Abu Omar: Jeff Stein, "CIA Officer in Italy Rendition Flap Enters New Phase," CQ Politics: SpyTalk (blog), Sept. 17, 2009, http://blogs.cqpolitics.com/spytalk/2009/09/cia-officer-in-italy-rendition.html.

For one report that Castelli supposedly misled CIA headquarters about the danger posed by Abu Omar: John Crewdson, "Italy says CIA may have had distorted view of cleric," *Chicago Tribune*, Jan. 8, 2007.

For Matthew Cole's interview with Bob Lady: Cole, *supra.*

For Lady's visit to Geneva in 2006: "Rest and Recuperation for CIA," *Intelligence Online* no. 525, Indigo Publications, June 9, 2006, http://www.intelligen ceonline.com/archives/p_som_archives.asp?num=525&year=2006&rub =archives.

For the essay that was all but certainly written by Lady under the nom de plume of his father: William Lady, "Coyotes From the Same Hill," *Dead Mule* (online), Oct. 1, 2005, http://www.deadmule.com/content/2005/10/01/ coyotes-from-the-same-hill/.

For Lady's interview with Fazzo: Fazzo, *supra.*

For Joseph Romano's statement "should be an embarrassment to Italy . . .": Matthew Cole, Avni Patel, and Brian Ross, "Convicted CIA Spy Says 'We Broke the Law,'" ABC News, Nov. 4, 2009, http://abcnews.go.com/Blotter/ exclusive-convicted-cia-spy-broke-law/story?id=8995107.

For the *Wall Street Journal*'s statement "one more dubious milestone . . .": "The War Against the War on Terrorism," *Wall Street Journal,* Nov. 6, 2009.

For Obama's executive order: Barack Obama, Executive Order 13491, "Ensuring Lawful Interrogations," Jan. 22, 2009.

Among the many reporters who misread Obama's executive order were two sagacious foes of torture, Glenn Greenwald and Scott Horton. See Scott Horton, "Renditions Buffoonery," *Harper's* (online), Feb. 2, 2009, http:// www.harpers.org/archive/2009/02/hbc-90004326; Glenn Greenwald, "The L.A. Times, Obama & renditions," *Salon: Glenn Greenwald* (blog), Feb. 2, 2009, http://www.salon.com/opinion/greenwald/2009/02/02/renditions/. Horton and Greenwald soon returned to their usual good sense on torture policy.

For Leon Panetta's statement "If we render someone . . .": David Ignatius, "Obama's Fine Print On Security," *Washington Post,* Mar. 29, 2009.

For the recommendation of Obama's task force: "Special Task Force on Interrogations and Transfer Policies Issues Its Recommendations to the President," press release 09-835, Ofc. of Public Affairs, U.S. Dept. of Justice, Aug. 24, 2009, http://www.justice.gov/opa/pr/2009/August/09-ag-835.html.

Index

Page numbers beginning with 283 refer to notes.